To Be One Thing

To Be One Thing

*Personal Unity
in Kierkegaard's Thought*

GEORGE CONNELL

MERCER

ISBN 0-86554-156-6

To Be One Thing:
Personal Unity in Kierkegaard's Thought
Copyright © 1985
by Mercer University Press, Macon GA 31207
All rights reserved
Printed in the United States of America

All books published by Mercer University Press
are printed on acid-free paper that exceeds
the minimum standards set by the
National Historical Publications and Records Commission.

Library of Congress Cataloging in Publication Data
Connell, George, 1957–
To be one thing.
Includes bibliographical references and index.
1. Kierkegaard, Søren, 1813-1855—Anthropology.
2. Self (Philosophy)—History—19th century. I. Title.
B4378.S4C66   1985   126   85-4812
ISBN 0-86554-156-6

CONTENTS

INTRODUCTION ix

PART I
The Emergence of the Theme
of Personal Unity, 1835–1838 1

    CHAPTER I
    Personal Unity and Romantic Theories of Science 3
    CHAPTER II
    Unity as an Aesthetic Principle 19

PART II
The Flight from Sameness:
The Aesthetic Self's Refusal
to Be One Thing 39

    CHAPTER III
    From the Journals to the Authorship 41
    CHAPTER IV
    The Varieties of Turbulence:
        Descriptions of Change in A's Manuscripts 55
    CHAPTER V
    The Final Synthesis:
        Art and Nature in "Diary of a Seducer" 83

PART III
Ways of Being One Thing 107
CHAPTER VI
The Common Characteristics of Unified Selfhood 109
CHAPTER VII
The Negative Oneness of the Ironist................................. 117
CHAPTER VIII
Duty and Continuity:
The Historical Oneness of the Ethical Self 137
CHAPTER IX
Oneness as Repentance:
The Unity of the Religious Self 155
CHAPTER X
Unified Through Faith:
The Oneness of the Christian Self 177

CONCLUSION... 191

INDEX... 195

It holds true for the catch-penny artists and those who are caught by them, that variety is the highest law of life. But in connection with the truth as inwardness, in connection with a more incorruptible joy of life, which has nothing in common with the craving of the life-weary for diversion, the opposite holds true; the law is: the same, and yet changed, and still the same.
—Concluding Unscientific Postscript, 254-55
—Samlede Værker, 9:240

INTRODUCTION

Father in Heaven! What is man without Thee! What is all he knows, vast accumulation though it be, but a chipped fragment if he does not know Thee! What is all his striving, could it even encompass a world, but a half-finished work if he knows not Thee: Thee the One, who art one thing and who art all! So may Thou give to the intellect, wisdom to comprehend one thing; to the heart, sincerity to receive this understanding; to the will purity which wills only one thing. In prosperity may Thou grant perseverance to will one thing; amid distraction, collectedness to will one thing; in suffering, patience to will one thing. Oh, Thou that giveth both the beginning and the completion, may Thou early, at the dawn of day, give to the young man the resolution to will one thing. As the day wanes, may Thou give to the old man a renewed remembrance of his first resolution, that the first may be like the last, and the last like the first, in possession of a life that has willed only one thing.[1]

---

[1] Søren Kierkegaard, *Purity of Heart is to Will One Thing*, trans. Douglas V. Steere (New York: Harper and Row, 1956) 31; *Samlede Værker*, ed. A. B. Drachmann, P. A. Heiberg, and H. O. Lange, rev. P. P. Rohde, 20 vols. (Copenhagen: Gyldendal, 1962) 11:15. Throughout this work, it will be the 3d edition of the *Samlede Værker* (henceforth *S.V.*) to which I shall refer.

With these words, Kierkegaard both opens and closes his edifying discourse, *Purity of Heart is to Will One Thing*, thus practicing the Socratic principle he so often repeats, "To say the same things about the same things."[2] The repetition of this prayer at the beginning and end of this small but powerful work has a significance beyond agreement with the Socratic maxim. It is the formal counterpart to and reflection of the content of both the prayer and the work as a whole.

And that content is striking indeed. In a world in which variety is all but equated with excitement and freshness, just as sameness is thought tantamount to monotony and boredom, the desire to know, to will, to be one thing seems as strange as the man who gave expression to it. Not only does the prospect of such a state strike us as tedious, it seems odd to pray so vehemently for that which comes most easily. Almost anyone can achieve substantial proficiency in a given endeavor if he narrowly devotes himself to it. It is the all-American athlete who is also a Rhodes scholar or the virtuoso violinist who is also a great painter who captures our attention. Everyone learns to speak his mother tongue, but we wonder at the man fluent in a dozen languages.

Kierkegaard's surprising desire is intimately bound up with his view of man as a synthesis of the finite and the infinite. Among other things, this view involves the belief that man is a synthesis of the temporal and the eternal. By virtue of his finite, temporal aspect, man shares the lot of all creatures. He is born, lives a life extending through a finite number of successive moments of time, and dies. In the case of creatures who without qualification belong to the finite, the story ends here. Is man any different? Is he by virtue of his infinite, eternal aspect immortal?

In Kierkegaard's view, the story can end differently only if it has differed from the story of the plant or animal throughout its course. Only if the eternal is constantly present in that life through every change to which the self is subjected as temporal and finite will the self endure through the final change of death. "Immortality cannot be the final alteration that crept in, so to speak, at the moment of death as the final stage. On the contrary,

---

[2]See, for example, Søren Kierkegaard, *Concluding Unscientific Postscript*, trans. David F. Swenson and Walter Lowrie (Princeton: Princeton University Press, 1941) 253; *S.V.*, 9:238. The source of this phrase is Plato's *Gorgias*, 491a.

it is the changelessness that is not altered by the passage of years."³ That is, immortality is not a change that happens to the self upon death, but the quality of changelessness and eternality that "must have been present in each moment of its life."⁴

This eternal, changeless element of the human self is *not* for Kierkegaard a substantial, immortal soul, invisibly serving as a substratum for the variegated parade of aspects the self shows in the course of its life. Such a self would be at least partially withdrawn from the Heraclitean realm of existence, a state of affairs Kierkegaard repeatedly denies. "However much the subject has the infinite within himself, through being an existing individual, he is in the process of becoming."⁵

Given this condition, the changelessness characteristic of the eternal can never be a possession. It can only be the outcome of a struggle that ceases only with death. Kierkegaard writes, "Existence (*Existens*)⁶ is the child born of the infinite and the finite, the eternal and the temporal, and is therefore a constant striving."⁷

What form is this laboriously maintained changelessness to take? Since no element of the self may be exempted from the dialectic of becoming, this changelessness cannot be present in any simple, straightforward manner but must take the form of continuity, that is, self-identity through

---

³*Purity of Heart*, 35; *S.V.*, 11:18.

⁴Ibid.

⁵*Postscript*, 85n; *S.V.*, 9:80n.

⁶In the translation of Kierkegaard's works into English, an important distinction made in the Danish language is lost. Where we use the single word *existence*, Danish distinguishes between *Tilværelse* and *Existens*. The former word indicates simply presence in time and space. *Existens*, a loan word from Latin, is reserved to indicate the form of existence found in the striving, spiritually alive human being. See Søren Kierkegaard, *Journals and Papers* (henceforth *J. and P.*), ed. Howard V. Hong and Edna H. Hong, 7 vols. (Bloomington: Indiana University Press, 1967-1978) 1:535n, and Mark Taylor, *Kierkegaard's Pseudonymous Authorship* (Princeton: Princeton University Press, 1975) 6n.

⁷*Postscript*, 85; *S.V.*, 9:79. It is interesting that this is the passage cited in the *Terminologiske Ordbog* accompanying the 3d edition of the *Samlede Værker* to illustrate Kierkegaard's use of *Existens*. See *S.V.*, 20:66.

change. It is just such self-identity that is the goal of the constant striving referred to above. "[T]he difficulty facing an existing individual is how to give his existence the continuity (*Continueerlighed*) without which everything simply vanishes."[8]

Immortality, then, should not be a good simply wished for and wondered about but rather a selfsameness laboriously maintained on the basis of the existing individual's passion for and infinite interest in that good. When severed from the task of maintaining unity in one's life, the question of immortality becomes an inhuman farce.

> [T]he question about immortality is made fantastically ludicrous . . . when people who have fantastically made a mess of everything and have been every possible sort of thing, one day ask the clergyman with deep concern whether in the beyond they will be the same—after never having in their lifetimes been the same for a fortnight and hence have undergone all sorts of transformations. Thus immortality would indeed be an extraordinary metamorphosis if it could transform such an inhuman centipede into an eternal identity with itself which 'being the same' amounts to.[9]

Immortality is a condition of the still-living self; it is the constantly reacquired presence of the eternal in the human self in the form of the Parmenidean qualities—oneness, self-identity, and changelessness—each quality receiving expression in a manner compatible with the self's temporal existence. The first of these three qualities is, of course, the one emphasized in *Purity of Heart*.

When we look more closely at the discussion of this quality of oneness, it becomes clear that there are two distinct ways in which Kierkegaard uses it to characterize the properly ordered self. First, as temporal, the self is forced to live moment by moment. If it would exist in such a way as to deserve the description "one," it must gather all the discrete moments of its life into a unity. This form of being one, having a history in the eminent sense of the word, is a possibility reserved for man, but it is also an obligation.

In the life of the Individual the task is to achieve an ennoblement of the

---

[8]*Postscript*, 277; *S.V.*, 10:19.

[9]*Postscript*, 157; *S.V.*, 9:146-47.

successive within the simultaneous (*Samtidighed*). To have been young, and then to grow older, and finally to die, is a very mediocre form of human existence; this merit belongs to every animal. But the unification of the different stages of life in simultaneity is a task set for human beings.[10]

The second form of unity Kierkegaard discusses is the unity of the self he terms "willing one thing." This phrase indicates the mode or manner of self that stands in contrast to double-mindedness.[11] The self in which the eternal and the temporal are properly integrated is, according to Kierkegaard, truly unified and at one with itself. The self in which this integration has not occurred is divided, chaotic, and at war with itself. For such slaves, the cry of the Gerasene demoniac, "My name is Legion; for we are many" (Mark 5:9), is their own.

As the discussion now stands, it would appear that a monomaniacal obsession of any description would serve to give the self the oneness characteristic of immortality. This, according to Kierkegaard, is an illusion. In his view, the self can truly will one thing only if its object is an essential unity, since the will or self necessarily shares the essential character of the object toward which it is directed.[12] Only one object, the Good,[13] has the unity, simplicity, and changelessness requisite to endow the will with these qualities. Kierkegaard supports this assertion with a thoroughly Platonic analysis of other possible objects of will.

---

[10]*Postscript*, 311; *S.V*, 10:50.

[11]*Mode* and *manner* are the terms Jeremy Walker uses to discuss the state of self Kierkegaard describes as "willing one thing." He writes, "Two possible examples of the idea of the will's mode or manner are the strength or weakness of one's will, for example, the degree of one's determination or the strength of one's commitment, and the unity, or internal conflict of one's will." Jeremy D. B. Walker, *To Will One Thing* (Montreal: McGill-Queens University Press, 1972) 113. Kierkegaard takes the term *double-minded* from James 1:8 and 4:8.

[12]In chapter 5 of his book, Walker discusses this principle, which he calls "the principle of homogeneity or 'harmony.' " *To Will One Thing*, 122.

[13]"The Good" here is to be understood as synonymous with "God." See ibid., 5 and Gregor Malantschuk, *Fra Individ til den Enkelte* (Copenhagen: Reitzels, 1978) 127.

> [P]leasure and honor and riches and all that this world have to offer only appear to be one thing. It is not, nor does it remain one thing, while everything else is in change or while [the willing self] is himself in change. It is not in all circumstances the same. On the contrary it is subject to continual alteration. . . . Neither can [the self] be said to will one thing when that one thing which he wills is not in itself one: is in itself a multiplicity of things, a dispersion, the toy of changeableness and the prey of corruption!
>
> [The appearance that such worldly goods are one] is a sense-deception, as when a swarm of insects at a distance seems to the ear like a single voice. . . .
>
> The fact is that the worldly goal is not one thing in essence because it is unreal. Its so-called unity is actually nothing but emptiness hidden beneath manyness. . . . No, the worldly goal is not one thing. Diverse as it is, in life changed into its opposite, in death into nothing, in eternity into damnation: for the one who has willed this goal![14]

Given such an understanding of worldly goods together with the principle that the will assumes the essential character of its object, it becomes clear why Kierkegaard believes that the unity of the self on which immortality depends can only result from the unqualified devotion of the self to the Good, and, thus, why he prays so vehemently for the purity of heart to will one thing.

In the preceding pages, I have sketched the reasoning that lies behind the prayer quoted at the opening of this introduction. That reasoning uses a number of venerable philosophical principles, principles that Kierkegaard handles with the agility of a mature and talented dialectician. While the isolation of these principles and the identification of their genealogies is an interesting and valuable activity, a study limited to these tasks would fail to grasp the full significance of the text. Such a study could produce an exhaustive anatomical description of the work but would miss the central idea that animates the fabric of assertion, argument, prayer, and entreaty that comprises *Purity of Heart*.

The thesis of this study is that one of the grounding principles of Kierkegaard's thought is his claim that the self must constitute itself as an es-

---

[14]*Purity of Heart*, 56-60; *S.V.*, 11:32-34.

sential unity in the face of the disruptive action of the world.[15] In *Purity of Heart*, this idea is maturely and eloquently expressed in terms familiar to all within the Western philosophical tradition. The idea, itself, however, is a fundamental way of apprehending the universe that is an essential part of who Kierkegaard is as a person and a philosopher. It is a philosophical idea in the sense that William James identifies in the first lecture of *Pragmatism*: "[T]he philosophy which is so important in each of us is not a technical matter, it is our more or less dumb sense of what life honestly and deeply means. It is only partly got from books; it is our individual way of just seeing and feeling the total push and pressure of the cosmos."[16]

As a thoroughly reflective person, as one who writes, "I still accept an imperative of knowledge,"[17] even after rejecting the sufficiency of intellectual endeavor as a way of life, Kierkegaard struggles to make his "sense of what life honestly and deeply means" less rather than more dumb. Throughout his life as a thinker and a writer, he seeks to express his conviction that selfhood and unity are essentially interrelated and to make use of this principle as a tool in his "authentic anthropological contemplation" to bring enlightenment to the human condition.

---

[15]It is uncanny that Hegel in his discussion of "unhappy consciousness," the form of consciousness often associated with Kierkegaard, nearly predicts that a person such as Kierkegaard would use just such a principle as his point of departure. "The simple Unchangeable . . . and the protean Changeable . . . are, for Unhappy Consciousness, alien to one another; and because it is itself the consciousness of this contradiction, it identifies itself with the changeable consciousness, and takes itself to be unessential Being. But as consciousness of Unchangeableness, or of simple essential Being, it must at the same time set about freeing itself from the unessential, i.e., itself." (sec. 208) G. W. F. Hegel, *Phenomenology of Spirit*, trans. A. V. Miller (Oxford: Oxford University Press, 1978) 126-27; see also Mark Taylor, *Journeys to Selfhood* (Berkeley: University of California Press, 1980) 196.

[16]William James, *Pragmatism* (New York: Signet, 1955) 17-18.

[17]*J. and P.*, 5100; *Søren Kierkegaards Papirer* (henceforth *Pap.*), ed. P. A. Heiberg, V. Kuhr, and E. Torsting, rev. Niels Thulstrup, 22 vols. (Cophenhagen: Gyldendal, 1968-1970) 1 A 75. (This collection of papers is arranged somewhat unusually. In references to it, the first number will be the volume, the following letter will be the section of that volume, and the number following will identify the specific selection itself, not the page on which it appears.)

It is to this written work in its great volume and variety that I must turn in sustaining my thesis; only in showing the pervasiveness of the idea, in pointing out its recurrence in various forms in Kierkegaard's letters, journals, and published works, can I hope to establish its foundational role. A mere catalog of these many individual appearances of the theme is insufficient, however. Kierkegaard's particular expressions must be viewed against the backdrop of his comprehensive engagement with the theme of personal unity.

This orientation, this concern to see the individual discussions of unity in terms of the larger picture, represents a major element of this study's originality. As a reading of the following chapters will reveal, my analysis draws on and benefits from the work of others at many points. Scholars have noted the role of the idea of unity in a number of aspects of Kierkegaard's thought, and to them I am indebted. However, because these individual moments of elucidation have not been brought together, because Jørgensen's work on Kierkegaard's aesthetic theory, Taylor's description of the ethical self's achievements, Elrod's investigations of the ontological underpinnings of the authorship, Malantschuk's discussions of the evolution of the methodology of pseudonymity, and so forth, treat only particular aspects of the theme's development, its true dimensions and importance have remained unappreciated; the idea of unity as deployed in Kierkegaard's writings has not been seen in its unity.[18]

---

[18]Carl Jørgensen, *Søren Kierkegaard,* 5 vols. (Copenhagen: Arnold Busck, 1964); Mark Taylor, *Journeys to Selfhood;* Gregor Malantschuk, *Kierkegaard's Thought,* trans. Howard V. Hong and Edna H. Hong (Princeton: Princeton University Press, 1971). The secondary literature on Kierkegaard has grown to such vast proportions in the past few decades that any new contribution must either be selective in its use of that literature or else become a study of the study of Kierkegaard. I have opted for the former alternative. Broadly stated, my policy has been to employ those studies that begin from compatible methodological presuppositions and that are in either Danish or English. The former part of the policy filters for relevance; the latter takes into account the virtue of accessibility, first, the accessibility of English language sources to my readers and, second, the special access Danish scholars have to the language and historical context of their countryman's thought. Regrettably this leads me to overlook the contributions of French and German scholars.

Personal Unity in Kierkegaard's Thought

Just as no listing of individual passages can capture the coherence of Kierkegaard's development of the theme, no simple compilation of these critical insights will suffice. Following the lead Kierkegaard provides in his own dissertation, I propose to establish my somewhat elusive thesis by an "integral calculation," by "triangulating" on it.[19] The chapters that follow are organized into three parts, each of which uses a distinct method to approach one phase of Kierkegaard's writings.[20] Considered separately, each of the groups of chapters is a self-contained discussion of one aspect of Kierkegaard's development and deployment of the idea of unity. Each is further significant within the whole in that it helps to convey the depth and breadth of the idea's presence in Kierkegaard's thought. This latter role is, necessarily, filled in a largely indirect manner. Just as viewing a statue requires an observer to move around it, to change his perspective so as to bring other aspects of the whole into view, thus allowing an appreciation that transcends any of the particular visual impressions, so here the variety of methods and materials should convey a more profound sense of the idea's place in Kierkegaard's mind than could any one-dimensional study, no matter how exhaustive. This complementarity goes beyond examining different bodies of writing in different ways; each group of chapters, in form, content, or both, corresponds to one of the three essential moments of Kierkegaard's relationship to the idea.

The first two chapters investigate Kierkegaard's earliest attempts to clarify the conviction dimly present but strongly felt within him. For assistance in this task, he draws on the ideas, terminology, and metaphors of other thinkers of his day who were also engaged with the idea of unity. These early writings show a Kierkegaard ready to *adopt* from others what

---

[19]Søren Kierkegaard, *The Concept of Irony*, trans. Lee Capel (Bloomington: Indiana University Press, 1965) 50, 365.

[20]My study employs three of the four methods of approach Aage Henriksen discusses in his historical survey of Kierkegaard scholarship, *Methods and Results of Kierkegaard Studies in Scandinavia: A Historical and Critical Study* (Copenhagen: Munksgaard, 1951). The approach I do not employ, the biographical, has been overworked, is reductionistic, and makes a mockery of its subject's strenuous endeavors to let his authorship stand apart from his personal existence.

he can use, but equally prepared to *adapt* ideas to meet his own needs.[21] The character of these early texts calls for the use of an "external criticism" in which influences are traced and different philosophers' writings are compared and contrasted so as to reveal Kierkegaard's debts and original contributions. Some have castigated such "intellectual genealogy" as reductionistic and untrue to its subject matter;[22] in fact, this method reflects an important dimension of Kierkegaard's thought. He always saw freedom as dialectical, involving the acceptance, appropriation, and responsible adaptation of one's given situation. No thinker exists outside a particular location in time and space; while this context is not a sufficient basis for understanding a thinker, it is a necessary one. My inquiry in these chapters into the inspirations of Kierkegaard's thought as well as into his innovations formally reflects his conviction that man is a synthesis. In the process, it casts light on an important side of Kierkegaard, the man. While he is often seen solely as an isolated individual, here the Kierkegaard alert to and involved with the ideas and concerns of his time stands before us.

The remainder of the book proceeds on the basis of a common thesis: each of the stages of existence and their subdivisions can be understood in terms of the idea of unity either by determining the particular expression of unity and continuity characteristic of that stage or by seeing the way the stage in question stands opposed to the imperative to be one thing. That is, the decisive character of all selves is shaped by the stance they adopt toward the imperative of oneness.

Chapters 3-5 examine the self who rebels, who refuses to be one thing: the aesthete. This phase of study takes as its primary source the first volume of *Either/Or*. The variegated and apparently disordered character of this work is not an obstacle to the project but a great opportunity. My thesis, in serving as the key by which order may be found where others have

---

[21]This use of the philosophical writings of others is in keeping with the form of philosophical study recommended by Kierkegaard's friend and teacher, Poul Martin Møller. One of Møller's many aphorisms reads, "The essential benefit the genuine philosopher receives from the study of philosophy's history is that he is led to an expression for the dark idea (*'den dunkle Ide'*) which lives within him." Quoted by Jørgensen, *Søren Kierkegaard*, 1:94. (My translation.)

[22]See, for example, the introduction to Per Lonning, *Samtighedens Situation* (Oslo: Land og Folk, 1954).

denied its existence, by establishing a claim to heuristic value, is powerfully confirmed.

I proceed in these chapters on the basis of a strictly applied "internal criticism," regarding *Either/Or* 1 as an integral whole to be investigated on its own terms. In employing this method, I follow the examples of F. J. Billeskov-Jansen, Aage Henriksen, and, in the United States, Louis Mackey, who have demonstrated that approaching Kierkegaard's writings as works of literature rather than philosophical texts is often the most fruitful method.[23] Here form, or more precisely, the narrative structure of *Either/Or* 1, proves to be the key to understanding the work's content.

This examination of the aesthete reveals a crucial side of Kierkegaard's personal relationship to the idea of oneness. The vividness and intensity with which he brings this form of existence to life shows that he has felt its draw powerfully. His temptation in this direction serves as the dialectical counterforce to his conviction that oneness and stability of self are crucial. The power of this latter belief originates in the dynamic tension between the two.

Whereas in the second group of chapters a single work is selected for study and is examined on its own basis—that is, its pseudonymity is scrupulously respected—in the remaining chapters, chapters 6-10, the method adopted is that most commonly used in current Kierkegaard scholarship: a synoptic approach seeking a single anthropology, philosophy, and/or theology that drives the authorship as a whole. This approach has the great disadvantage of failing to take Kierkegaard's employment of pseudonymity seriously. However, the use of it in these chapters is justified and even mandated by my project. Here, I describe Kierkegaard's "phenomenology" of selves that acknowledge and obey the imperative to be one thing. I first describe abstractly the necessary characteristics of such a self and then trace the progressively more perfect fulfillment of these requirements in the various forms of selfhood. That each form's salient achievement remedies the fatal weakness of its predecessor makes apparent the developmental character of this succession of forms. All this can only come to

---

[23]F. J. Billeskov-Jansen, *Studier i Søren Kierkegaards Litterære Kunst* (Copenhagen: Rosenkilde og Bagger, 1951); Aage Henriksen, *Kierkegaards Romaner* (Copenhagen: Gyldendal, 1955); Louis Mackey, *Kierkegaard: A Kind of Poet* (Philadelphia: University of Pennsylvania Press, 1971).

light in a comprehensive survey of Kierkegaard's writings. Accordingly, I look beyond the bounds of the authorship in this chapter, making use of both Kierkegaard's dissertation, *The Concept of Irony*, and the late religious works. By uncovering, in these many varied works, a cohesive line of thought on the subject of unity, I seek to prove the foundational character of this theme in Kierkegaard's works.

PART I

The Emergence of the Theme of Personal Unity, 1835-1838

CHAPTER I

Personal Unity and Romantic Theories of Science

The Theme of Unity in the Gilleleje Journal

By late spring, 1835, it had become painfully obvious to the twenty-two-year-old Søren Kierkegaard that his life was disordered, directionless, and in danger of becoming mired in such a state. His studies at the University of Copenhagen, where he was entering the fifth year of a three-year program of theological study, had become increasingly desultory as the years passed and gradually drifted beyond the sphere of theology altogether. As he gave no sign of taking or even preparing for his final examinations, his comrades expected and his family feared that he would settle into the life of a *studiosus in perpetuum*.

Kierkegaard, however, was not to drift quietly into such a life. During the late spring and the summer of 1835, he turned his already substantial reflective powers upon himself in order to assess thoroughly his condition, his possibilities, and his task in life. As he writes in a letter of this period to P. E. Lind, he intends "to direct toward myself that concave mirror with which I have attempted until now to comprehend life around me."[1] This self-assessment was to serve as the basis for a resolution that would restore order and direction to his life.

Kierkegaard's father chose this auspicious moment to provide his prodigal son with funds for a summer vacation at Gilleleje, an idyllic fishing village at the northernmost point of the island of Zealand. The escape from the bustle of Copenhagen proved a great boon to Kierkegaard's project of self-assessment. Amidst the descriptions of places visited, sights seen, and people met that fill the pages of the Gilleleje journal, are two documents that stand apart from all his writings until then as indicative of the self-reflective and expressive powers he would later unveil.[2] These documents are especially significant for this study in that they represent Kierkegaard's first real attempts to develop the theme of unity. He struggles to express his need for a project that will unify and direct his life. His first attempt fails, thus leaving it to the second document to repudiate and correct the statements of the first. This repudiation does not reduce the importance of the first document, however. Kierkegaard's failure in it to distinguish between two different forms of unity reveals much about the early

---

[1] Søren Kierkegaard, *Letters and Documents*, trans. Henrik Rosenmeier (Princeton: Princeton University Press, 1978) 49.

[2] The importance of these documents has been widely recognized by students of Kierkegaard. Lowrie, for instance, writes that "the journal of this tour, which is the very beginning of his serious journals, contains the fullest and most perspicuous account of his state of mind that he ever wrote in his youth." Walter Lowrie, *Kierkegaard* (London: Oxford University Press, 1938) 107. See also p. 77. Capel notes, "The central document signifying the beginning of Kierkegaard's quest for intellectual integrity is the remarkable Gilleleje Journal." Lee Capel, Historical Introduction to *The Concept of Irony* by Søren Kierkegaard (Bloomington: Indiana University Press, 1965) 17; see also James Collins, *The Mind of Kierkegaard* (Chicago: Henry Regnery Company, 1953) 25-27; Gregor Malantschuk, *Kierkegaard's Thought*, trans. Howard V. Hong and Edna H. Hong (Princeton: Princeton University Press, 1971) 12; Niels Thulstrup, *Kierkegaard's Forhold til Hegel* (Copenhagen: Gyldendals, 1967) 23; Carl Jørgensen, *Søren Kierkegaard*, 5 vols. (Copenhagen: Arnold Busck, 1964) 1:42-53.

sources of images, terminology, and inspiration used by him to develop the theme of unity.

The first of the Gilleleje documents to be considered is a letter written to the brother-in-law of two of Kierkegaard's sisters, Peter Wilhelm Lund (two of Kierkegaard's sisters married two of Lund's brothers). The letter was actually written 1 June shortly before the trip to Gilleleje. It was later transcribed into the journal of that trip as the occasion for writing the second document. Lund, then working in Brazil, was an accomplished zoologist and paleontologist educated in Copenhagen and Kiel. He had returned to Denmark for three months in 1831, during which time Kierkegaard had conversed at length with him.[3] Why Kierkegaard chose to write so self-revealing a letter to Lund is unclear. Commentators have speculated that Lund's distance and his clear sense of his own task in life led to the choice.[4]

In the letter, Kierkegaard moves quickly from a recollection of the conversations he enjoyed with Lund to a consideration of the problems facing youth on the threshold of manhood, that is, the problems he finds himself facing. Choosing images well suited to a letter to a biologist, he writes:

> Our early youth is like a flower at dawn, cupping a lovely dewdrop, reflecting pensively and harmoniously on its surroundings. But soon the sun rises over the horizon and the dewdrop evaporates; with it vanish life's dreams, and now the question is (to use once more the flower metaphor) whether one is able, like the oleander, to produce a drop that can stand as the fruit of his life. This requires, above all, that a person find the soil where he really belongs, but that is not always easy to discover.[5]

The remainder of the letter shows that by "find the soil where he really belongs," Kierkegaard means determining the activity, the discipline, the vocation for which he as an individual has a particular aptitude. In Kierkegaard's view, persons can be classified into three groups according to the way they face this task.

---

[3]Jørgensen, *Søren Kierkegaard*, 1:19, 42.

[4]See, for example, Lowrie, *Kierkegaard*, 107.

[5]*J. and P.*, 5092; *Pap.*, 1 A 72.

> In this respect there are fortunate temperaments so decisively oriented in a particular direction that they go steadily along the path once assigned to them without ever entertaining the thought that perhaps they should really be taking another path. There are others who let themselves be so completely directed by their environment that they never become clear about what they are really working toward. Just as the former class has an internal categorical imperative, so the latter class has an external categorical imperative. But how few there are in the former class and to the latter I do not wish to belong. The majority will get to try out in life what the Hegelian dialectic really means.[6]

What Kierkegaard means by "the Hegelian dialectic" is not immediately apparent. Niels Thulstrup in his exhaustive study of the development of Kierkegaard's knowledge of Hegel, *Kierkegaards Forhold til Hegel*, examines this passage and concludes that nothing more than unfamiliarity with Hegel at this point in time can be inferred from it.[7] It is clear from the rest of the letter that Kierkegaard here refers to those who are forced to struggle in the face of uncertainty to determine "the soil where [they] really belong." Thulstrup notes that Hegel's dialectic is far removed from such an intensely personal concern.

Kierkegaard describes the situation of this third class as Faustian, taking Faust as "doubt personified." Context dictates that "doubt" be taken here to mean failure, inability, or refusal to subordinate all one's interests to the pursuit of one interest in particular.[8] Kierkegaard concludes the first part of the letter by clearly placing himself in this third class of Faustian doubters.

> Here I stand before a big question mark. Here I stand like Hercules, but not at a crossroads—no, here there are a good many more roads to take and thus it is much more difficult to choose the right one. It is perhaps my misfortune that I am interested in far too much and not decisively in any

---

[6]Ibid.

[7]Niels Thulstrup, *Kierkegaard's Forhold til Hegel*, 56-57.

[8]See Knud Jensenius, *Nogle Kierkegaard Studier* (Copenhagen: Nyt Nordiske Forlag, 1932) 14.

one thing; my interests are not subordinated to one but instead all stand coordinate.⁹

In the second half of the letter, Kierkegaard examines two fields of endeavor, the natural sciences and theology, with an eye to determining whether he should devote his life to one of these disciplines. In both cases, Kierkegaard places unity at the forefront of his discussions as the sine qua non of any science, be it natural, human, or divine. In the case of the natural sciences, he belittles the "people who have made a name for themselves in the literature by their assiduousness in collecting." Such researchers have a multitude of details but nothing more. The true scientists are those "who through their reflection have found or are trying to find that Archimedean point which is nowhere in the world and from that point have surveyed the whole and have seen the details in their proper light."[10]

In the following paragraphs, Kierkegaard attacks theological rationalism in the same way he attacked the "assiduous collectors."

> [R]ationalism . . . does not create a system but a Noah's ark . . . in which the clean and the unclean animals lie down side by side. . . . That is why it virtually attaches itself to Christianity, bases its formulations on scripture and sends out a legion of Bible passages in advance of every single point, but the formulation itself is not penetrated by it.[11]

Orthodoxy, in Kierkegaard's view, has the organic unity lacking in rationalism; in fact, he considers it to be such an essential unity that it must stand or fall as a whole. This perception is in large part responsible for his ambivalent attitude toward Christianity in these years. As he says here, many of the individual propositions of doctrine are unobjectionable to him, but his doubts about others oblige him for the present "to let the main foundations stand *indubio*."[12] This statement at least in part explains his

---

[9]*J. and P.*, 5092; *Pap.*, 1 A 72.

[10]Ibid.

[11]Ibid.

[12]Ibid.

dissatisfaction with his present status as a theological student, apart from which the letter to Lund is incomprehensible.

The striking presupposition that lies behind this letter is that the personal unification Kierkegaard seeks is to be won through a career decision. This claim is confirmed in the first paragraph of the journal entry composed at Gilleleje on 1 August. Kierkegaard writes thus of his state of mind at the time of the composition of the letter to Lund: "I therefore believed that I would possibly achieve more tranquility by taking another line of study, by directing my energies toward another goal."[13] More is involved in this belief, which he rightly rejects as erroneous, than the naiveté and career consciousness typical of youth. Kierkegaard had implicitly believed that the activities of synthesis, which he identifies as central to genuine intellectual pursuits, give rise not only to unity in the accumulated information of a field of study but also in the self of the person so employed. He approaches an explicit statement of this belief at one point in the letter to Lund. After criticizing the "assiduous collectors" and praising the true scientists who have found the Archimedean point from which to view all details as parts of the whole, Kierkegaard remarks, "As far as [the latter] are concerned, I cannot deny that they have a very salutary effect on me. The tranquility, the harmony, the joy one finds in them is rarely found elsewhere."[14]

In stark contrast to the letter to Lund, the predominant theme of the Gilleleje entry is that the unity of a system of knowledge is not and cannot serve as the source of the unity of the individual subject. As in his later works, especially the *Postscript*, Kierkegaard describes a system of knowledge as essentially public: Even if one creates it, it stands outside of one indifferent to and uninvolved with the coherence or chaos that is within one.

> [O]f what use would it be to me to be able to develop a theory of state, getting details from various sources and combining them into a whole, and constructing a world I did not live in but merely held up for others to see?[15]

---

[13]*J. and P.*, 5100; *Pap.*, 1 A 75.

[14]Ibid. I follow Rosenmeier's translation here.

[15]Ibid.

Personal Unity in Kierkegaard's Thought

Kierkegaard's rejection of the intellectual path to self-integration is the immediate occasion for a statement that captures the essence of his thought. Upon reading the following passage, one can only wonder at the firm grip Kierkegaard had on his central message nearly eight years before launching his authorship with the publication of *Either/Or*. This passage makes plausible Gregor Malantschuk's claim that the development of Kierkegaard's thought was essentially complete by the beginning of the authorship.[16]

> What I really need is to get clear about *what I must do*, not what I must know, except insofar as knowledge must precede every act. What matters is to find a purpose, to see what it really is that God wills that *I* should do; the crucial thing is to find the truth which is truth *for me*, to find *the idea for which I am to live and die*. . . . This is what I needed to lead a *completely human life* and not merely one of *knowledge*, so that I could base the developments of my thought not on—yes, not on something called objective—something which in any case is not my own, but upon something which is bound up with the deepest roots of my existence (*Existents*), to which I cling fast even though the whole world may collapse. *This is what I need, and this is what I strive for.*[17]

The close connection between the Kierkegaardian dictum, "Truth is subjectivity," and the conviction that the self must constitute itself as an essential unity is especially apparent here. In a marginal note to the Gilleleje entry, Kierkegaard asks, "What is the truth but to live for an idea?" Obviously, this is a prototypical form of the more famous dictum from the *Postscript*.

But what exactly is involved in living for an idea? In this context, it is sufficient to answer that in living for an idea a unification internal to the self is effected. Instead of finding the Archimedean point from which a multitude of isolated details may be viewed as a whole as in the case of the sciences, the self finds the task or project wherein all of its moments and actions may be held as a unity. This task relates to the whole person, to the person both as knower and doer, whereas the idea that serves to fuse a mass of details into a system relates to a person only as knower. All systems of

---

[16]Gregor Malantschuk, *Kierkegaard's Thought*, 7, 8, 12.

[17]*J. and P.*, 5100; *Pap.*, 1 A 75.

knowledge remain outside the self both in the sense of not relating to the whole self and in the sense that such a system is essentially public. In contrast, personal unity is essentially private in that each self must win unity for itself by actually coming to live for an idea. In this living for an idea, the idea is made as inward as possible; it becomes "something which is bound up with the deepest roots of my existence," giving the continuity and unity of self, the self-identity, that will allow the self to stand fast, "even though the whole world may collapse."

Despite his rejection of the connection between the unity of a system of knowledge and the unity of a self, Kierkegaard continues to draw on the former for terminology and images with which to discuss the latter. For example, immediately after characterizing a system as a body of knowledge that has a "focal point wherein all radii are collected," he writes, "I, too, have certainly looked for this focal point."[18] The sentences that follow leave no doubt that in this second use of "focal point," he is referring to an idea that may serve to unify his personal life.

It is apparent that in his earliest writings, Kierkegaard naturally associates the unity characteristic of systems of knowledge and the personal unity that is every self's task. At first, this association is so effortless that he assumes that the creation of the former would result in the creation of the latter. Even after rejecting such a belief, he continues to treat the two forms of unity as similar enough that the former yields metaphors by which the latter may be understood. These findings are surprising considering Kierkegaard's later criticisms of "the system." It is therefore appropriate to ask why, at least at this early stage of his development as a thinker, he made this association and what, if any, manifestations are to be found of it in his later works.

Romantic Philosophy of Nature
and the Idea of Unity

Even the most cursory examination of the intellectual milieu in which Kierkegaard matured yields the beginnings of an answer to the first of these questions. Little Denmark lay within the ambit of a cultural world that was defined by its larger neighbor to the south, Germany. For some time, this world had been dominated, perhaps even possessed, by the idea of unity.

---

[18]Ibid. (My translation.)

German philosophy focused its attention on this idea with Kant's disclosure that the formal unity of thought is a necessary condition of consciousness. The idea was already at work as an aesthetic principle in the writings of Goethe and Herder.[19] Only with the joint literary and philosophical movement of romanticism, however, did this idea assert itself as absolute. The best examples of the romantic development of this idea are perhaps to be found in the writings of Friedrich Schlegel and Schelling, respectively.[20]

Schelling's ideas were introduced to Denmark in 1803 with Henrik Steffens's *Indledning til philosophiske Forlæsninger* (*Introduction to Philosophical Lectures*). One need not look far in these lectures to find the idea of unity in all its power. In the second paragraph of his first lecture, Steffens requires of his listeners the knowledge expected of any educated man: an interest in solving the riddles of existence (*Tilværelse*) and the ability to "grasp every individual part together as a whole, to posit the absolute whole, the *One* as the real, and with this comprehensive intuition to exclude every foreign idea which is not necessarily thought in connection with the whole."[21]

Among those attending Steffens's lectures was Fredrik Christian Sibbern. Although not initially impressed, Sibbern went on to accept Schelling's philosophy as mediated by Steffens as the basis for much of his thought. This process was complete by 1813 as can be seen by the glowing

---

[19]Jens Himmelstrup, *Kierkegaard's Opfattelse af Sokrates* (Copenhagen: Arnold Busck, 1924) 23.

[20]"The thought of organic unity is the key to the romantic world view as a whole. The essential mark by which we can recognize this thought is a wish to see and grasp the phenomenon as a totality, and in this lies hidden the whole romantic quest for oneness. The thought is most clearly and thoroughly developed in Schelling. But Friedrich Schlegel from the beginning of his thought is also directed toward this goal. It is in reality Schlegel's program which Schelling realizes when he shows Nature and Spirit, world and man, to be a living unity in his *System des transcendentalen Idealism* (1800)." Ibid. (My translation.)

[21]Henrik Steffens, *Indledning til philosophiske Forelæsninger* (Copenhagen: Gyldendals, 1968) 5. (My translation.)

terms Sibbern uses to speak of his visit of that year with Schelling in Munich.[22]

Sibbern later became professor of philosophy at the University of Copenhagen and one of Kierkegaard's teachers. Of his teachers, Sibbern and Møller are among the select group not scorned by him and stand almost alone in receiving his warm praise. Kierkegaard developed a personal relationship with both men, though a somewhat closer one with Møller. Because of Møller's early death, it was Sibbern who served as the first reader of Kierkegaard's thesis, *The Concept of Irony*.[23] The evidence points to Sibbern as the immediate source of Kierkegaard's knowledge of the idea of unity as a philosophical principle.

Still-existing class rolls indicate that Kierkegaard attended Sibbern's lectures on logic in the summer of 1831.[24] An inspection of the book Sibbern developed out of his lectures on logic, *Logik son Tænkelære (Logic as a Doctrine of Thought)*, reveals the pervasive presence of the romantic belief that thought reaches its goal of knowledge only with an intuition of the absolute in which all multiplicity and separation are dissolved. Sibbern is by no means hostile to careful analysis and categorization of the given in all its multiplicity. He does, however, deny ultimacy to such thought. Analytic thinking is a necessary prelude to pure intuition (*blot Anskuelse*), but no more than that.

> We are here concerned with a given multiplicity (*Mangfoldighed*) which in order to be fully known must become the object of (a) a thoroughgoing and ordering separation (*Adskillen*), but this must be followed up in such a way that the knowledge of multiplicity (*Mangfoldighedserkjendelsen*) goes up into (b) a knowledge of oneness and wholeness (*en Eenheds-og Heelheds-erkjendelse*) by means of a self-constituting insight.[25]

---

[22]"Sibbern was most deeply influenced by Schelling and Steffens—or, as P. L. Møller expresses it, by Steffens's 'Christianized Schellingianism.' " Jens Himmelstrup, *Sibbern* (Copenhagen: J. H. Schutz, 1934) 76. (My translation.)

[23]Capel, Historical Introduction to *The Concept of Irony*, 10.

[24]Thulstrup, *Kierkegaard's Forhold til Hegel*, 38.

[25]Fredrick Christian Sibbern, *Logik* (Copenhagen: Paa Forfatterens Forlag,

Kierkegaard apparently had ample opportunity to learn of the contemporary philosophy's association of knowledge with the unification of parts in a perfect whole. It is, as yet, unclear why he associates the unity of a body of knowledge with the personal unity he seeks. Is Kierkegaard alone in making this association or is his thought following a path already worn by others?

A further inspection of Sibbern's works reveals that the young Kierkegaard's friend and teacher vigorously and explicitly asserts such a connection in *Om Erkjendelse og Granskning: Til Indledning i den akademiske Studium* (*On Knowledge and Research: An Introduction to the Academic Studium*). While the conception of knowledge and scientific methodology presented here is essentially the same as that seen in *Logik som Tænkelære*, this work's stated goal of introducing new students to the academic life makes appropriate comments not proper to a study of logic on the relationship between thought and life.

Three passages from this work are representative of the ways Sibbern treats the topic of personal unity and its relationship to the project of knowing the whole as the whole. The first of these passages is found in the preface to the work. Here, Sibbern addresses only the negative aspects of the relationship. The inquirer's status as an existing individual makes him prey to the distracting, disturbing, and warping powers at work in the world. To the extent that these forces gain control over his personal life, the inquirer is rendered incapable of achieving the desired intuition of the One. Thus, personal life is considered only insofar as it presents a possible obstacle to the completion of the task at hand.

> It is now our task to cast light from all sides on [the inquirer's (*den Studerendes*)] life-form, and to remind ourselves what it really is for which we, as inquirers, strive and ought to strive, what we, in the midst of a life in which so much diverts and confuses, pulls to one-sidedness, detains and delays, ought steadily to keep in view. When we succeed in this, a singular middle-point (*et ejendommeligt Middelpunkt*) shows itself around which

---

1859) 16-17. (My translation.) This work is a later, substantially revised version of *Logik som Tænkelære*. It is cited here rather than the 1835 edition that Kierkegaard owned because it expresses more succinctly the same thought. For an expression of the same thought in the earlier edition, see *Logik som Tænkelære* (Copenhagen: Paa Forfatterens Forlag, 1835) 27, 69.

the multiplicity that presents itself to observation may be collected into a unity (*samles til Eenhed*)[26]

The next passage treats the theme of personal unity more positively. It shows the personal unity of the inquiring self and the organic unity of knowledge to be closely analogous and mutually dependent.

> What speculation and the intuition (*den Skuen*) for which the Idea uninterruptedly stands in its totality as the One and the All from which all goes out and all returns is for science, having an ideal in sight, having the ideal in yourself and being inspired by and for it, is in the domain of the purely personal and individual. The ideal here referred to is the absolutely complete Science as the Idea's full, nothing lacking, presentation in which the whole will be seen in its infinite connections and significances. We have need of such a vision to reassure us in the face of the inadequacy of that which we have already achieved, to strengthen us in our fragmentary work and to determine that work with an eye to the goal of completeness. By means of such a vision, the partial results we already have point on to the final goal whose reality we already perceive and as it were already possess because we are on the way to it.[27]

As noted above, the forms of unity are here mutually dependent. Scientific unification is only possible when thinkers unify their lives around the ideal of its achievement. It would also appear from this passage that personal unification is only possible through dedication to the idea of the complete science.

Despite the reciprocity observed here, personal unity is subservient to the goal of the complete science. The sense of the passage is that the self should constitute itself as a unity around this ideal so that the intellectual goal might be reached. In the letter to Lund, Kierkegaard's reasoning runs in the opposite direction. While agreeing that scientific and personal unity are analogous and mutually dependent, his foremost interest is in the latter. He feels the need to bring some order to his scattered personal life and hopes that the activity of synthesizing disconnected bodies of information

---

[26]Fredrick Christian Sibbern, *Om Erkjendelse og Granskning* (Copenhagen: Fredrick Brummer Forlag, 1822) vi-vii. (My translation.)

[27]Ibid.

will reflect itself in his own soul. He is not devoted to any one science, but rather to the activity of constructing a science in general.

There is, then, a difference in emphasis between Sibbern and the Kierkegaard of the letter to Lund, but the two essentially agree in their understanding of the relation between thought and life. By the time of the Gilleleje entry, however, Kierkegaard rejects the notion that the two forms of unity are mutually dependent even if he continues to consider them analogous in many ways. With this issue decided, Kierkegaard declares that it is the internal, subjective unity won through absolute commitment to an idea that is essential, not the external, objective unity of a system of knowledge. It might be thought that in coming to this conclusion, Kierkegaard breaks radically with Sibbern. It is, however, more accurate to say that Kierkegaard isolates and more thoroughly develops the personalistic or even proto-existential additions Sibbern makes to Schelling's thought: the most stunningly mature passage from Kierkegaard's Gilleleje entry echoes, in part almost word for word, the third of the passages from *Om Erkjendelse og Granskning*. It will be recalled that Kierkegaard writes:

> What really matters is to find a purpose, to see what it really is that God wills that I shall do; the crucial thing is to find a truth which is truth for *me*, to find *the idea for which I am willing to live and die*.[28]

Compare this statement with the following one by Sibbern:

> There must be something of which man is so convinced, as of his own existence, that he will *live and die upon its truth*.[29]

The concern for the concrete life of the individual subject that shines through this last statement of Sibbern's is, in fact, characteristic of his thought as a whole. That concern is allowed only limited expression in the scientific and logical works dealt with above but asserts itself more decisively in Sibbern's works on religion, ethics, psychology, and art. This concern is, in fact, characteristic of Danish philosophy in general. In case

---

[28]*J. and P.*, 5100; *Pap.*, 1 A 75.

[29]Fredrick Christian Sibbern, *Om Erkjendelse og Granskning*, 178. The similarity between these two passages is pointed out by Malantschuk, *Kierkegaard's Thought*, 114. I follow the Hongs' translation of this passage.

after case, Danish thinkers follow the philosophical trends prevailing abroad but stamp the thus-received thought with a personalistic character all their own. The Danish historian of philosophy, Harold Høffding, comments on this tendency in his *Danske Filosofer* (*Danish Philosophers*).

> That Danish thought has its own peculiar character can be seen by comparing it with Swedish thought. Sweden's intellectual life has received the same influences from abroad as Denmark's, but these influences have been appropriated and developed by the Swedes in a different manner and in a different direction than by us. Speculation and mysticism have played a much larger role in Sweden than in Denmark and in the process, a desire for systematic completeness has asserted itself with them, which never found solid ground with us. Danish thought has essentially been borne by psychological and ethical interests and has again and again developed thoughtful critiques of system-building.[30]

An example of this tendency in Danish thought is the case of Niels Treschow. Treschow, who was one of Sibbern's teachers, introduced Kant's philosophy to Denmark in the 1790s. While he substantially agrees with Kant, he takes exception to the German's formalism in his treatment of the self. Treschow believes that the value and dignity of the individual self are only comprehensible if each such individual has an "essential character" or "core" that remains unchanged through all the alterations the self is subjected to as temporal. The purely formal unity of the self in Kant's philosophy, the possibility of joining "I think . . ." to any of the self's representations, lacks, according to Treschow, all relation to the individual qua individual. Treschow asks whether

> every human being as well as the species itself has a certain fundamental form or essential character which in the midst of all life's circumstances remains the same? Is the individual something other than a play of shifting forms or new determinations in which nothing is imperishable other than that which he has in common with all other selves, that is, with universal human nature? Or are these changes only successive developments of a core . . . which continues to maintain its essential character. Is the final goal toward which each self, even if unconsciously, strives that pattern, in truth

---

[30]Harold Høffding, *Danske Filosofer* (Copenhagen: Gyldendals, 1909) 1-2. (My translation.)

an infinite idea, after which he (as an individual) must be formed so that despite all multiplicity and apparent conflict, he has an internal oneness and imperishable steadfastness in himself? It is clear that only in the latter case does each individual have an indescribable value; in the former case, the species alone has that value.[31]

The similarity between Treschow's concern that the individual self constitute a changeless and unified entity in the midst of change and multiplicity and the concerns of Kierkegaard and Sibbern discussed above is striking. There is also a noticeable similarity in terminology. Both Treschow and Kierkegaard speak of an idea internal to the self that makes possible the oneness of the self in the face of multiplicity. Sibbern uses the word *ideal* in much the same way.

Despite these similarities, Treschow addresses the issue of the unity and continuity of the self in a different and less effective manner than Kierkegaard. Treschow argues in *Forelæsninger over den Kantische Philosophie* (*Lectures on Kantian Philosophy*) that the soul must be a simple substance and therefore immune to destruction.[32] To establish the integrity of the individual self in such a way is to return to the project of certain Medievals, notably Duns Scotus, who sought with the doctrine of *haecceitas* to reconcile the soul's incorruptibility as a form with its essential individuality.[33] Kierkegaard rejects all such notions of a substantial self, even when an effort is made to make room for individuality. Such theories make self-identity a possession, a given, rather than a task.

In addressing the question of why Kierkegaard so naturally associates the unity of a system of knowledge with the personal unity of a self, I have shown that concern for both forms of unity and a tendency to associate them

---

[31]Niels Treschow, "Gives der noget Begreb eller Nogen Ide om enslige Ting?" in *Vid. Selsk. Skr.* (*Videnskabelige Selskabs Skrifter*?) 1810, cited by Anders Thuborg, *Den Kantiske Period i Danske Filosofi: 1790-1800* (Copenhagen: Gyldendals, 1951) 27-28. (My translation.)

[32]Niels Treschow, *Forelæsninger over den Kantische Philosophie* (Copenhagen: Gyldendals, 1798) 203, 205, 213, 215. (My translation.)

[33]For a brief analysis of this concept, see Efiem Bettoni, *Duns Scotus*, trans. B. Bonansea (Washington DC: Catholic University of America Press, 1961) 60-65.

were rife in the intellectual circles in which he moved as a young student at the university. What, if any, manifestations of this association are to be found in his later writings?

An inspection of those writings reveals that while continuing to regard unity as a sine qua non of both a science and a self, Kierkegaard comes not only to deny the interdependence of the two forms of unity but also to cease to consider them analogous. In fact, in the *Postscript* Kierkegaard explicitly and vehemently asserts their dissimilarity. The unity to which science aspires is systematic; the incompleteness and constant becoming of existence render such a system impossible. Since the unity characteristic of a self must be compatible with the self's status as an existing being, it is clear that the self's oneness must be of a qualitatively different nature. As this study will later investigate the various forms this personal unity takes, it is enough for the moment to note that Kierkegaard's association of the two types of unity is confined to the earliest stages of his development as a thinker.

CHAPTER II

Unity as an Aesthetic Principle

Scientific, systematic unity is not the only form of "external" unity recognized by Kierkegaard. Throughout his career as a thinker, he was convinced that every true work of art is an essential unity. This conviction stands out as a rare common element in his varied and rather fragmentary ventures in art criticism. As Marete Jørgensen writes in *Kierkegaard som Kritiker* (*Kierkegaard as Critic*):

> [For Kierkegaard] the primary criterion for a successful work of art (or performance) is the presence of unity and coherence (*enhed og sammenhæng*); . . . the individual parts must be motivated by and illuminate the dominant idea of the whole.[1]

---

[1] Marete Jørgensen, *Kierkegaard som Kritiker* (Copenhagen: Gyldendals, 1978) 60. (My translation.)

Whereas Kierkegaard's youthful enthusiasm for the sciences and their synthetic operations is replaced by hostility as he matures, his interest in and love for art continues throughout his life. Obviously, the coherence of a work of art is "external" in contrast to the "internal" unity of a properly ordered self; to this extent, it resembles the unity of a system of knowledge. The question is whether Kierkegaard regards these two varieties of external unity as so alike that they share the independence of and indifference to personal, internal unity characteristic of science, or whether he sees the unity of a work of art as somehow more integrally connected with personal unity.

Answering this question requires further determination of Kierkegaard's understanding of art. The following journal entry, though specifically related to poetry (*Digtning*), that is, art whose medium is language, serves nicely to communicate Kierkegaard's view of art in general.

> All poetry is glorification (i.e. transfiguration) [*Forklarelse*: transfiguration] of life by way of its clarification [*Forklarelse*] (in that it is explained, illuminated, developed, etc.). It is truly remarkable that language has this ambiguity.[2]

In one of the few pieces published in English on Kierkegaard's aesthetics versus his treatment of the aesthetic stage of existence, Stephen Crites explains such transfiguration/clarification as the purification and isolation in a work of art of ideas already present in actuality. The artist by means of imagination transfers these ideas from the hurly-burly of existence, in which they are never perfectly instantiated, into the lucid, timeless, and ideal world of art. Just as these ideas must be separated from actuality in order to enter the realm of ideality, each observer of art must at least temporarily lay aside the vestments of his actuality in order to enter the realm of ideality in which aesthetic experience takes place.

It is entirely appropriate, Kierkegaard thought, to approach art as a time-

---

[2] *J. and P.*, 136; *Pap.*, 2 A 352, cited by Rune Engebretsen, *Kierkegaard and Poet-Existence with Special Reference to Germany and Rilke* (Ph.D. diss., Stanford University, 1980) 114.

less observer, since one's aesthetic satisfaction consists precisely in being brought into a relation to pure ideas through an appropriate medium.[3]

In such a view, works of art, like systems of knowledge, are essential unities unrelated to the unity of the existing self. This finding coincides with Kierkegaard's statements in the *Postscript* associating speculation and aestheticism on the basis of their desertion of actuality for ideality. In fact, speculation is identified as a variety of aestheticism, the latter category being expanded from its modern restriction to things artistic to coincide with its etymological association with perception and observation in general (*aisthanomai*—to perceive, to notice, from *theaomai*—to watch, to gaze at).[4]

While this characterization of Kierkegaard's view of art finds copious support in the authorship, it clashes violently with the approach to art taken in several works of criticism lying outside the boundaries of the authorship.[5] The best example of such a work is *Af en Endnu Levendes Papirer* (*From the Papers of One Still Living*).

---

[3]Stephen Crites, Introductory Essay to *A Crisis in the Life of an Actress* by Søren Kierkegaard, trans. Stephen Crites (New York: Harper and Row, 1967) 28.

[4]Ibid.

[5]One of the texts I include in this latter group is *The Two Ages*. In placing it outside the authorship proper, I follow the scholarly consensus. However, it appears that Kierkegaard takes exception to such a view in his journal entry of 9 August 1851, in which he records and comments on a conversation with Bishop Mynster. Since the continuity of his works was the topic of discussion, Kierkegaard's comments can be construed simply to mean that *The Two Ages* takes its place within the overall Kierkegaardian project as it is described in *The Point of View for My Work as an Author* rather than as placing the work within the authorship in the technical sense of the term. This is indicated by Kierkegaard's issuing of this work under his own name. Curiously, he speaks in this entry as if *The Two Ages* were pseudonymously published. "I did make the remark [to Mynster] that this review is essentially part of the whole authorship and that I attributed it to another because there were things I wanted to have said but at that time felt unable to say them as well myself." *J. and P.*, 6804; *Pap.*, 10 A 558, cited by the Hongs in an appendix to Søren Kierkegaard, *The Two Ages*, trans. Howard V. Hong and Edna H. Hong (Princeton: Princeton University Press, 1978) 151.

Af en Endnu Levendes Papirer is Kierkegaard's "debut book," appearing in September 1838, almost five years before the publication of *Either/Or*. In this slight but ponderously written work, Kierkegaard undertakes a study of Hans Christian Andersen's activity as a novelist. He measures Andersen's work against the standard of organic unity and finds it desperately lacking. Surprisingly, given Crites's description of Kierkegaard's aesthetics, Kierkegaard concludes that Andersen is unable to produce an organically unified work of art because he lacks a life-view (*Livanskuelse*),[6] and is, therefore, disunified in his personal existence. This conclusion appears to return to the view that internal and external unities are essentially related, but here external unity (the unity of a work of art) depends on the internal, personal unity of its creator. This order of dependence reverses that seen in the letter to Lund, where the hope was expressed that the construction of external unity would reflect itself in the ordering of the self.

By making the personal unity of the author an essential concern of a work of criticism, Kierkegaard's practice is at variance with the theory of art attributed to him by Crites. Is Crites in error or does Kierkegaard fail to abide by his own aesthetic principles? The answer to this question will also be the answer to the original question as to Kierkegaard's understanding of the relationship between art and the artist. If Crites is right and *Af en Endnu Levendes Papirer* is an aberration, the unity of a work of art stands indifferent and unrelated to its creator or beholder much as a scientific system does. If, however, this little work truly represents his aesthetic theory, then Kierkegaard distinguishes between the two forms of external unity and admits a more integral, though as yet indeterminate, link between art and artist than between theory and theorist.

---

[6]*Livsanskuelse* is defined in the multi-volume *Ordbog over den Danske Sprog* as "the individual human being's (purely subjective) view of and thoughts on life; the human being's stance in the whole process of world development, attitude toward the after-life, etc." The word apparently entered the Danish language in the early nineteenth century and was formed by "Danisizing" the German *Lebensanschauung*. I follow the Hongs in translating it as "life-view," but Capel's rendering of it as "an organic view of life" underlines the dimension of unity and totality essential to the concept.

Frithiof Brandt in his *Den Unge Søren Kierkegaard* (*The Young Søren Kierkegaard*) interprets his subject's emphasis on Andersen's person in a way favorable to the former alternative. Following his usual practice of explaining Kierkegaard's writings in terms of his interactions with contemporaries, Brandt sees the discussion of Andersen's personal inadequacies as part of a feud between the two giants of Danish literature. He argues that the appearance of Andersen's *Lykkens Galoscher* (*The Galoches of Fortune*) in May 1838, in which Kierkegaard is caricatured as a parrot constantly screeching Heibergian slogans, changed Kierkegaard's intention in *Af en Endnu Levendes Papirer* from serious criticism to personal vendetta.[7]

After viewing the paltry image Brandt conjures forth, it is a relief to read Aage Henriksen's response:

> One feels an urge to protest in the name of reason and decency; this is not the way it happens. Even humans can be underrated. And at any rate cogent proofs, preferably confessions, are required before we can hope to hit the mark on aiming so low. There exist no confessions.[8]

Beyond the initial presumption of good faith owed any writer, there is considerable evidence against dismissing, as a departure from his theory, Kierkegaard's consideration of Andersen's person. The principle that the presence or absence of unity in a work of art is to be explained by the presence or absence of a unifying life-view in its creator is applied throughout *Af en Endnu Levendes Papirer*, even when Andersen is not under discussion. Kierkegaard not only deduces the presence but also the character of the life-view held by Thomasine Christine Gyllembourg, the anonymous author of *Hverdagshistorien* (*A Story of Everyday Life*), on the basis of the unity and coherence he observes in that author's works. Kierkegaard sets these works beside Andersen's in order to make manifest the inadequacies of the latter. Seven years later in *The Two Ages*, he returns to the works of

---

[7]Frithiof Brandt, *Den Unge Søren Kierkegaard* (Copenhagen: Munksgaard, 1929) 126-26, 130-31, 137.

[8]Aage Henriksen, *Methods and Results of Kierkegaard Studies in Scandinavia: A Historical and Critical Study* (Copenhagen: Munksgaard, 1951) 103.

Fru Gyllembourg to reaffirm his deep respect for them and, in the process, his adherence to the aesthetic principles of *Af en Endnu Levendes Papirer*.[9]

A further suggestion that Crites's interpretation of Kierkegaard's aesthetics is incomplete, if not in error, is that in both *Af en Endnu Levendes Papirer* and *The Two Ages* Kierkegaard takes the position that the task of the author is not simply to entertain but, more fundamentally, to communicate a view of life that will, directly or indirectly, clarify reality for his readers. The artist is to use his art to bring to life a particular stance toward existence, a distinctive and comprehensive view of how things stand and how one ought to act. In the process of presenting this specific life-view, he also communicates at a more general level the possibility of an ordered life. Even if the reader rejects the particular life-view offered, he is stimulated to clarify his own outlook on life by determining where and how he differs. Thus, whether he agrees or disagrees, the artistic representation of a life-view encourages the reader to rise above the muddled manyness of daily life to a coherent view of things. Ideally, the life-view thus developed will come to structure the reader's actual existence as decisively as it orders the author's novel.

It should come as no surprise that Kierkegaard voices such a theory of art since it describes his own practice in the authorship, especially in its more novelistic instances. In creating ideally consistent representative personages—A, Johannes the seducer, Judge William, Constantine Constantius, Quidam, and so forth—and letting them come to voice, Kierkegaard shows the various possible life-views from within. He consistently describes his intention as, first, to let each way of existing stand forth as a distinct alternative. This mode of presentation forces a choice on readers who have previously and inconsistently moved haphazardly from one way of living to another; he precipitates an either/or out of a both/and.

In the definition of poetry cited above as indicative of Kierkegaard's view of art as a whole, the functions of transfiguration and clarification, both rendered by the Danish *Forklarelse* were preeminent. It is now ap-

---

[9] "What I first wrote was in the nature of a review or, more correctly, an effusive discourse on these novels. Since then I have not tried my hand as a reviewer. Now, after seven years, I want a second and a last try at it. . . . I trust (the unknown author) will find me unchanged, or, if possible, changed in the repetition." *The Two Ages*, 23; *S.V.*, 14:25.

parent that the equivocality of *Forklarelse* is deeper than Kierkegaard indicated in that journal entry. The *Forklarelse* discussed by Crites involves the separation of ideal forms from actuality; that is, clarification is achieved by abandoning actuality for the ideal realm of art. In *Af en Endnu Levendes Papirer* and *The Two Ages* as well as other works, *Forklarelse* indicates the transfiguration and clarification *of* actuality by means of a withdrawal and return that allows the development of a structuring and ordering lifeview.

This second equivocality of *Forklarelse* indicates a fundamental split between the approaches to art taken in Kierkegaard's writings.[10] A further investigation of this split is critical in determining his resolution of the question of the relationship of internal and external unities. The first Kierkegaardian aesthetic presents the unity of a work of art as uninvolved with the personal unities of the artist and the audience. The second aesthetic asserts a relationship between the unity of a work of art and the personal unities of both the artist and the audience.

Since the second of the two aesthetics has apparently gone unnoticed in English language scholarship (and is substantially unrecognized even in Danish secondary literature) and because much clarification is still needed of the relationships postulated by this aesthetic between the work of art, the artist, and the audience, this investigation will begin with a closer examination of *Af en Endnu Levendes Papirer*.[11] Other works will be ex-

---

[10] The existence of this split is the principal thesis of Marete Jørgensen's *Kierkegaard som Kritiker*. Jørgensen classifies Kierkegaard's various writings on art into two categories. Those that embody the approach to art discussed by Crites she calls "the aesthetic critique." Those whose theoretical basis is in essence that of *Af en Endnu Levendes Papirer* constitute "the ethical critique."

[11] Though he places his name on the title page of this book as responsible for its publication, Kierkegaard attributes the work to an undisclosed friend whom he describes as his "alter ego." While an eloquent testimony to the tremendous gap between the public and the private Kierkegaard at this point in time (he presented himself as a witty, sociable, brilliant, young protégé of Heiberg while so overwhelmed with melancholy that he was contemplating suicide), it also represents an important step on the way to the pseudonymous authorship.

I will not recapitulate the scholarly battles that have been fought over the work's mysterious title, but refer the interested reader to the following sources: Frithiof

amined insofar as this serves to illuminate the at times obscure and attenuated argument of this work.

Kierkegaard sets the stage for his critique of Andersen by "orient[ing] [himself] in [the contemporary] novel and short story literature."[12] Considering that Kierkegaard writes during the golden age of Danish literature, it might seem strange that in this orientation he considers only the works of Steen Steenson Blicher and Fru Gyllembourg. This procedure is understandable, however, in light of his rather formalistic aesthetics, which is concerned less with literary history than with using actual examples to illustrate ideal types. Blicher's work is cited here as an example of lyric prose while Fru Gyllembourg's writings represent epic prose.

As is so often the case with Kierkegaard, his thought here turns on an axis whose poles are immediacy and reflection. Reversing the order postulated in Hegel's aesthetics, but following the Danish Hegelian aesthetician Heiberg, Kierkegaard identifies lyric art with immediacy, epic and dramatic art with reflection.[13] By considering the works of Blicher and Gyllembourg, Kierkegaard establishes the characteristics of aesthetically valid immediate and reflective art, thus setting the boundaries of the aesthetically illegitimate no-man's land within which he intends to place Andersen.

As noted above, Kierkegaard sees essential unity as the common characteristic of all true works of art. This quality is stressed in the positive comments he makes about the works of Gyllembourg and Blicher. Though these comments are brief, especially in the case of Blicher, they are sufficient to prove that to Kierkegaard, unity manifests itself in qualitatively different ways in these two types of art.

In discussing Gyllembourg's work, Kierkegaard continually claims that it is her personal development of a life-view that is responsible for her suc-

---

Brandt, "Af en Endnu Levendes Papirer," in *Syv Kierkegaard Studier*; P. P. Rohde, "Den Endnu Levende," in *Gaadefulde Stadier paa Kierkegaard's Vej* (Copenhagen: Rosenkilde og Bagger, 1974); Malantschuk, *Kierkegaard's Thought*, 186; Carl Jørgensen, *Søren Kierkegaard*, 1:96; Henriksen, *Methods and Results of Kierkegaard Studies in Scandinavia*, 103-105.

[12]*S.V.*, 1:24, cited by the Hongs in an appendix to *The Two Ages*, 123. (Unless otherwise indicated, all quotations from this work are my translations.)

[13]*S.V.*, 1:336, 7.

cess as a novelist. Kierkegaard's principal use of "life-view," both here in *Af en Endnu Levendes Papirer* and throughout his writings, is to indicate an individual subject's all-embracing stance toward and understanding of the cosmos. The following passage illustrates an alternate but related use:

> Essentially, a life-view plays the part of providence in the novel; it is the novel's deeper unity which provides it with an interior center of gravity; it frees the novel from becoming pointless because the purpose is immanently present everywhere in the work of art.[14]

Here, "life-view" indicates the structuring idea of the novel rather than the idea defining the life and thought of a person. From his willingness to employ the same term in both cases, it is obvious that Kierkegaard considers the two types of unifying idea to be closely related. In fact, he indicates that the two differ only in regard to the media in which they are deployed.

> [This study of Gyllembourg's work] takes place . . . out of consideration of the life-view contained therein, which just as surely has its corresponding element in existence as its presupposition.[15]

Thus, the act of creation in the case of reflective art is essentially a *re-creation* in an external medium of the idea or life-view that orders the personal life of the artist.[16] This statement explains both why consideration of the person of the artist is appropriate in the critical appraisal of a work of art and why art differs from science in its relationship to the personal lives of its practitioners. Because reflective creation is essentially re-creation, an artist who undertakes to create a work of art without having achieved

---

[14]Ibid., 1:39, cited by Malantschuk, *Kierkegaard's Thought*, 186.

[15]*S.V.*, 1:24; Malantschuk, *Kierkegaard's Thought*, 124.

[16]As this principle stands, it is entirely too restrictive. Later, Kierkegaard loosens it somewhat by allowing an author to bring to expression a life-view that he has previously held as well as that which he currently holds. This is still a very restrictive theory of art, but we must give Kierkegaard credit for practicing what he preaches. He steadfastly refuses to write about any stage of existence he has not personally lived. (Writings from the hand of Anti-Climacus are the exception that proves this rule.)

beforehand a life-view will only reproduce his own disunity and confusion in his product, thus foreordaining its failure as a work of art. This intimate relationship between the internal and external unities is characteristic of art and not science because more than a difference in medium is involved in the distinction between the unity of a person and the unity of a scientific system. The world of the novel, the art form to which Kierkegaard always refers in his discussions of the aesthetic role of a life-view, is such a human world, it lies so close to our subjective, personal encounter with reality, that the same unifying idea may be deployed in both realms. In fact, much of the pleasure of reading fiction results from the experience of a world like the one in which we dwell, but which shows a comprehensibility and coherence we ideally could, but seldom do, enjoy in our daily experience.

The structuring ideas of the natural sciences, mathematics, and logic are qualitatively different and altogether unsuited to expression in a human medium. The human sciences constitute an uncertain middle ground, a point nicely indicated by the dispute in the philosophy of history over whether history is a science that should aim to establish and apply covering laws or is the coherent retelling of past events along the lines of a novel.

While a life-view is a structuring idea with a personal, subjective component alien to the structuring idea of the sciences, as an idea, it has an intellectual dimension foreign to immediacy and immediate art. Thus, the unity characteristic of immediate art must be different from that of reflective art. Though Kierkegaard's chosen representative of lyric prose, Blicher, receives only limited treatment in *Af en Endnu Levendes Papirer*, the treatment he does receive is sufficient to show that the unity of lyric art is a function of mood rather than idea.

> Instead of the life-view present in the short-stories of the author of *Hverdagshistorien* . . . there stands forth here a profound poetical mood wrapt in the misty veil of immediacy.[17]

Kierkegaard's most illuminating comments on mood as the unifying factor in immediate art are addressed not to the subject of lyric prose but to the even more immediate art form: music. In "The Immediate Stages of the Erotic" of the first volume of *Either/Or*, the young aesthete, A, discusses the distinction between opera and drama, the former being the mu-

---

[17]*S.V.*, 1:28.

Personal Unity in Kierkegaard's Thought

sical and, hence, immediate form of theater, the latter being reflective and genuinely linguistic. A points out that while in dramatic art a definite idea bonds the discrete moments of the depicted situation into "a unity of action," "that which preserves the unity in the opera is the keynote which dominates the whole production."[18]

After indicating the characteristics of successful immediate and reflective art through his sketch of Blicher and Gyllembourg's work, Kierkegaard turns to the principal task of *Af en Endnu Levendes Papirer*: the criticism of Andersen as an artist. While the emphasis here is on the evaluation of his activity as a novelist, Andersen's earlier lyric productions also receive attention. Kierkegaard argues that the resemblance these pieces bear to the writings of Blicher is only superficial. Andersen tries to evoke the *folkelig,* but where Blicher is "a full-toned organ for folk-consciousness," Andersen "moves through a scale of tones as easily waked as they are again silenced."[19] The result is that Andersen's lyric writings are the same "weave of accidental moods" in which Andersen, as a person, finds himself snared. Neither immediately nor reflectively imbued with a single, unifying mood, Andersen's lyric productions fail as art.

Just as he fails to measure up to Blicher in the realm of lyric art, Andersen fails to measure up to Gyllembourg as a novelist. Andersen's novels are the same jumble of accidental, unsynthesized elements as his lyric productions. While Kierkegaard documents this assertion at some length in the last third of *Af en Endnu Levendes Papirer*, it is his explanation of Andersen's failure that is of interest to this study. According to Kierkegaard, "Andersen altogether lacks a life-view,"[20] and is therefore condemned as a person and an artist to reflect the inconstancy and disorder of existence.

Kierkegaard considers two defenses of Andersen that might be brought against his criticism of *Af en Endnu Levendes Papirer*. Kierkegaard's responses to these defenses illuminate his critical position.

---

[18]Søren Kierkegaard, *Either/Or*, vol. 1, trans. David F. Swenson and Lillian M. Swenson; vol. 2, trans. Walter Lowrie, 2d ed. rev. Howard A. Johnson (Princeton: Princeton University Press, 1971) 1:116-17; *S.V.*, 2:110-11.

[19]*S.V.*, 1:29.

[20]Ibid., 1:34.

The first defense offered is that it is unfair to demand a finished and comprehensive life-view of one so young as Andersen. Kierkegaard willingly admits that Andersen is young but excludes this bit of personal information as irrelevant to the project of aesthetic criticism. "[W]e are here concerned only with Andersen as a novelist."[21]

Kierkegaard's willingness to sort his subject's personal characteristics into those belonging to Andersen qua novelist and those that are purely personal and hence irrelevant brings us face to face with the rather paradoxical heart of the aesthetic of *Af en Endnu Levendes Papirer*. The irrelevance of the author's purely personal characteristics is in keeping with the aesthetic principle that the work of the art should be an essential unity. The work should be sufficient to itself and not require for its appreciation information about the author's history, intentions, likes, dislikes, ideology, and so forth. The paradox is that not despite but because of such a theoretical basis *Af en Endnu Levendes Papirer* continually returns to the subject of Andersen's person. Marete Jørgensen comments on the way in which demanding artistic unity leads to a consideration of the author's life-view or lack thereof.

> Generally, one can say of Kierkegaard's method that it is very work centered. He takes his point of departure in the work and finds there the steering idea behind the work; that is to say he analyzes that which creates the work's unity—and by the same token . . . [he investigates] the places where the unity is broken, the places where the work's inner contradictions come forth. Since unity is created on the basis of the author's life-view, [the critic] can in this way come to analyze [that life-view]. . . . The work is thus criticized on its own premises.[22]

Here, the author's life-view is said to be appropriate subject matter for critical discussion on the basis of its special causal relation to the integrity of the work of art. While an artist's purely personal characteristics may also affect his work of art, the life-view's special status as a necessary condition of artistic unity sets it apart as the one aspect of the artist germane to the critical discussion of his creation.

---

[21]Ibid., 1:35.

[22]Marete Jørgensen, *Kierkegaard som Kritiker*, 107. (My translation.)

The second defense is that Andersen does in fact have a life-view. As even Kierkegaard admits, "there is one idea that persistently recurs in Andersen's novels."[23] This idea is that creative personalities, geniuses, must be favorably treated by fortune, must enjoy conducive circumstances and surroundings, in order to produce. This theme is especially dominant in *Kun en Spillemand* (*Only a Fiddler*), Andersen's thinly veiled autobiographical novel, which Kierkegaard singles out for detailed criticism in *Af en Endnu Levendes Papirer*.

Such a view is inimical to Kierkegaard's already firmly established sense of defiant individualism. He calls such a notion "thorough-going womanishness,"[24] and accuses it of no more deserving the title *life-view* than skepticism deserves to be called a theory of knowledge. He argues that Andersen portrays not a genius, whose power is only intensified by the challenges of misfortune, but a "sniveller."[25]

No matter how deep his moral outrage at Andersen's fundamental idea in *Kun en Spillemand*, Kierkegaard must show why this idea is *aesthetically* inferior to the ideas behind successful novels or else shift his criticism from an aesthetic to an ethical plane. Kierkegaard believes that Andersen's idea cannot be the basis of a successful novel because it cannot properly mediate between the artist and his work, because it is part and parcel of an improper relationship between the author and his creation. According to Kierkegaard, this idea is not the sublimate but the reflex of An-

---

[23] *S.V.*, 1:37.

[24] Ibid., 1:38.

[25] So deep is Kierkegaard's offense at Andersen's "theory of perdition" that Georg Brandes, in the first serious critical work on Kierkegaard published, attributes to this offense the overall acrimony and harshness of *Af en Endnu Levendes Papirer*. "[T]he fundamental thought in Andersen's novel struck Kierkegaard at a decisive point in his own thought-life, had offended him almost personally by inciting that which was best in him, his courage in relation to the external. What infuriated him was the doctrine Andersen had produced on genius, a doctrine of passivity, that genius needed care, sympathetic surrounding and a certain tepid warmness in order to put forth fruit, and that without this support it would or must go under." Georg Brandes, "Søren Kierkegaard: En Kritiske Fremstilling i Grundrids," in *Samlede Værker* (Copenhagen: Gyldendals, 1899) 2:272-73; cited by Frithiof Brandt, *Den Unge Søren Kierkegaard*, 124-25.

dersen's experience in life, a fact that coincides with the doctrine of passivity contained in the idea.

> A great number of admittedly poetic wishes, longings, etc., after having been held back within Andersen for a long time by the prosaic world, seek to immigrate to that little world accessible to poetic spirits, where the true poet celebrates his Sabbath in the midst of life's travail. But hardly have these arrived and been incorporated in new individuals before the pixies already loudly proclaim their arrival, in other words, before a long train of depressing observations about life [appear] either in the form of [lamentations about] blind fate or the evil in the world (namely reality) which choke the good. [These observations] grow with the luxuriance of the tares in the gospel while Andersen sleeps. In vain [he] works against them, but he soon abandons his efforts and, turning to the opposite side, irritated and annoyed as he is with the real world, he seeks in the dispiritedness [*Forknyttelse*] of his poetic creation satisfaction for his own dispiritedness.[26]

Restated in clearer and less picturesque language, Andersen, when faced with unfortunate circumstances as a child, develops his imagination as a means of escaping an unpleasant reality. It is on the basis of his powerful imagination that Andersen becomes a writer and ultimately a great literary success. While the original use of imagination was the creation of more pleasant fantasy worlds, a hostility to reality and a concomitant sense of being wronged by fortune soon makes its way over to the fictional realms, changing imagination's task from simple escapism to a maudlin exercise in self-pity. Kierkegaard thus explains the recurrent theme of genius's need for the tender care of fortune and the repeated teary-eyed submission of Andersen's stand-in, Christian, to all manner of unfortunate circumstances.

Andersen's use of the novel to pursue purely personal agendas destroys the novel's integrity. It places author and novel in an immediate relation to each other when they should stand as separate, mutually independent unities. So close is Andersen's person to his fictional creations that Kierkegaard remarks, "[His] novels stand in so physical a relation to him that their coming into existence is not so much to be seen as

---

[26]*S.V.*, 1:33.

a production as an amputation."[27] Andersen's identification with his surrogate in the novel is so complete that, "when the hero dies, Andersen dies with him," losing control of the novel and managing only a morose sigh over their common fate as the work's conclusion.

Kierkegaard argues that Andersen's lack of a life-view and his improper relation to his artistic creations are essentially related. The following passage, which was partially cited above, makes this point:

> Essentially, a life view plays the part of providence in a novel; it is the novel's deeper unity which provides it with an interior center of gravity; it frees the novel from becoming arbitrary or pointless, because the purpose is immanently present everywhere in the work of art. When, on the other hand, such a life-view is lacking, the novel seeks at the expense of poetry to insinuate some theory or other (dogmatic, doctrinaire novels) or else stands in a finite and accidental relation to the author's flesh and blood . . . (subjective novels).[28]

He goes on to say,

> [T]he poet must first and foremost win for himself an authentic personality. . . . [O]nly such a dead and transfigured personality . . . is able to produce—not angular, earthly, palpable persons . . . [in whose works] is found a residue of the author's finite character which like an impertinent person or badly reared child often speaks in the improper places.[29]

It is clear that Kierkegaard's critical interest in the person of the author, his life-view or lack thereof, stems directly from his insistence that a work of art be an essential unity. The life-view that the author and the work share, while insuring that, "the particular production will not have a merely external relation to the poet,"[30] also frees the two from each other. It is the structuring idea that mediates between, that both joins and separates, the two. It frees the novel by filtering out any accidental or purely personal

---

[27]Ibid., 1:41.

[28]Ibid., 1:39. I use in part the Hongs' translation of this passage which appears in Malantschuk, *Kierkegaard's Thought*, 186.

[29]Ibid., 1:39-40.

[30]*The Concept of Irony*, 337; *S.V.*, 1:327.

aspects of the author that might have been included. It frees the author in that it constantly reminds him that his novel is, after all, only a novel by preventing him from transforming it into a magical realm into which he may escape and with the stroke of a pen resolve or dissolve his personal problems.

An objection might be raised here by recalling the assertion that persuasion and not entertainment is the primary goal of art according to the Kierkegaardian aesthetic of *Af en Endnu Levendes Papirer*. How can Kierkegaard see the role of the novel as persuasion and yet reject as aesthetically invalid "the doctrinaire novel"? The answer is that Kierkegaard never understands by "persuasion" an attempt by one person to force his views on another, whether it be by art or any other means. He writes in *The Two Ages*:

> What does it mean to persuade, how does one define this concept philosophically and affirm its noble character, paying attention to the fact that here it is not a matter of a relationship between two individuals but of the relationship of a life-view to a recipient.[31]

Here, again, the life-view appears in its liberating, separating role. By means of the life-view, the novel stands apart from its author, thus allowing the true relationship of an individual (the reader) to a life-view (in its fictional embodiment) that he can choose to accept or reject rather than the false relationship in which one person tries to impose a life-view on another. The deep connections between Kierkegaard's theory of art and his more general theory of communication are evident here.

Why, then, are two distinct aesthetics to be found in Kierkegaard's writings? It will be remembered that both approaches to art make unity the sine qua non of successful art. While the aesthetic employed in the critique of Andersen gives an account of artistic unity and thereby identifies its necessary conditions, the "aesthetic critique"[32] lacks the theoretical basis to say more about the source of this unity than that the artist is "fortunate." Marete Jørgensen is correct in attributing this difference between the two aesthetics to a difference in perspective. While the "ethical critic"

---

[31]*The Two Ages*, 20; *S.V.*, 14:22.

[32]Marete Jørgensen, *Kierkegaard som Kritiker*, 30.

(that is, the aesthetician who follows the principles of criticism employed in *Af en Endnu Levendes Papirer* and similar works) writes from an existential position high enough to comprehend the functions and importance of a life-view, the "aesthetic critic" does not. The instances of aesthetic criticism that Marete Jørgensen identifies are for the most part writings attributed to representatives of the aesthetic stage, notably the young aesthete A and Constantine Constantius. These aesthetes are described as "possibilities of a personality," exactly as Andersen is characterized in *Af en Endnu Levendes Papirer*. Like Andersen, they have failed to develop a life-view and are thereby precluded from comprehending its role in artistic production. Also like Andersen, they are incapable of producing works of art that meet the standards of unity by which they themselves judge art. This inability is especially evident in the fragmentary, disordered, and parasitic character of A's writings in the first volume of *Either/Or*.

The difference in the existential position of the practitioners of the two aesthetics also underlies their divergence from each other as regards their desire for unity in a work of art. The ethical critic sees art as the clarification *of* existence. By means of a life-view contained in the work of art, the chaos of existence is tamed and order won, even if only in a fictional realm. The reader is challenged in the process to adopt the life-view as his own or to reject it in favor of an alternative, but at any rate to order his own life. Such art departs from the real for the ideal only as to inspire a return to the real.

For the aesthete, on the other hand, art constitutes an ideal realm removed from reality where he may flee and thus avoid the trials and sorrows of existence. This is exactly the escapism characteristic of Andersen's art. Such a "resolution" of the dilemmas posed by existence is analogous to that attributed by Johannes Climacus to self-forgetful objective thinkers. Both seek fulfillment of their aspirations by simply abandoning, be it by imagination or abstraction, the existential, temporal component of themselves.

Despite this similarity to the intellectual desertion of existence so roundly condemned in the *Postscript*, Crites does not believe that Kierkegaard rejects the approach to art taken by the aesthete. In fact, he describes it as Kierkegaard's own.

> If an aesthetic treatment of ethics and religion must necessarily and fundamentally distort the ethical and religious life, it is nevertheless obvious

that no such problem exists for an aesthetic treatment of art. It is entirely appropriate, Kierkegaard thought, to approach art as a timeless observer, since one's aesthetic satisfaction consists precisely in being brought into relation to pure ideas through an appropriate medium.[33]

Crites's position is impossible to maintain in light of the fact that such a view of art is endorsed only in pseudonymous writings while numerous works bearing Kierkegaard's own name, notably *Af en Endnu Levendes Papirer*, *The Concept of Irony*, and *The Two Ages* condemn it. It is more plausible to assert as does Marete Jørgensen that the aesthetic of these last mentioned works is Kierkegaard's own, while that employed by the pseudonyms is symptomatic of an improper existential stance and thus rejected by Kierkegaard.

A necessary qualification of this conclusion may be made by anticipating a possible objection to it on the basis of a passage in the introduction to *The Two Ages*. Speaking of Fru Gyllembourg's art, that is, art that satisfies the criteria for successful art laid down in the ethical critique, Kierkegaard writes:

> Where poetry to all intents and purposes stops, this author begins. For poetry does not essentially reconcile with actuality; by means of imagination it reconciles with the ideality of imagination, but this reconciliation in the actual individual is precisely the new split with actuality.[34]

This quotation appears to endorse Crites's position by identifying poetry with those writings that bear one away from reality rather than those that are calculated to stimulate the adoption of a life-view by which to live. Thus, only the former could be called art while the latter constitutes some form of hortatory communication. This extreme and counterintuitive conclusion is rendered unnecessary by an inspection of the Danish text. "Poetry" in the above passage renders the Danish *Poesi* but is also used elsewhere to translate *Digtning*. It is this latter term that Kierkegaard uses to indicate all art whose medium is language. *Poesi* has a more restricted range of application. Marete Jørgensen defines this term in the following passage:

---

[33] Stephen Crites, Introduction to *Crisis in the Life of an Actress*, 28.

[34] *The Two Ages*, 14-15; *S.V.*, 14:17.

The concept, *Poesi,* includes both un[self]conscious, immediate poetry (*Digtning*) . . . as well as conscious, escapist poetry (*Digtning*) [which is] a reflective abandonment of reality.[35]

When Kierkegaard says that Gyllembourg's fiction lies outside of *Poesi,* he is in no way denying its status as art. He is simply locating it within the domain of successful reflective, linguistic art. Within the scope of *Poesi* lie both genuine, immediate art, for example, that of Blicher, and reflective, escapist art, as in the case of Andersen. Kierkegaard's rejection of escapist art is not a rejection of all *Poesi;* room must be made for aesthetically valid immediate art. Such art in no way communicates a life-view, but since it does not represent an evasion of existential responsibilities and is not the product of an attempt to make art fulfill nonaesthetic needs, it is to be appreciated and enjoyed for what it is.

Thus, Kierkegaard does consider the unity of works of art to be essentially if not immediately connected with the unity of the artist as a person. Setting aside immediate art, the development of a life-view is a necessary precondition of the existence of essential unity in the work of art because only by means of this life-view may the artist and the work of art stand as mutually free and independent unities. Art thus differs importantly from the sciences. Nonetheless, art, like the sciences, stands apart from the self and can never accomplish the all-important ordering of the self. Its possibilities are exhausted with its presentation to the self of the possibility of order.

Having traced Kierkegaard's early consideration of art and science in developing his understanding of the self's project of becoming one thing and having determined the ways in which the self's unity differs from, resembles, and is involved with the unities characteristic of these two fields of human endeavor, this study will now turn exclusively to the inner unity of the self, the subject most important to Kierkegaard. As noted in the introduction, each of the stages, subdivisions of the stages, and intermediate positions in the Kierkegaardian "phenomenology" may be characterized by its way of accepting or rejecting the imperative of self-unification. I begin the task of providing such a characterization in the next three chapters with a discussion of the aesthete's rebellious manyness.

---

[35] Marete Jørgensen, *Kierkegaard som Kritiker*, 98. (My translation.)

PART II

The Flight from Sameness: The Aesthetic Self's Refusal to Be One Thing

CHAPTER III

From the Journals to the Authorship

Kierkegaard's treatment of the aesthete in the authorship stands out as particularly elusive and indirect, even by the standards of "irony's magister." The best source of information about the aesthete and his peculiar agenda with change, *Either/Or* 1 is one of Kierkegaard's most brilliant books but also one of his most enigmatic. As the following pages will show, this obscurity is at least partially alleviated when *Either/Or* is viewed as the fruit of a long and sometimes frustrating process of thought and research through which the young Kierkegaard struggled and which he recorded in his journals. By following these journal entries, this chapter will trace an unbroken line of development from the interests described in the preceding chapter to the content and methodology of the authorship in general, and *Either/Or* 1 in particular.

Kierkegaard's journal from the fall of 1835 shows that he returned to Copenhagen firm in the convictions he had reached at Gilleleje. He reaffirms his belief that truth is not solely a characteristic of abstract bodies of knowledge but, more importantly, of concrete human beings. On the basis of this insight, he closes his first period of theological reflection, concluding that Christianity and philosophy differ essentially from each other. On 17 October, he writes:

> *Philosophy and Christianity can never be united*, for if I am going to hold fast to what is most essential in Christianity—namely, redemption, and if it is really going to amount to anything, it must of course be extended to the whole man.[1]

Despite his appreciation of Christianity's relation to the whole, concrete man, Kierkegaard holds himself at arm's length from it during this period, maintaining what Lowrie calls an attitude of "critical aloofness."[2] As the autumn progresses, this attitude gives way to aloofness, pure and simple. He ceases to attend classes in the theological faculty and in early November commences a seven-month silence in his journal on the subject of Christianity.[3]

It is at this time that Kierkegaard begins in earnest the study of literature and aesthetics that occupies him until 1838. While no doubt reflecting at the personal level a rebellion against the oppressively pietistic atmosphere of his father's house, it is best understood as an expression of his interest in the concrete. He immerses himself in the romantic prose and poetry of Germany and Denmark, conducts an extensive study of the folk and fairy tales of Europe, and acquaints himself with relevant theoretical and critical works. From these studies, he gathers the material for his later treatments of the aesthetic stage of existence and, even more significantly, develops the essential methodological underpinnings of his authorship.

In order to understand the influence Kierkegaard's reading exercised upon his methodology, we must remember the twin demands for consistency and concreteness expressed in the Gilleleje entry. There, Kierkegaard states his need for an idea around which to organize his life and

---

[1] *J. and P.*, 3245; *Pap.*, 1 A 94.

[2] Walter Lowrie, *A Short Life of Kierkegaard* (Princeton: Princeton University Press, 1944) 89.

[3] Carl Jørgensen, *Søren Kierkegaard*, 1:56.

thereby give it unity. In that same entry, however, he acknowledges that he continues to stand under an "imperative of knowledge";[4] he feels obligated to give intellectual expression to his existential insight. Meeting this challenge involves, first, the selection of existentially relevant ideas as subject matter for investigation. That is, his studies must center around those ideas that can serve as organizing forces in the lives of individuals. Beyond investigating the appropriate subject matter, his project of inquiry must proceed according to an appropriate methodology. A purely abstract examination, whatever its subject matter, may prove irrelevant to man's existential concerns and thus serve merely to divert and dissipate. Therefore, Kierkegaard's project must proceed as concretely as possible.

It is not in theology or philosophy, but rather in literature and aesthetics that Kierkegaard receives his primary methodological impulse. He meets, first, in Schleiermacher's *Vertraute Briefe ueber die Lucinde* and, shortly thereafter, in Goethe's *Wilhelm Meister* the presentation of ideas in the persons of fictional characters. In the case of Schleiermacher, Kierkegaard notes that the characters are little more than representatives of "different stand-points" in the debate over Schlegel's *Lucinde*. Of *Wilhelm Meister* he writes that, "by the end of the novel the view of the world which previously existed outside of Wilhelm, now is embodied and living within him."[5]

While he finds in Jean Paul's *School for Aesthetics* a theoretical rationale for Goethe's, Schleiermacher's, and numerous other contemporary authors' practice of identifying a character with an idea,[6] Kierkegaard develops a grounding of his own out of his study of mythology. In an undated entry from 1836, he writes:

Mythology is the compacting (suppressed being) of the idea of eternity (the eternal idea) in the categories of time and space—in time, for example,

---

[4]*J. and P.*, 5100; *Pap.*, 1 A 75.

[5]*J. and P.*, 1455; *Pap.*, 1 C 73; cited by Malantschuk, *Kierkegaard's Thought*, 25; See F. J. Billeskov-Jansen, *Studier i Søren Kierkegaard's Litterære Kunst* (Copenhagen: Rosenkilde and Bagger, 1951) 222-23.

[6]Johannes Richter (Jean Paul), *The Horn of Oberon: Jean Paul Richter's School for Aesthetics*, trans. Margret R. Hale (Detroit: Wayne State, 1973) 148-63.

Chiliasm, or the doctrine of a kingdom of heaven which begins in time, *in space, for example, an idea construed as being a finite personality*.[7]

Thus, the presentation of ideas as persons is as old as human imagination. It remains a valid way to present an idea even today inasmuch as mythological consciousness differs from that of the poet only in that it takes its own productions for actual beings while the poet is aware of the ideal nature of his creations. Kierkegaard expresses this idea by saying that mythology is "a hypothetical statement in the indicative" case whereas poetry (*Digtning*) is a statement in the subjunctive.[8] The practice of expressing ideas in concrete, personal form could hardly receive a more profound theoretical basis than Kierkegaard has provided in showing that the finitization and concretization of ideas is the very heart of literary art.

Drawing heavily on the lessons learned in his study of literature, Kierkegaard gives a preliminary sketch of his project of "authentic anthropological contemplation"[9] in a journal entry of 20 September 1837:

> [T]he work [which] I believe ought to be written . . . [is] the history of the human soul (as it is in an ordinary human being) in the continuity of the state of the soul (not in the concept) consolidating itself in particular mountain-clusters (that is, noteworthy world-historical representatives of life-views).[10]

This entry represents an early blueprint of the authorship, or, perhaps more accurately, of the concrete line of the authorship.[11] Kierkegaard proposes to write a "phenomenology" of human spirit based not upon concepts but

---

[7] *J. and P.*, 2799; *Pap.*, 1 A 300. (My emphasis.); see also Søren Kierkegaard, *The Concept of Irony*, 132-33, and Malantschuk, *Kierkegaard's Thought*, 22-23.

[8] *J. and P.*, 2798; *Pap.*, 1 A 214; cited by Malantschuk, *Kierkegaard's Thought*, 22.

[9] *J. and P.*, 37; *Pap.*, 3 A 3; cited by Malantschuk, *Kierkegaard's Thought*, 12.

[10] *J. and P.*, 4400; *Pap.*, 2 A 163; cited by Malantschuk, *Kierkegaard's Thought*, 159.

[11] See Malantschuk, *Kierkegaard's Thought*, 214-15.

Personal Unity in Kierkegaard's Thought

on paradigmatic individuals and concrete representative types.[12] This methodology allows him to stay as close as possible to the concrete while satisfying his need as a thinker to pursue to the last consequence the implications of every life-view.

Kierkegaard had begun his investigation of representative mythological and literary types well before formulating the rationale for his overall plan of study. In the first pages of his journal, he takes up the theme of "the master-thief," a Robin Hood figure, who is "conscious of living for an idea." The master-thief breaks the law not to satisfy personal desires but rather to express his displeasure "with the established order." Thus, this exile from normal society is unlike his fellow thieves as well and is denied even that source of "encouragement and comfort."[13] This motif of the outsider recurs frequently in the figures Kierkegaard selects for study.

Kierkegaard makes occasional journal entries concerning the master-thief between September 1834 and March 1835, at which time the idea of Faust comes to replace it, both in the journals and in Kierkegaard's mind. The two ideas are not unrelated. Knud Jensenius writes:

> In "the master-thief" lie the seeds of [Kierkegaard's] interest in Faust, who is [also] one "for whom all conditions of life were so utterly askew and who had such a canted stance toward everything."[14]

Despite this similarity, the idea of Faust is far richer and engages Kierkegaard far longer than the idea of the master-thief. The fervor with which he throws himself into the study of Faust is evidenced by the reading notes, critical comments, and bibliographical information on this subject that figure so prominently in the C section of the journals from the spring of that year.

By the time of the 1 June letter to Lund, Kierkegaard had decided that Faust is "doubt personified," and on this basis, that Goethe's *Faust 2*,

---

[12]See Louis Mackey, *Kierkegaard: A Kind of Poet* (Philadelphia: University of Pennsylvania Press, 1971) 16, for a use of this observation to contrast Kierkegaard with Hegel.

[13]*J. and P.*, 5061-62; *Pap.*, 1 A 11-12.

[14]Knud Jensenius, *Nogle Kierkegaard Studier* (Copenhagen: Nyt Nordiske Forlag, 1932) 14. Jensenius quotes here *J. and P.*, 5086; *Pap.*, 1 C 54.

which had appeared just three years previously on the author's death, "certainly is a sin against the idea [since] Goethe lets Faust be converted."[15] This note of dissatisfaction with Goethe's *Faust* (both 1 and 2, but especially 2) is repeatedly sounded throughout the period of Kierkegaard's investigation of the Faust-idea, that is, from spring 1835 to summer 1837.

The letter to Lund is of further significance in the development of the Faust-idea in that it is here that Kierkegaard first explicitly uses it in assessing himself. Here, also, he describes the idea as representative of a necessary stage "in every intellectual development."[16] Before realizing his destiny, each person must pass through a period of uncertainty, which Faust, as personified doubt, represents. Kierkegaard considers himself to be in just such a period at the time of this letter's writing. His personal identification with the idea had, no doubt, additional and deeper, even if not explicitly mentioned, roots in his then ambivalent attitude toward Christianity.

This understanding of Faust as representing a stage in human development marks an important step toward writing "the history of the human soul . . . [as it] consolidat[es] itself in particular . . . mountain-clusters." In order to depict development, however, additional "noteworthy world historical representatives of life-views" must be identified and situated in the developmental scheme.

Already in March 1835, Kierkegaard connects the ideas, Faust, Don Juan, and the Wandering Jew (Ahasverus), in a way that suggests that he views all three as paradigms of distinct manners of existence.

> People often say that someone is a Don Juan or a Faust but rarely say that someone is the Wandering Jew. Should there not also be individuals who have embodied in themselves too much of the Wandering Jew?[17]

There is no indication in this entry that Kierkegaard views the three ideas as representing stages in a single line of development. That he does come

---

[15]*J. and P.*, 5092; *Pap.*, 1 A 72.

[16]Ibid.

[17]*J. and P.*, 2206; *Pap.*, 1 C 66.

to regard them as such is shown in his December 1835 description of the Faust-idea as the final stage in such a line.

> It is interesting to note that Faust (whom I perhaps more properly place in the third stage as the more mediate) embodies both Don Juan and the Wandering Jew (Despair).[18]

The identification here of the Wandering Jew as personified despair shortly proves the basis of a reevaluation of the ideas' relationships to each other. Already in November, Kierkegaard had further specified Faust's doubt as the doubt (*Tvivl*) unto despair (*Fortvivelse*).[19] It thus seems a natural step to designate Ahasverus and not Faust as the third and culminating figure in the line. Kierkegaard acknowledges that the order of progression is sensuality to doubt to despair but still maintains the preeminence of the figure of Faust by describing the Wandering Jew as the idea in which the Faust-idea completes itself, that is, by continuing to stress the mediate nature of the Faust-idea that he noted in the journal entry quoted above. Thus, Faust is no longer simply doubt personified as in the letter to Lund. He stands as the single mediate figure who by taking up Don Juan, "Faust 1," and Ahasverus in himself represents the whole of this process of development.

The consolidation of the "three great ideas" into a developmental scheme and the selection of Faust as the figure in which this line of development culminates is naturally followed by an attempt to situate this constellation in the broader perspective of "the history of the human soul." In March of 1836 Kierkegaard writes:

> Representing life in its three tendencies, as it were, outside of religion, there are three great ideas (Don Juan, Faust, and the Wandering Jew), and not until these ideas are mediated and embraced in life by the single individual, not until then do the moral and religious appear.[20]

In this entry, Kierkegaard has in all but name sketched the theory of the stages that he will later lay forth in the authorship. In those later writings,

---

[18] *J. and P.*, 1179; *Pap.*, 1 C 58.

[19] *J. and P.*, 1178; *Pap.*, 1 A 104.

[20] *J. and P.*, 795; *Pap.*, 1 A 150.

the aesthetic stage is described as the necessary first stage through which each individual must pass on the way to ethical and religious selfhood. It alone constitutes the stage of life "outside of religion," since Kierkegaard's ethical stage is really an ethico-religious stage. As both of these identifying characteristics are attributed in the above entry to the line of development represented by the three great ideas, there can be no doubt that it is out of his early investigators of the ideas, Don Juan, Faust, and Ahasverus, that Kierkegaard develops his notion of the aesthetic stage.

Kierkegaard's investigation of this segment of "the history of the human soul" first takes the form of a continuation of his Faust project. He works to develop a characterization of "the modern Faust," a figure with whom he closely identifies and whom he sharply contrasts with Goethe's Faust. In fact, his project develops as a polemic against Goethe's version of the legend, which he believes to reflect the shortcomings of the eighteenth century: pantheism, a superficial conception of evil, and a banal optimism that manifests itself in Faust's conversion.[21]

Kierkegaard's project comes to a sudden and traumatic end in the summer of 1837 with his reading of an article by Martensen on Lenau's *Faust*. Kierkegaard's former tutor and lifelong antagonist devastates him by anticipating each and every point he planned to make in his forthcoming work on Faust. All plans of publishing such a work abandoned, Kierkegaard looses his pen on a mission of vengeance against his Wagner, first in the highly satirical "Battle between the Old and New Soap-Cellars"[22] and then more subtly but no less bitingly in *The Concept of Irony*. The Faust study, however, does not serve merely to sharpen, in its collapse, Kierkegaard's already polemical nature. Though no work specifically devoted to Faust or the other two "great ideas" ever appears, the studies of 1835-1837 bear fruit, first, in the second half of *The Concept of Irony* and then, most spectacularly, in *Either/Or*.

Change and the Aesthete
in *Either/Or* 1

On 20 February 1843, *Either/Or* appeared in Reitzel's bookshop near the university. Shortly after, the equally impressed and perplexed reading

---

[21]See Carl Roos, *Kierkegaard og Goethe* (Copenhagen: G. E. C. Gads Forlag, 1955) 82-91.

[22]*J. and P.*, 5156; *Pap.*, 1 A 220.

public of Copenhagen realized that a new and as yet unidentified virtuoso of the Danish language had arisen in their midst. Had anyone known that Kierkegaard was the author of the work, they would have had cause for surprise. *Either/Or* points everywhere to a daring and self-confident mastery of language that in *The Concept of Irony* is but glimpsed and that is strikingly absent in *Af en Endnu Levendes Papirer*.

The newness of Kierkegaard's stylistic excellence does not alter the essential continuity of *Either/Or* with the journal entries of the preceding years. In presenting through the figures of the aesthete, A, and the ethicist, Judge William, the contrast between the aesthetic and ethical stages of life, Kierkegaard is putting into practice the methodology that had taken form as early as 1837. This is not to say that no methodological improvement has taken place. It is an advance in concreteness to let the representative figures depict the forms of life they typify through their own writings rather than by serving as the subject matter of a theoretical discussion. This change represents the completion of that which, in the main, was already formulated. (Kierkegaard's theory of communication plays at least as great a role in the selection of this format for the work as does his desire for concreteness, however.)

As its title suggests, *Either/Or* is a work shot through with tension and opposition. This opposition characterizes the work as a whole at the level of the opposition between the two life-views. In the first volume, A either avoids or rejects as beyond his concern actions and persons that fall within the sphere of the ethical. There lurks in this an implicit hostility to and derision of the ethical.

Judge William's opposition to the aesthetic form of life could not be more explicit. He discusses at great length the failings of aesthetic existence and the triumphs of the ethical. His opposition takes on personal form in his reiterated invocations to A to mend his ways and cross over into the promised land of responsible married life.

What is true of *Either/Or* as a whole is true of volume 1 in a special way. In addition to its opposition to the ethical way of life, the aesthetic stage is characterized by deeply rooted tensions and fractures within itself. In the first place, the aesthetic stage shows a polarity without counterpart in ethical existence. It includes the immediacy innocent of all reflection represented by Don Juan and the unalleviated reflectivity of Johannes the seducer. Significantly, Don Juan is the subject of the first essay after the tone-setting "Diapsalmata," while Johannes appears in the first volume's final segment. This arrangement symbolically expresses that the two Johns constitute

> the ideal *terminus a quo* and the equally ideal *terminus ad quem* of the aesthetic life. . . . Inspired to enthusiasm by the one, recoiling in dread from the other, the aesthete strikes between them the precarious unhappy equilibrium of his own life.[23]

The roots of the aesthete's inner conflict lie deeper yet. This conflict goes to the heart even of the two ideal figures who represent the opposed poles of the stage. In fact, it traces back to the very figures from which Kierkegaard formed his concept of the aesthetic stage: Don Juan, Faust, and Ahasverus. These figures were selected for study because they represent with ideal consistency the "tendencies of life outside religion."[24] Continuity and unity of self are only possible, however, when the self stands in a proper relationship to the Good (God) and thus exists within the sphere of religion. By nature discontinuous and inconsistent, but ideally continuous in this discontinuity and consistent in this inconsistency, the "three great ideas" illustrate the fundamental self-conflict that characterizes the stage for which they serve as prototypes.

Kierkegaard establishes the discordant tone that reverberates throughout *Either/Or* 1 in the "Diapsalmata," a collection of aphoristic outbursts that serves as a mood-setting overture to the essays that follow. Time after time in these fragmentary comments, A points out the contradictory, the paradoxical, the self-opposed. Laughter originates in an inhibited cry of pain; "the melancholy temperament has the greatest comic sense"; "the object of desire is first attainable through its opposite." A long series of despairingly melancholy entries is interrupted by an outburst of ecstatic joy as A describes hearing strains of Mozart's "immortal overture." These divine tones are quickly traced to a pitiful pair of blind street musicians, who, led by a child, play with fingers red and blue from the cold for the coins of passersby. In a preceding Diapsalm A remarks appropriately, "The best

---

[23] Mackey, *Kierkegaard: A Kind of Poet*, 32.

[24] *J. and P.*, 795; *Pap.*, 1 A 150.

Personal Unity in Kierkegaard's Thought 51

proof of the wretchedness of existence is the proof that is derived from the contemplation of its glories."[25]

The oppositions and contradictions A observes around him are the external reflections of his more fundamental internal conflict. The first Diapsalm describes the terrible tension of poet-existence, the existence A ascribes to himself.

> What is a poet? An unhappy man who in his heart harbors a deep anguish, but whose lips are so fashioned that the moans and cries which pass over them are transformed into ravishing music.[26]

Kierkegaard comments in his journal on the significance of the tension evoked here.

> The first Diapsalm is really the task of the entire work, which is not resolved until the last words of the sermon. An enormous dissonance is assumed, and then it says: Explain it. . . .[27]

This task of explaining falls not to A but to B; A's task is to *live* the contradiction.[28] The above journal entry goes on to tell how the final Diapsalm illustrates the way in which A fulfills his task:

> The last Diapsalm tells us how a life such as this has found its satisfactory expression in laughter. He pays his debt to actuality by means of laughter, and now everything takes place within this contradiction. His enthusiasm is too intense, his sympathy is too deep, his love is too burning, his heart too warm to be able to express himself in any other way than contradiction.[29]

This contradiction at the very heart of the aesthete is expressed in a number of Diapsalmata as a paralyzed restlessness. Lacking the peace to rest or the power to act, A "feel[s] the way a chessman must, when the

---

[25]*Either/Or*, 1:28; *S.V.*, 2:31.

[26]*Either/Or*, 1:19; *S.V.*, 3:23.

[27]*J. and P.*, 5629; *Pap.*, 4 A 216; see also *Postscript*, 226; *S.V.*, 9:211.

[28]Mackey, *Kierkegaard: A Kind of Poet*, 16.

[29]*J. and P.*, 5629; *Pap.*, 4 A 216.

opponent says of it: That piece cannot be moved.'"[30] The opposed forces in A, whose standoff is so effectively suggested in this Diapsalm, are passionate wildness and immobilizing world-weariness. Split asunder at his very core, the aesthete can have no simple, single relationship, even in his unequivocal rebellion, to the imperative to be one thing. His life alternates between two widely disparate antitheses of continuity and unity. On the one hand, his is a life of chaotic discontinuity; it moves disconnectedly from one momentary passion to another. On the other hand, it is a dead sameness, a lifeless tedium, which in its hopelessly becalmed condition is a parody of the changelessness of genuine continuity.

These two sides of the aesthete, which are juxtaposed in so many of the Diapsalmata, reappear throughout *Either/Or* 1, often in separation from each other. The aesthete alternately appears as a source and embodiment of chaotic flux and as a lifeless parasite fastening dependently on outside sources of movement and change, the sustaining forces of the aesthete's life.

This shifting of aspect characterizes the immediate aesthete as well as the reflective and sets the interpretive task of this group of chapters. Why is *Either/Or* 1 the scene of such alternations of appearance, and what do these alternations tell us about the aesthetic sphere of existence and its relation to the imperative of being one thing?

At the most obvious level, this instability of aspect reflects the essential discontinuity of aesthetic life. The aesthete is so far from meeting the universal human obligation to maintain self-identify that he cannot even be univocally described in his failure. With a writer as careful and subtle as Kierkegaard, however, it is possible that the specific variations communicate a message about the aesthete at once more profound and more elusive than the message conveyed by the variations considered generally. Hence, I will examine the characterizations of the aesthete's relation to the forces of change in light of their contexts as well. Careful attention to the underlying structure of *Either/Or* 1 provides a key to understanding the pseudonyms and their inner contradictions. The pattern that emerges by using this key broadens and deepens our knowledge of the aesthete's peculiar agenda with change.

---

[30]*Either/Or*, 1:21; *S.V.*, 2:25.

The first step in substantiating this claim is to defend the notion that *Either/Or* 1 possesses an overall structure. It presents to immediate observation no such coherence, seeming rather to be a literary grab bag of greatly varied writings. Sven Clausen takes this immediate appearance as the reality of the work. In his "Forsinket Anmedelse af 'Enten-Eller' " ("Delayed Review of *Either/Or*"), he writes,

> All manner of things are thrown helter-skelter together.... One can with great certainty guess that Kierkegaard never wrote a song congratulating someone on his confirmation since it would have been included in *Either/Or* 1.[31]

Billeskov-Jansen upbraids Clausen for failing to see that the structurelessness of *Either/Or* 1 is exactly its carefully wrought structure. With fully thought out artistic design, Kierkegaard lets the work's form reproduce its content. Referring to Victor Eremita's introduction to the book, Billeskov-Jansen points out that B's papers reflect in their outward appearance and internal coherence the life-view B represents. Similarly, the widely varied and apparently accidentally ordered writings of A express his inconstant but brilliant manner of life.

What Billeskov-Jansen forgets in this explanation is that A is just as artful as he is unstable. A closer reading of Victor Eremita's remarks would have alerted him to the possibility of a hidden structure.

> The arranging of A's papers was not so simple. I have therefore let chance determine the order, that is to say, I have left them in the order in which I found them, without being able to decide whether the order has any chronological value or ideal significance.[32]

It is exactly this bracketing of the question of structure, the assignment by default of the task of ordering to the absent and inaccessible A, the impossibility of knowing whether A ordered them by accident or design, that should make one suspect that Kierkegaard has more in mind with the order of the essays in *Either/Or* 1 than a simple formal reflection of A's disorder.

---

[31] Cited by Billeskov-Jansen, *Studier i Søren Kierkegaards Litterære Kunst*, 26. (My translation.)

[32] *Either/Or*, 1:7-8; *S.V.*, 2:13-14.

This suspicion is confirmed in a pair of marginal comments in Kierkegaard's personal copy of the book.

> Probably no one will suspect that *Either/Or* has a plan from the first word to the last, since the preface makes a joke of it and does not say a word about the speculative.
>
> Some think that *Either/Or* is a collection of loose papers I had lying around on my desk. Bravo!—As a matter of fact, it is the reverse.[33]

The grounds having been established for suspecting that such an underlying structure exists, it remains to describe the structure and show how it provides the interpretive key to understanding *Either/Or* 1's variable characterizations of the aesthetic stage as they relate to change and changelessness.

The order that underlies the apparent chaos of *Either/Or* 1 becomes visible only if we take the pseudonymity of the work seriously. The book is not only *about* the aesthetic way of life, it is also *by* an aesthete. While no commentator would deny this in word, unfortunately, a large number do so in deed. They mine the essays for descriptions of aesthetes of various forms from which to construct an account and analysis of the aesthetic stage. In doing so, they violate the text's integrity. They seize exclusively on the object side of the subject-object relationship around which the work is built. They are thus rendered oblivious to the subtle changes that take place in this relationship between the aesthete as subject and the acsthete as object, between the aesthete as observer and recorder and the aesthete as the observed and recorded representative of a way of living, in which the structure of *Either/Or* 1 is to be found. It will be shown that from an initial relation of radical otherness, the two poles are gradually mediated into an identity. Through the process, a "phenomenology" of the aesthetic stage is provided showing the gradual transition from the most primitive to the most developed forms within the stage. The Hegelian character of this way of presenting the aesthetic stage is obvious, but whether it signals a debt, a parody, or both will not emerge until later. The task now is to examine the essays and interpret in light of the emerging structure the perplexingly various characterizations of the aesthete as regards change and changelessness.

---

[33] *J. and P.*, 5628, 5627; *Pap.*, 4 A 214-15.

CHAPTER IV

The Varieties of Turbulence: Descriptions of Change in A's Manuscripts

Between Victor Eremita's editorial remarks and Johannes the seducer's infamous diary lie first the already discussed Diapsalmata and then half a dozen widely varied "essays," all from the hand of an unknown aesthete designated for convenience's sake as A. These six manuscripts range from impassioned art criticism, to almost sermonical addresses to a secret club of aesthetes, to a theoretical treatise on the proper conduct of aesthetic existence. Together they provide an admirably inclusive survey of the aesthete's many masks, moods, and methods. As others have cataloged these phases of the aesthete, I will concentrate in this chapter on identifying the structural development disclosed as the essays progress and on using this information to cast light on the aesthete's varying comments on the role of change in his life.

"The Immediate Stages of the Erotic or the Musical Erotic"

In this first essay of the volume, A argues passionately to establish Mozart's *Don Juan* (*Don Giovanni*) as first among equals in the pantheon of classic works of art. Defining a classic as a work in which content perfectly corresponds to form, as one in which "the idea reposes with transparent clearness in definite form,"[1] A argues that the idea, Don Juan, who personifies "sensuous genius" (*sandselige Genealitet*), can be presented properly only in the medium of music. His reason is that sensuous genius is ideally immediate in content, and "Music always expresses the immediate in its immediacy."[2] So essential is the medium of music to the idea of Don Juan that only in this medium can the idea truly represent sensuous genius. As immediate, this idea admits of no conflict or opposition since the essential characteristic of the immediate is the absence of relation.[3] In any medium besides music, however, Don Juan takes the form of an individual and is "*eo ipso*, in conflict with his environment."[4] In contrast, "the music does not represent him as person or as individual, but only as Power."[5] In the opera, Don Juan strides forth as a natural force, as the principle of desire, perfectly immediate in his abstractness, immediately victorious in his unopposed power.

As might be expected, given the deeply rooted self-opposition that characterizes the aesthetic stage, this picture of happy correspondence of form and content and of immediacy free of the conflicts and tensions of reflective consciousness is incomplete. Don Juan bears the stamp of a birth at odds with his very essence. This knight of infinite immediacy owes his existence to Christianity, the principle that posits him as the principle of sensuousness precisely by excluding sensuousness, the force that sets the

---

[1] *Either/Or*, 1:52; *S.V.*, 2:53.

[2] *Either/Or*, 1:68; *S.V.*, 2:68.

[3] Søren Kierkegaard, *Johannes Climacus: or De Omnibus Dubitandum Est*, trans. and intro. T. H. Croxall (Stanford: Stanford University Press, 1958) 147.

[4] *Either/Or*, 1:106; *S.V.*, 2:101.

[5] Ibid.

flesh free as a distinct force precisely by introducing spirit, the antithesis of flesh. In the following passage, A describes sensuousness as it existed before Christianity's arrival and, in the process, shows that only in opposition and exclusion can the sensuous attain the status of principle as it does in Don Juan.

> Sensuousness, then, already existed in the world but without being spiritually determined. How then has it existed? Psychically. It was in this manner that it existed in paganism, and, in its most perfect expression, in Greece. But sensuousness psychically determined is not opposition, exclusion, but harmony and accord. But precisely because sensuousness was harmoniously determined, it appeared, not as a principle, but as an enclitic assimilated by assonance.[6]

The paradoxical origin of Don Juan, who as immediacy incarnate represents the absence of all relation, in a relation of exclusion and opposition reflects itself in the content and form of the idea. The idea's content is desire. As A notes in his account of the stages of the immediate, desire, properly speaking, emerges only through the diremption of desire and its object. These are innervatingly and suffocatingly united in the embryonic desire represented by the Page in "Figaro."

> [I]n this stage . . . the desire is so indefinite, its object is so little separated from it, that the object of desire rests androgynously within the desire, just as in plant life the male and female parts are both present in one blossom. Desire and its object are joined in this unity, and they both are of neuter gender.[7]

This phenomenon of androgyny characterizes the psychical sensuousness of the Greeks as well. Not the feminine, but "beautiful individuality" constitutes the object of desire.[8] Only with the coming of Christianity and the consequent diremption of the harmonious unity of soul and body is desire sharpened and focused into its determination as Don Juan. Immedi-

---

[6]*Either/Or*, 1:60; *S.V.*, 2:60-61.

[7]*Either/Or*, 1:76; *S.V.*, 2:74.

[8]*Either/Or*, 1:87; *S.V.*, 2:85.

acy, which Kierkegaard defines as indefiniteness,[9] and, thus, as the lack of separation, arises through a series of separations, first of desire and its object, then of soul and body.

This paradox repeats itself in the idea's form. As noted, "Music always expresses the immediate in its immediacy."[10] Despite its immediacy, however, music is born of the same conflict as desire. The coming of Christianity and the consequent positing of spirit causes the separation of the sensuous and the significant, which had previously been united in poetry. Spirit takes prose as its own, elevating significance to exclusive dominion and, in the process, reducing the sensuous component of language to mere instrumentality.[11] The sensuous dimension of language is thus posited as an independent medium: music.

The paradoxical, self-contradictory nature of Don Juan underlines his ideal nature. He is a figure who could never exist except *for* another. He lives his tumultuous life in a gap that exists not in time or space but only for reflection. Don Juan is born of Christianity's exclusion of the sensuous and dies with its judgment of the sensuous as sin. Thus, A rightly describes the "daemonic in aesthetic indifference" as "only the matter of a moment."[12] Don Juan's whole existence rests upon a logical distinction between two moments that could never actually be separated.

But he does exist *for* reflective consciousness, first for the Middle Ages, then for Mozart and his audiences, and now for A. It is in this last relationship that the essay's subject-object structure is to be found.

A's relation to Don Juan and hence the subject-object structure of the essay follows the same pattern of opposition and distinctness emerging from harmony and indistinctness that so characterizes the Don. Declaring an unbounded, childlike enthusiasm for Mozart's *Don Juan,* A shows his existence to be thoroughly interpenetrated by the opera. This communion, which is as murky as it is sublime, is replaced by separation as A turns to the task of understanding.

---

[9]*De Omnibus Dubitandum Est*, 147.

[10]*Either/Or*, 1:68; *S.V.*, 2:68.

[11]*Either/Or*, 1:65; *S.V.*, 2:65.

[12]*Either/Or*, 1:89; *S.V.*, 2:86.

> That which you have loved with youthful enthusiasm and admired with youthful ardor, that which you have secretly and mysteriously preserved in the innermost recesses of your soul, that which you have hidden in your heart: *that* you always approach with a certain shyness, with mingled emotions, when you know that the purpose is to try to understand it. . . . The soul becomes sad, and the heart softens; for it is as if you were bidding it farewell, as if you were separating yourself from it, never to meet it again either in time or eternity.[13]

This separation is symbolically expressed later in the essay. A says that whereas once he "would have given anything for a ticket" to the opera, he now prefers to stand outside the auditorium in the corridor.

> [The opera] is better understood at a distance. . . . It is a world by itself, separated from me; I can see nothing, but I am near enough to hear, and yet so infinitely far away.[14]

This metaphor of distant observation is best developed in A's description of music and language as adjoining kingdoms. As reflective, A inhabits the realm of language and is excluded from that of music. After first ironically attributing this exclusion to his status as layman and amateur, A goes on to describe his project of coming to know the realm of music by tracing its boundaries with the kingdom of language from the side of the latter kingdom. Thus, though he acquaints himself with the realm of music, he is completely barred from entering it himself.[15]

The picture that emerges of a radical cleft between A and Don Juan captures the subject-object structure of the essay. The greatest possible disparity within the aesthetic stage characterizes this relationship. Don Juan, the immediate aesthete, is the object of observation by A, the reflective aesthete. One is pure activity, ceaselessly and tirelessly pursuing his female prey; the other is pure subject, playing the part of Leporello, observing, recording, and vicariously enjoying his counterpart's activities.

This structure provides the basis for understanding the essay's variable characterizations of the aesthetic stage as regards change and changeless-

---

[13]*Either/Or*, 1:58-59; *S.V.*, 2:58-59.

[14]*Either/Or*, 1:119; *S.V.*, 2:113.

[15]*Either/Or*, 1:64; *S.V.*, 2:64.

ness. Given that Don Juan is the observed and A the observer, it is not surprising that only the immediate aesthete is extensively described in this regard.

Time and again throughout "The Immediate Stages of the Erotic," A characterizes sensuous genius as a tumultuous principle. "It is an energy, a storm, impatience, passion"; "It is . . . force, life, movement, constant unrest, perpetual succession."[16] Of the Venusberg, he writes:

> There sound only the voices of elemental passion, the play of appetites, the wild shouts of intoxication; it exists solely for pleasure in eternal tumult. The first born of this kingdom is Don Juan.[17]

These portrayals of the immediate aesthete as the embodiment of chaotic flux represent the primary vision of the essay. The antithetical characterization of the aesthetic as dead changelessness peeks out occasionally, however. As opposed as these descriptions are, they are dialectically related since change pressed to its final extreme becomes changelessness.

As the ideal seducer and quintessentially faithless lover, Don Juan loves only in the moment. Because he is an unopposed elemental force, he is "absolutely victorious." "To see her and to love her [is] one and the same."[18] His conquest is instantaneous. As faithless as he is seductive, he in the next moment pursues another; the previously conquered woman is but a mark in Leporello's ledger book. This endless round of conquest and desertion represents the ultimate in instability. There is no coherence or connection between any two moments of Don Juan's life. On closer inspection, however, this utter changeability reveals itself as constant repetition[19] and unrelieved stasis.

---

[16] *Either/Or*, 1:55, 70; *S.V.*, 2:56, 69.

[17] *Either/Or*, 1:88; *S.V.*, 2:85-86.

[18] *Either/Or*, 1:93; *S.V.*, 2:90.

[19] This is not, of course, the repetition characteristic of ethical and, especially, Christian existence. See the following chapter for further discussion. It suffices here to point to Constantine Constantius's ill-conceived return to Berlin in *Repetition* to indicate that aesthetes are incapable of fathoming this concept in its true meaning.

To see her and to love her is the same thing; it is in the moment, in the same moment everything is over, and the same thing repeats itself endlessly.

[Don Juan] constantly finishes, and constantly begins again from the beginning, for his life is the sum of repellent moments which have no coherence, his life as moment is the sum of moments, as the sum of the moments is the moment.[20]

This identification of an "atomic multiplicity" of moments and a single moment stems from the absolute discreteness of each moment in the immediate aesthete's life. As divorced from the past and future, and thus confined to a "present" that only parodies a genuine, historically situated present, Don Juan exists in a *nunc stans*, an eternal now, which in its invariance born of impotence constitutes a parody of the eternal.[21] Unable to continue what he has begun in a previous moment, each moment is a monotonous repetition of every other. Sensuous genius "remains always the same, it does not unfold itself, but it storms uninterruptedly forward as if in a single breath."[22]

Since there is both an aspect of wild, chaotic flux and of unalleviated stasis in A's description of the immediate aesthete, why does the former characterization dominate? Again and again, the note of power, storm, turbulence, and exuberance is struck. The contrasting theme, when heard at all, is only hinted at as an afterthought. This is literally the case, for each passage indicating the repetitive quality of Don Juan's life either immediately or closely follows a characterization of that life in the opposite terms.[23]

---

[20]*Either/Or*, 1:93-95; *S.V.*, 2:90, 91.

[21]See Søren Kierkegaard, *The Concept of Anxiety*, trans. Reidar Thomte (Princeton: Princeton University Press, 1980) 85; *S.V.*, 6:173.

[22]*Either/Or*, 1:70; *S.V.*, 2:69. As a natural force, Don Juan, like nature, "is too abstract to have a dialectic with respect to time in a stronger sense." Søren Kierkegaard, *Philosophical Fragments*, trans. David F. Swenson, intro. Niels Thulstrup, rev. Howard V. Hong (Princeton: Princeton University Press, 1962) 94; *S.V.*, 6:70.

[23]See, for example, *Either/Or*, 1:70; *S.V.*, 2:69.

This disproportionate emphasis upon the aspect of chaotic flux stems from A's relationship to his subject matter. Above, I noted that no greater polarization can be imagined than that demonstrated in *Either/Or* 1's framework of the aesthete writing about the aesthetic. This disparity is best shown in A's status as reflective aesthete and Don Juan's as immediate aesthete. The gap between the two is ideally accentuated by A's appearance in the essay only in the role of observer. He speaks only of the Don, saying nothing of himself except insofar as he describes his relation to the opera and its central figure. That is, he only observes or observes himself observing. Thus, pure observer stands over against pure activity, since Don Juan in his immediacy diverts no energy from action to self-examination.

In a passage echoing his own role as fascinated observer and recorder, A writes that Leporello, spellbound by the immediate life of Don Juan, is so assimilated that he "almost become[s] the voice" of his master.[24] This is the function A repeatedly describes as his own. Casting aside all claim to originality, he says, "What I have to say on this subject I owe to Mozart alone." He assures any doubter that "not only the little which I here present is found [in the opera] but infinitely more."[25] Faithfully serving as Don Juan's voice involves more, or, perhaps more accurately, less, than bringing to linguistic expression the opera's idea. Such expression in an alien medium is necessarily corrupting. A's speech is successful only insofar as it is self-negating; he uses language to induce others to hear that which is nonlinguistic.

> I shall constantly ferret out the musical in the idea, the situation, and so on, distilling its very essence, and then when I have made the reader so musically receptive that he seems to hear the music though he really hears nothing, then I shall have completed my task, then I become mute, then I say to the reader as to myself: listen.[26]

---

[24]*Either/Or*, 1:124; *S.V.*, 2:117.

[25]*Either/Or*, 1:58; *S.V.*, 2:58.

[26]*Either/Or*, 1:85; *S.V.*, 2:83. Billeskov-Jansen points out that in one brilliant passage (*Either/Or*, 1:102; *S.V.*, 2:97-98), A uses language as music by relying upon its texture and rhythm rather than significant content to convey his message. Billeskov-Jansen, *Studier i Søren Kierkegaards Litteraere Kunst*, 34.

This passage shows A turned so totally and receptively toward the Don that he has no other goal than to turn others toward the immediate seducer as well. What is the reason for this total devotion, which appears in A's passionate descriptions, in Leporello's faithful keeping of the ledger book, in the women's total surrender, and even in Donna Elvira's tireless pursuit of her seducer? It is that Don Juan is the power of life and all turn toward him to soak up the energy radiating from him.

> Don Juan is the hero of the opera, the chief interest centers in him; not only so, but he lends interest to all the other characters. This must not be understood, however, in a merely superficial sense, for this constitutes the mysterious in the opera, that the hero is also the animating force in the other characters. Don Juan's life is the life-principle within them. His passion sets the passion of all the others in motion.
>
> As in a solar system the dark bodies which receive their light from a central sun are never more than half-illuminated, namely on the side which is turned toward the sun, so is this the case with the persons in the play—only that moment in their lives, that side which is turned toward Don Juan is illuminated, the rest is dark and obscure.[27]

It is now clear why "The Immediate Stages of the Erotic" stresses the active, turbulent, constantly changing aspect of Don Juan. Situated over against the "dark body" of a purely receptive and passive observer, the movement and change that are the aesthete's lifeblood can only originate in the natural vigor and turbulence of immediate life. A's enthusiasm and liveliness are not self-generated but derived; on his own he would languish. Thus, he passionately thanks Mozart, "to whom I owe it that I did not pass through life without having been stirred by something."[28]

In this first essay of *Either/Or* 1, change springs from the natural, the immediate. The reflective aesthete can do no more than receive that which is generated in the dynamo of immediate life. While expressing a truth about the aesthetic stage, the essay does not present the entire truth. It presents an implicit thesis about change and changelessness in the aesthetic stage that must be supplemented and corrected in other essays. This incompleteness is indicated in the opera itself. Pointing to an antithetical truth, the

---

[27]*Either/Or*, 1:118, 123; *S.V.*, 2:112, 116.

[28]*Either/Or*, 1:47; *S.V.*, 1:48-49.

Commandant reappears in the work's conclusion displaying a reflective consciousness in no need of an external source of power and reducing Don Juan to impotence by confronting him with the past, which the Commandment as a returned spirit represents.[29]

Addresses to the *Symparanekromenoi:* "The Ancient Tragical Motif," "Shadowgraphs," and "The Unhappiest Man"

The necessity of immediacy's passing, already symbolically expressed in the Commandant's triumphant invasion of Don Juan's homeland, the opera, is further expressed in these three essays by A's turning his attention from immediacy to reflective forms of aesthetic existence. This new direction involves the partial mediation of the split between the aesthete as describer and as described in that both are now reflective. Nonetheless, A stands over against his subjects here much as he did with Don Juan. He continues in the role of observer, taking as his object an other from whom he receives energy and stimulation. In fact, his parasitism is more obvious and more demonic in these essays. In place of the good-natured adulation and fascination of "The Immediate Stages of the Erotic," these essays reveal a perverse voyeurism, an unnatural curiosity that pries relentlessly into the secret sorrows of reflective sufferers. This darkening of tone and the continued dependence on an external source of life are symbolically expressed in A's appearance here as a member of and speaker to the *Symparanekromenoi*, "the society of the already dead."

In "The Ancient Tragical Motif," A uses a relatively ignored dimension of the Kierkegaardian stages—their correspondence to historical epochs—to shift his discussion smoothly from the immediate aesthetic to the reflective. He juxtaposes these two forms of consciousness by comparing the ancient and modern ages. Although this comparison focuses first on the political domain, A quickly moves to dramatic art as the site for this confrontation of epochs.

The immediacy characteristic of Greek consciousness manifests itself in tragedy in that

> the action (*Handling*) does not issue exclusively from character, that the

---

[29]*Either/Or*, 1:112, 123; *S.V.*, 1:106, 116.

action does not find its sufficient explanation in subjective reflection and decision, but that the action itself has a relative admixture of suffering (*Liden*) [passion, *passio*].[30]

That is, the individual is not what he is solely on the basis of his own actions and decisions. The substantial realities to which he is immediately related decisively affect the action's outcome. The elements of fate, family, history, the unpredictable acts of gods not bound by ethical constraints, and so forth, constitute the "fatalistic element" in tragedy represented by the chorus.[31]

While often showing that disasters befall those who are only partially responsible for them, ancient tragedy is much milder than modern. In fact, it is for this reason that it is milder. The individual's guilt is only relative in ancient tragedy. Though he comes to a bad end, he is not fully responsible as he is in modern tragedy. In the latter,

> absolutely nothing of the immediate remains anymore. Hence, modern tragedy has no epic foreground, no epic heritage. The hero stands of falls entirely on his own acts.[32]

As a result of this difference, ancient tragedy is characterized by sorrow (*Sorg*), the suffering born of guilt in its "aesthetic ambiguity," while modern tragedy is characterized by the "bitter pain (*Smerte*) that accompanies the total transparency of guilt." Sorrow is an immediate state, an unreflective response to guilt or suffering. What it lacks in sharpness and definition, it makes up in depth. On the other hand, "Pain always implies a reflection over suffering which sorrow does not know." Thus, guilt as the object of explicit awareness and the product of free action gives rise to pain.[33]

---

[30]*Either/Or*, 1:141; *S.V.*, 2:132.

[31]"Whether the chorus approaches the epic substantiality or lyric exhaltation, it indicates, as it were, the more which will not be absorbed in individual reality." Ibid; see also *The Concept of Irony*, 162, and *S.V.*, 1:171, where Hegel is cited as the source of this understanding of the chorus.

[32]*Either/Or*, 1:141; *S.V.*, 2:133.

[33]*Either/Or*, 1:145-46; *S.V.*, 2:137-38.

Having distinguished between the two forms of drama and the states of mind characteristic of them, A tells us that modern tragedy is a thoroughly "mistaken endeavor."[34] By eliminating all ambiguity as to guilt, by rendering the individual entirely responsible for his own downfall, modern dramatists abrogate the tragic in their tragedies. The tragic consists precisely in a balance between activity and passivity, action and suffering, guilt and innocence. When sorrow is eliminated, guilt becomes "totally transparent"; that is, when the first element of each of the above pairs is posited as absolute, guilt is determined as sin, the scene is set in an ethical and not an aesthetic universe, and the tragic is banished.

> Between these two extremes [of action and suffering] lies the tragic. If the individual is entirely without guilt, the tragic interest is nullified, for the tragic collision is thereby enervated; if on the other hand, he is absolutely guilty, he can no longer interest us tragically. Hence, it is certainly a misunderstanding of the tragic, when our age strives to let the whole tragic destiny become transubstantiated in individuality and subjectivity.... [O]ne would throw [the tragic hero's] whole life upon his shoulders, as being the result of his own acts, would make him accountable for everything, but in doing so, one would also transform his aesthetic guilt into an ethical one. The tragic hero thus becomes bad; evil becomes precisely the tragic subject; but evil has no aesthetic interest, and sin is not an aesthetic element.[35]

The portraits that A presents to the *Symparanekromenoi* in this and the following two essays are attempts to fill the void left by modern dramatists. The first of these tragic figures is "the modern Antigone." Contrasting this figure with the Antigone of Greek tragedy, A shows his fellow deceased how the characteristic feature of modern consciousness, reflection, may heighten rather than eliminate the tragic.

The original Antigone is, of course, characterized by immediacy. The surd of parental guilt, which is the force driving her, her brothers, and Creon to the tragic conclusion, falls outside of her control and even largely outside her consciousness. A writes that this Antigone "is not at all concerned

---

[34]*Either/Or*, 1:142; *S.V.*, 2:134.

[35]*Either/Or*, 1:142; *S.V.*, 2:133-34.

about her father's unhappy destiny. This rests like an impenetrable sorrow over the whole family."[36]

The modern Antigone is set radically apart from her Greek counterpart by her conscious knowledge of her father's guilt. In her youth, she has only "dim suspicions (*dunkle Hentydninger*) of this horrible secret."[37] As long as she has only immediate presentiments, she remains in a state of sorrow, just like her Greek sister. With mature development, however, comes certain knowledge of her father's guilt and with it a new state of mind.

This new state of mind is characterized by constant unrest. As she becomes explicitly aware of her father's guilt, she makes this guilt the object of her reflection. In this reflection lies the truly modern aspect of this Antigone. She is like her ancient counterpart in all other respects, however. By virtue of her piety, she takes her father's guilt as her own. Thus, there is a residue of immediacy in her. This retention of immediacy indicates that her reflectivity is only relative. Infinite reflectivity would reflect her out of all guilt not her own and, in the process, out of the tragical and into the ethical.[38]

Bringing together in her person both the immediate, inherited guilt and a reflection not too developed to coexist with it, the modern Antigone greatly heightens the tragic. Her form of consciousness forces her to reflect upon that which ultimately defies reflection: the opaque block of inherited guilt. This reflection, in the form of anxiety (*Angest*), constantly transforms the sorrow, which naturally results from tragic guilt, into pain, the reflective form of suffering. Besides adding the dimension of pain to tragedy without thereby eliminating the integral element of sorrow, this psychic configuration produces a tragic figure whose essence is unrest and

---

[36]*Either/Or*, 1:153; *S.V.*, 2:144.

[37]*Either/Or*, 1:152; *S.V.*, 2:143.

[38]That is to say that in suppressing altogether the passive dimension of guilt, all responsibility comes to rest squarely on the agent's shoulders. It would thus be determined as ethical guilt. Whether the individual acknowledges his guilt, that is, whether he makes the transition from the aesthetic to the ethical stage is beyond the power of reflection to determine; it requires an act of will. Thus, there is no inconsistency in Kierkegaard's letting infinitely reflecting aesthetes appear later in this book.

disquiet. As reflection can never penetrate inherited guilt, the process of transforming sorrow into pain never exhausts the source of sorrow. Thus arises the dialectic that sets the modern Antigone's soul in unending motion.

> [H]er sorrow is not a dead, immovable possession; it moves constantly, it gives birth to pain and is born in pain.
> Here is the modern: unrest in her sorrow, ambiguity in her pain.[39]

The modern Antigone's form of consciousness is especially significant to this study. For the first time in *Either/Or* 1, movement is born of reflection and not immediacy. Since he has already identified anxiety as a reflection, A clearly ascribes the dynamic force of the modern Antigone's soul to reflection when he writes that "anxiety is the energy of the movement."[40]

A corresponding shift has taken place in A's characterizations of the immediate. Whereas up to this point, the dynamic, stormy, and changeable aspect of the immediate has been stressed almost to the exclusion of its alternative, now he writes that sorrow, the immediate form of suffering, is saved from being a "dead, immovable possession" only by the play of reflection upon it.[41] It is significant that the reflective aesthete's diversion of his attention from the natural and immediate to the reflective coincides with his recognition of reflection's capacity to generate movement. His absorption with the latter and description of the immediate as essentially static indicates that in the internal turbulence generated by reflection, A finds a more complete satisfaction for his demonic hunger for change and motion.

In the following essay, A presents for the voyeuristic pleasure of the *Symparanekromenoi* "shadowgraphs" of three tragic figures. These three

---

[39]*Either/Or*, 1:156, 159; *S.V.*, 2:146, 149.

[40]*Either/Or*, 1:152; *S.V.*, 2:143.

[41]The unalloyed sorrow of the Greek Antigone is described by A as "in complete and profound harmony." *Either/Or*, 1:146; *S.V.*, 2:137.

figures have in common a "reflective sorrow" (*Sorg*)[42] born of their lovers' deceit. The term *reflective sorrow* appears to be inherently contradictory given the respective definitions of "sorrow" and "pain" supplied in "The Ancient Tragical Motif." This opposition reflects the inner conflict of the psychic state it denotes. "Reflective sorrow" is here used to name an unhappy combination of activity and passivity, of reflection and that which defies reflection, a state of mind that obviously recalls "the modern Antigone." As in Antigone's case, the juxtaposition of opposed factors sets the soul in unceasing motion and unrest.

> Reflective sorrow (*Sorg*) . . . cannot be represented artistically . . . because it never is, but is always in the process of becoming (*den er nemlig aldrig tilværende men bestandig i Vorden*).
>
> [I]t lacks inner repose, and is constantly in movement; although this motion does not enrich it with any new content, yet the agitation is nevertheless essential.[43]

The passive dimension of reflective sorrow lies in its origin. Except in pathological cases, this state of mind arises because of an "objective sorrow," that is, because the self *suffers* a blow of fate. As in the case of Antigone, the ceaseless round of reflection to which these figures are doomed is initiated by an external force. Under closer inspection of the occasions of this suffering, however, differences from Antigone begin to emerge. Antigone's reflection had as its object her father's guilt, a guilt that became her own, that became the object of ceaseless reflection, only because of her pious acceptance of it. The immediate relation between father and daughter on which this transference of guilt depends cannot endure the full development of reflection. Thus, Antigone's liberation from the anxious conversion of sorrow into pain could be accomplished simply by pushing reflection to its limits.

Such is not the case with reflective sorrow. The object of reflection, the objective occasion for this state of mind, is not simply alien and opaque to reflection as in the case of the substantial block of inherited guilt; it is

---

[42] I depart here from the Swensons' translation by continuing to render *Sorg* as "sorrow." Their use of both "grief" and "sorrow" to translate the single Danish word is unwise since A has attributed a special technical significance to it.

[43] *Either/Or*, 1:170, 168; *S.V.*, 2:160, 158.

an unanswerable challenge, a paradox, to it. All three tragic heroines discussed in this essay are deceived lovers. But, as A tells us, "deception is for love an absolute paradox."[44] While each of the three cases of deception proves to be a paradox in a different way, it is true of them all that reflection is kept endlessly occupied because it is impossible for both the egoistic and the sympathetic component of love simultaneously to coexist with the deception.

In terms that strikingly parallel those of Johannes Climacus's discussions of the Paradox—the incarnate God—and reflection's inability to "digest" it, A writes that only by an act of will can the process of reflection resulting from this collision of love's two moments be halted. Such a decisive act, however, would propel the sufferer out of the aesthetic stage and, therefore, beyond both A's interest and comprehension.

> The paradox is unthinkable, and yet love persistently attempts to think it, and determined by the momentary dominance of one factor or another, it constantly seeks to think the paradox, often in contradictory fashion, in the ever-unsuccessful effort to understand it. This process of reflection pursues an endless path, and can come to an end only if the individual arbitrarily (*vilkaarlig*) breaks it off by bringing something else into play, a resolution of will, but in so doing the individual brings himself under ethical categories, and loses his aesthetic interest. What he cannot win by reflection, he attains by resolution of the will: finality and rest (*Ende og Hvile*).[45]

So far is A from dwelling on such an exit from the state of reflective sorrow that he seeks rather to follow it out to its most advanced form, to plumb its ultimate depths. It is to this task that he turns in "The Unhappiest Man." Speaking for the last time to the *Symparanekromenoi*, he opens a contest for the title from which the essay gets its name and which the society of the deceased shall judge.

The general characterization of unhappiness within which the following reflections maneuver is drawn, not without a touch of irony, from Hegel. According to Hegel,

---

[44]*Either/Or*, 1:177; *S.V.*, 2:166.

[45]*Either/Or*, 1:178; *S.V.*, 2:166.

The unhappiest person is one who has his ideal, the content of his life, the fullness of his consciousness outside of himself. He is always absent, never present to himself.[46]

Obviously, all four of A's tragic heroines fall within this description. It is not possible, however, to grant any of them that at once dreadful and coveted title, the unhappiest man. This impossibility is best understood by following A's determination of the concept "unhappy" through to its logical conclusion in the concept "unhappiest."

Given that unhappiness consists in being absent from oneself, having one's ideal outside of oneself, it is clear that this state can take either of two forms with regard to time. One may be absent from oneself in the past, that is, one's life may be totally bound up in remembering, or one may be absent from oneself in the future, in which case one's whole life consists in hope. Of the two, the former is to be regarded as the more unhappy. A future in which one is absent may one day become present; the past, however, has already been present, but never more shall be. Due to the irretrievable absence of the past, A concludes that "in a certain sense the future is nearer the present than the past."[47]

Despite this relative advance, the person who lives in his memory is no more to be granted the laurels than is one who lives exclusively in hope. Both these states are present, if not in the present, then in the past and future respectively. A truer absence is found in those who remember a past that never was or who hope for a future they know will never be. A gives examples of these two unfortunate states. First, he paints a picture of a man who, deprived of a normal childhood, nonetheless as an adult remembers (*erindre*) fondly this state after coming to know it in others. As an instance of a man who lives in hope of an impossible future, he describes one who learns to love life and wish for its pleasures only after his own life has passed by.

Following his precedent of characterizing memory as "the real element of the unhappy," A places the former above the latter in the contest for the title. He, however, reserves the prize for an unhappiness more ab-

---

[46]*Either/Or*, 1:220; *S.V.*, 2:204.

[47]*Either/Or*, 1:221; *S.V.*, 2:205.

solute. He describes this final stage of unhappiness as a combination of the last two varieties.

> Let us imagine a combination of the two types of unhappiness already described. . . . There can be but one combination of these two types, and this happens when it is memory which prevents the unhappy individual from finding himself in his hope, and hope which prevents him from finding himself in his memory.[48]

Such a person is ideally unhappy since he is ideally absent from himself. Having neither present, past, nor future in which to live, "he has no contemporary time to support him."[49] An infinitely displaced person, he is a model member of the *Symparanekromenoi*, the society of the living dead.

> He cannot become old, for he has never been young; he cannot become young, for he is already old. In one sense of the word he cannot die, for he has not really lived; in another sense he cannot live, for he is already dead.[50]

What is the origin of this unfortunate state? A notes early in the essay that "a single blow, be it ever so heavy, cannot possibly make a man the unhappiest of all."[51] He explains this by noting that no single misfortune may rob one of both memory and hope, of past and future. If it takes one of the two, the other will be left.

Later, A writes of Job that "He lost all, but not at a single blow; for the Lord took, and the Lord took, and the Lord took."[52] Still, Job does not take the title "the unhappiest man." That he doesn't should make us suspect that his unhappiness is not merely quantitatively but qualitatively distinct from other forms of unhappiness.

This is, in fact, the case. In "The Rotation Method," just such a condition of existence is described as originating not in a blow or a series of

---

[48]*Either/Or*, 1:223; *S.V.*, 2:206.

[49]*Either/Or*, 1:224; *S.V.*, 2:208.

[50]*Either/Or*, 1:224; *S.V.*, 2:207.

[51]*Either/Or*, 1:221; *S.V.*, 2:204.

[52]*Either/Or*, 1:225; *S.V.*, 2:209.

blows or any combination of external forces and events; it can only be brought about by the person himself, intentionally and from within. It is a state born of art: the art of forgetting and recollecting, the art of living without hope.[53]

The paradoxical, opposed character of the aesthete could not be more vividly illustrated. It is now apparent that the condition of supreme unhappiness is the condition of aesthetic omnipotence for which A aims in "The Rotation Method." The loss of all presence, the detachment from all that is earthly and concrete, allows one "to play battledore and shuttlecock with the whole of existence,"[54] and thus to keep the wolf of boredom from the door. The remarkable equation of the unhappiest of men with the happiest with which A concludes his final address to the *Symparanekromenoi* perfectly captures the dual nature of the aesthete's life. In him are combined the highest raptures of pleasure and deepest abysses of melancholy.

In pointing beyond itself to the later essays of *Either/Or* 1 and by providing contrast, "The Unhappiest Man" serves to make apparent the patterns that have prevailed in earlier essays. First, in depicting a mode of aesthetic consciousness that is intentionally produced by the aesthete himself, that is, by showing an aesthete who is a product of his own art, A reveals the "naturalness" of all previously described forms of aesthetic consciousness. This point is obvious in relation to Don Juan; he is himself a force of nature. In the cases of the reflective Antigone, Marie Beaumarchais, Donna Elvira, and Margret, their characteristic states of mind had their origins outside of them. They passively receive either the blow of inherited guilt or the slap of deception, which suffices to initiate the motion of reflection in them. Activity has no other place here than as a possibility, and this possibility exists only for the latter three figures.

The second outstanding feature of the qualitatively new form of aesthetic consciousness described in "The Unhappiest Man" is its self-reflexiveness. As his own work of art, he is essentially preoccupied with himself and only secondarily or instrumentally related to that which is other. This self-absorption becomes evident when it is noted that the unhappiest

---

[53]*Either/Or*, 1:288; *S.V.*, 2:270.

[54]*Either/Or*, 1:290; *S.V.*, 2:271.

man is the perfect representative of the *Symparanekromenoi*. In speaking of him, A is speaking of himself. This practice of focusing one's attention on oneself is continued in all subsequent essays of the volume, thus representing a significant mediation of the opposition between the aesthete as describer and as described, between the aesthete as subject and as object. As Hegel makes clear, such opposition and the difference that spawns it can only be eliminated in self-reflection. Thus, this first instance of the self taking itself as object offers the promise of the fully realized mediation with which the volume closes in "The Diary of a Seducer."

In contrast, the essays considered up to this point have been marked by an outward directedness on the part of the describing aesthete. In "The Immediate Stages of the Erotic," A functions only as observer and describer. His comments about himself concern himself only as observer and describer of the Don and the opera in which he is immortalized. The subject-object dichotomy that this essay displays is partly mediated in the following addresses to the *Symparanekromenoi* in that a reflective aesthete now directs his attention toward and writes about reflective aesthetes. The resulting configuration involves an identity of type between the two poles, but as numerically distinct representatives of the type, describer and described remain different from and opposed to each other.

Restricted to the role of passive observer, A consistently appears in these first essays as a parasite, drawing on the life and energy, the motion and change, that dwells as a natural force in the aesthetes under his observation. I have already characterized this relationship as it appears in the first essay. It is no less obvious in the series of addresses to the *Symparanekromenoi*. The unholy zeal with which these voyeurs seek to gaze into the hidden sufferings of others reflects their need to be stirred up from their dead impotence, from the paralysis of excessive reflection, by the observation of any process of motion and change, even if it is the monotonous oscillation inherent in reflective sorrow. The "sympathetic dread" of these living dead is the means by which they, like vampires, make their meal upon the lifegiving blood of others' sufferings. This dependence represents an element of passivity and receptivity that A attempts to suppress in the next two essays.

"The First Love" and "The Rotation Method"

The most unambiguous and univocal expression of the aesthete as reflective self-producer, as his own work of art, is found in "The Rotation

Method." The essential characteristic of this form of aesthetic consciousness, as far as this study is concerned, is its self-generation of the change and motion on which all aesthetes depend. All previously discussed forms of aesthetic existence have either naturally embodied change, motion, and turbulence or have parasitically relied for life on another aesthete who does. Now, however, a new aspect of the aesthete's agenda with change emerges: change as the product of art.

There is in "The Rotation Method" an increased sophistication on A's part that allows him to see that all change is not created equal and that the avoidance of boredom requires a particular sort of change. Past is the time when A could rejoice in natural flux and disorder; this shows itself in the characterization of the world that lies behind his understanding of boredom: "Boredom depends on the nothingness which pervades reality."[55] Despairing of any satisfaction of his needs from the world around him, A looks exclusively within himself for relief from boredom.

Just as this essay is the first in which change is clearly the product of art, so it is the first in which artful change, change that is produced in accordance with a reflectively held principle, is identified as the only adequate satisfaction of the aesthete's needs.

> Everyone who feels bored cries out for change. With this demand I am in complete sympathy, but it is necessary to act in accordance with some settled principle.[56]

It is from this principle that the essay draws its title "The Rotation Method" (*Vexeldrift*). In its most elementary formulation, this principle appeals to the aesthete's connection of enjoyment and change to establish that the avoidance of boredom requires one to vary one's enjoyments.

Before describing the proper method of rotation, A tells us what does *not* qualify as artful variation. When the principle of rotation is interpreted in a "vulgar and inartistic" manner, when one attempts to vary one's pleasures in an external and superficial way, "one may find oneself driven deeper and deeper into the mire in the effort to escape."[57] This is the case with all those who change the field instead of the crop, to continue in the

---

[55] *Either/Or*, 1:287; *S.V.*, 2:268.

[56] *Either/Or*, 1:287; *S.V.*, 2:269.

[57] Ibid.

agricultural metaphor, that is, all those who seek to avoid boredom either by traveling or by constantly seeking new forms of diversion. Eventually, one either runs out of places to visit or sees that there is no essential difference between them and so boredom prevails. Similarly, one can only temporarily drive off boredom by varying one's amusements, because one becomes increasingly jaded and in need of continually more splendid and diverting entertainments. This process of hedonistic escalation soon outruns human capacity. After burning Rome for curiosity's sake (I draw here on A's version of Roman history), what is Nero to do next?

The sophisticated practitioners of the rotation method follow the farmer in shifting not fields, but crops and methods of cultivation. The goal is to maintain the same circumstances, the same people, the same activities as constantly fresh sources of enjoyment and amusement. Since the externals remain the same, the change must be in the enjoyer himself. Thus, the true rotation method is intensive rather than extensive.

In describing this intensive method of hedonic cultivation, A writes that "every particular change will always come under the general categories of *recollecting* and *forgetting*."[58] "Recollecting" and "forgetting" have for A different meanings than are usually assigned to them. They identify the positive and negative moments of the state of consciousness already described in "The Unhappiest Man." In recommending the art of recollecting as the key to sound aesthetic life, A is calling for the elimination of all presence. In keeping with the common use, recollecting involves for A a consciousness of that which is distant and removed. A makes it clear that the normal temporal character of this distance is not essential to his use of the term when he writes, "it gives one a very peculiar feeling in the midst of one's enjoyment to look back upon it for the purpose of recollecting it."[59]

The act of regarding the present as already past evokes the temporal dislocation of "the unhappiest man." Here, however, A points out the distinct aesthetic advantages of such a state. To limit oneself to recollected enjoyments is both to enjoy and to maintain a distance from that which is being enjoyed. This distance and freedom is a necessary precondition of the variation of self called for by the rotation method.

---

[58]*Either/Or*, 1:288; *S.V.*, 2:270.

[59]*Either/Or*, 1:289; *S.V.*, 2:271.

Since recollecting is a way of relating to a temporally present enjoyment, "forgetting is an art which must be practiced beforehand."[60] Forgetting is the negative moment of this state of mind; it involves the distancing of the enjoyment, the limitation of personal involvement with that which is being enjoyed. This stance makes it possible for the aesthete to appreciate from afar, to recollect.

One can only experience in such a noncommittal, tentative way if one has surrendered all hope, for "whoever plunges into his experiences with the momentum of hope will recollect in such wise that he is unable to forget."[61] This individual is too immediately and unreservedly caught up in his experience to forget it properly, that is, to ever set it at such a distance that it might be recollected. Therefore, to master the art of forgetting, and, thus, lay the basis for recollecting is,

> from the beginning . . . [to] keep the enjoyment under control, never spreading every sail to the wind in any resolve . . . to devote oneself to pleasure with a certain suspicion, a certain wariness.[62]

Just as the single art producing the state of mind characteristic of this reserved enjoyer has both positive and negative dimensions, so are there positive and negative dimensions of its relation to the change the aesthete craves. As has been seen, the only change capable of repelling boredom for any length of time is intensive; it involves the variation of the aesthete himself. The distancing, the removal of presence, the elimination of immediacy, which the art of forgetting and recollecting accomplishes, is the key to this intensive variation.

While it is essential to avoid "sticking fast in some relationship of life" such that one is daily pressed into contact with the same person or circumstances, the practitioner of the rotation method accepts, as the cruder aesthete does not, the limits, both practical and ideal, on the variation of the occasions of his enjoyment and diversion. He finds himself in a given locale that, in itself, affords a finite number of hedonic possibilities. Such finitude would quickly give rise to boredom were it not for the positive as-

---

[60] *Either/Or*, 1:289; *S.V.*, 2:270.

[61] Ibid.

[62] *Either/Or*, 1:289; *S.V.*, 2:271.

pect of the art of forgetting and recollecting: the arbitrary assignment of meaning. The initial negative moment of the art distances and frees the aesthete sufficiently from the circumstances in which he finds himself that the immediately given, public significance of events and persons does not bind him. He is thus in a position to assign whatever significance he pleases and thereby to determine his own enjoyment.

> One does not enjoy the immediate but something which he arbitrarily imports into it. You go to see the middle of a play, you read the third part of a book. By this means you insure yourself a very different enjoyment from that which the author has been so kind as to plan for you.[63]

In expounding his technique of "systematic arbitrariness," the very core of the rotation method, A details his attempt to assuage exclusively by means of art his hunger for change. All attention is directed toward his method. The controlling supposition is that if the method is perfected, if the aesthete conducts himself in a sufficiently artistic manner, then variation and change will be adequately provided and boredom avoided. The finite number of immediately available occasions for enjoyment and diversion are rendered infinitely productive by the aesthete's art since one and the same person or event may be enjoyed in any number of ways. When one arbitrary vision of one's surroundings grows tedious, one simply seizes upon some new accidental feature to elevate to all-importance. "The eye with which you look at reality must constantly be changed."[64]

"The Rotation Method" represents a radical antithesis to the vision of "The Immediate Stages of the Erotic" concerning the relation of the aesthete to change. In A's first essay, change is presented as natural force; in the essay presently under discussion, it is exclusively the product of principle-governed action. As I have frequently asserted, each essay's vision of the aesthete's relation to change varies with its subject-object structure. This assertion is confirmed here in the way that the subject-object structure of "The Rotation Method" differs from that of "The Immediate Stages of the Erotic."

The contrast is in fact twofold. First, whereas in the earlier essay, the observing, recording aesthete directs all of his attention toward Don Juan,

---

[63]*Either/Or*, 1:295; *S.V.*, 2:276.

[64]*Either/Or*, 1:296; *S.V.*, 2:276.

in the later essay, A is concerned with the theory of social prudence by which he himself acts. This redirection of attention represents a move from an extroversion in which the subject takes the radically other as its object to the introversion of self-reflection.

The technique of systematic arbitrariness points toward the second disparity in the subject-object structures of the two essays. The artistic omnipotence of A in "The Rotation Method" has as its counterpart the total emptying of the objects of his enjoyment. These objects are stripped of all inherent, immediately given significance and reduced to mere blank screens onto which A projects whatever meaning he desires. Using a somewhat different metaphor to say the same thing, A writes:

> Forgetting is the true expression for an ideal process of assimilation by which experience is reduced to a sounding-board for the soul's own music.[65]

In contrast, "The Immediate Stages of the Erotic" places A over against not an object to which all must be given but rather one from which all is taken. In the earlier essay, A repeatedly states that all that he knows, says, and feels he owes to the infinite richness of the opera.

In the final paragraph of "The Rotation Method," A admits the sketchiness and excessive abstractness of his discussion. "It is impossible here to go into detail, for no theory can adequately embrace the concrete."[66] Though effectively masked by a thoroughgoing irony, "The First Love" represents a concrete application of the technique abstractly presented in the essay it precedes.

"The First Love" is composed of three distinct sections: first, general comments on the category "occasion"; second, a description of the occasion(s) of the present critique; and, finally, the actual critique of the play by Scribe from which the essay draws its name.

While it is exclusively in the third part of the essay that the method of arbitrariness is applied, as such, the opening section of the essay is also significant. It describes the occasion (*Anledning*) as the negatively productive moment that leads forth (*lede an*) literary productions out of noth-

---

[65] *Either/Or*, 1:290; *S.V.*, 2:271.

[66] *Either/Or*, 1:296; *S.V.*, 2:276.

ing. The occasion is too accidental to qualify as the ground or cause (*Grund eller Aarsag*) of the production. Nonetheless, it is essential; A asserts that no balanced literary work can come into existence without it.

The concept "occasion," as thus far described, nicely subsumes the objects enjoyed by the practitioner of rotation. While A requires some situation in which to practice the art of arbitrariness, there is no positive contribution of that situation to A's enjoyment. Thus, the objects of A's enjoyment are negatively productive, accidentally related to the enjoyment, but nonetheless essential to it. They are its occasions.

Though "The First Love"'s analysis of the concept "occasion" is a source of enrichment for our knowledge of the rotation method, A ironically obscures this fact. He appears to continue to speak of the grounds and causes of literary production, be that production creative or critical. Since external grounds and causes are lacking in the rotating aesthete's enjoyment, there appears to be an asymmetry between these essays' visions of literary and hedonic production. In "The First Love," the play and all its constituent elements, the script, staging, casting, and so forth, are said to be too essential to be called occasions. In the essay's second part, a chance meeting, accidental encounters with copies of the play, and, ultimately, the spilling of an inkwell while reaching for an apricot are said to be the critique's occasions.

If A were straightforwardly stating this, it would be necessary to attribute importantly different theories of production to "The First Love" and "The Rotation Method." However, in reading the actual review of Scribe's play, it becomes apparent that this insignificant dramatic work is exactly and nothing more than the occasion of A's remarks, his protestations to the contrary notwithstanding. A speaks of Scribe as an immortal artist and of "The First Love" as his classic work in almost the same terms as he has earlier spoken of Mozart and *Don Juan*. There are even passages that obviously mimic some of the most brilliant passages from "The Immediate Stages of the Erotic." The difference is that whereas A was infinitely in debt to Mozart and *Don Juan,* whereas in the earlier essay he simply brought to voice the inherent riches of the work, in this essay A makes of a hack artist's bit of buffoonery an immortal work. That is, A makes something of nothing, projects significance onto that which previously lacked it, arbitrarily transforming given reality in order to amuse himself. Mackey perceptively notes the correspondence of A's literary practice in "The First Love" with his theory in "The Rotation Method."

An example of A's literary employment of the method of arbitrariness is his unpublished review of Augustin Scribe's one-act play, *Les premièrs amours*. Commentators have several times noted that Scribe's farce is unworthy of the attention—not to mention the pages! that "Kierkegaard" has lavished upon it. But it is a product of A's ingenuity and a typical product at that. He knows that the play is trivial, and reviews it for precisely that reason. Otherwise wholly nugatory, the little comedy serves as an occasion on which A can display to himself his own poetic cleverness—and revel in the conceit of doing something worthless in the most exquisite style. By seizing the occasion—any occasion—and turning it to capricious ends, he makes and unmakes his situation as it pleases him. He is at once the donor and recipient of his delights.[67]

Though "The First Love" contributes little directly to our knowledge of A's agenda with change, it is clear that it is in essential continuity with "The Rotation Method" in that it presents art as all-powerful. This unqualified assertion of art's power, however, needs to be qualified just as the assertion of the natural did in "The Immediate Stages of the Erotic." The dialectic of *Either/Or* 1 takes us beyond both of these onesided realizations of aesthetic existence in the final entry, "Diary of a Seducer," by joining the two antithetical visions in a higher synthesis. It is to this culminating moment of aesthetic existence that I now turn.

---

[67]Mackey, *Kierkegaard: A Kind of Poet*, 11.

CHAPTER V

The Final Synthesis: Art and Nature in "Diary of a Seducer"

After seeking life-giving change first in nature and then in art, the aesthete is now ready for a higher vision in which both are given their due, in which a more fundamental and complete turbulence is produced through the interaction of both principles. "Diary of a Seducer" supplies just such a vision. It is here that the seducer, the very embodiment of unalleviated reflectivity and absolute artfulness, and Cordelia, the unplucked flower of pure immediacy, are shown to complement each other perfectly.[1] Through a demonic dialectic, they achieve, albeit momentarily, a height of passion whose very possibility is unsuspected by ordinary human beings.

---

[1] Speaking of the "unfolding [of a] . . . whole divinely rich nature" in a perfect aesthetic moment, Johannes writes, "I am one of the few who can do this, she is one of the few who is fitted for this; are we not well suited to one another?" *Either/Or*, 1:380; *S.V.*, 2:356.

Throughout my discussion of *Either/Or* 1, I have asserted that the subject-object structure of each of the entries corresponds to the vision of the aesthete's relation to change represented there. In continuing to support this view, I will show that the final mediation of subject and object is to be seen in "Diary of a Seducer" as a counterpart to the depiction of quintessential aesthetic change as the product of art and nature.

The mediation of subject and object involves, of course, self-reflection in which the subject is its own object. Both "The Rotation Method" and, in a more limited manner, "The First Love," however, display this structure. In the latter, A describes at some length how he came to write the critique at hand, and, in the former, he scrutinizes the theory by which he attempts to conduct his life. Setting aside "The First Love" as a first, tenuous brush with self-reflective structure, how does "Diary of a Seducer" represent a more perfect mediation of subject and object than its immediate predecessor, "The Rotation Method"?

The difference between the two entries becomes apparent upon exploring what is involved in complete mediation. Not only is self-reflection involved but identity of function as well. That is, if perfect mediation is to be achieved, the roles of subject and object must not be different from each other. In "The Rotation Method," they are. As A himself points out, the essay is an abstract treatise. As its author, A assumes the role of an observer exacting rules and principles from the endeavors and activities in which it is his wont to engage. Thus, the essay involves a separation of A as observer and formulator and A as practitioner.

This separation is not present in "Diary of a Seducer." As a diarist, and more particularly as a diarist who consistently writes in the present tense as if the described events were even now occurring, Johannes strides forth simultaneously as agent and observer. His role formally reflects his nature. Not content to theorize, as does A, about the aesthetic life, he is always in action, or more descriptively, on the hunt. As a thoroughly reflective person, he never acts spontaneously, that is, without prior consideration and artful design. Thus, we see substantively in Johannes and formally in his Diary the ultimate aesthetic mediation of subject and object.

There is an appearance of inconsistency between the two mediations that take place in "Diary of a Seducer." The recognition that both art and nature contribute essentially to the climactic turbulence for which the aesthete yearns appears to imply that the aesthete is to some degree passive, receptive, and dependent. His art is needed to enhance nature, but he relies on nature for that which he cannot himself provide. This dependence on nature appears to involve a degree of extroversion inconsistent with perfect subject-object mediation. Hegel's vision of Absolute Knowing, with which the *Phenomenology* culminates, illuminates this point. There, perfect subject-object mediation involves the total elimination of otherness, as Spirit's externalization of itself is led back into full self-consciousness. In terms closer to the text at hand, it is hard to see how Johannes can reconcile the relative passivity and receptivity required of him by the one mediation with the absolute interpenetration of action with reflection required of him by the other.

This apparent conflict is circumvented by the inner complexity of the seducer's self and the corresponding complexity of his relations with reality beyond him. A supplies an important sketch of the structure of Johannes's enjoyment in his introduction to the Diary.

> In the first instance he enjoyed the aesthetic personally, in the second instance he enjoyed his own aesthetic personality. In the first instance the point was that he enjoyed egoistically and personally what in part was reality's gift to him and in part was that with which he himself had impregnated reality; in the second instance his personality was effaced, and he enjoyed the situation. In the first instance he constantly needed reality as occasion, as factor; in the second instance, reality was submerged in the poetic.[2]

At the first level, Johannes's enjoyment represents the mediation of art, "that with which he had himself impregnated reality," and nature, "reality's gift." Later, by "dropping back" a level, taking this initial dialectic as an object and thus "submerging it in the poetic," Johannes "recaptures a productive relation to the events,"[3] that is, realizes in himself the self-enclosedness associated with total subject-object mediation.

Having completed this preliminary sketch of the psychic configuration that constitutes the seducer's ideal and aim, I now turn to a more detailed analysis of each of the two levels of enjoyment, examining first the dialectic of art and nature that constitutes the first level of enjoyment and

---

[2]*Either/Or*, 1:301; *S.V.*, 2:283.

[3]Henriksen, *Kierkegaards Romaner*, 80.

then investigating the enjoyment-once-removed of the second level. This translates into examining, first, the interactions of Johannes and Cordelia as they unfold within the Diary and, then, turning to the more elusive question of the seen Diary's relation to the unseen diarist.

The Dialectic of Art and Nature

Whereas development has hitherto involved differences between essays, each of which represents a single subject-object structure and corresponding vision of the role of change in the aesthete's life, "Diary of a Seducer" is characterized by shifting emphases, drastic changes of aspect, and a continually developing relationship between Johannes, the Diary's subject, and the various objects of his attention, notably Cordelia. This internal complexity sets the Diary apart from the preceding essays, allowing it not only to complete but also to recapitulate in a compressed and somewhat altered manner the dialectic that has unfolded throughout *Either/Or* 1.

This dimension of recapitulation is manifest in the Diary's opening pages. Before any encounter with Cordelia, Johannes appears as an unobserved observer, impassively but unblinkingly gathering in visions of the anxious "sweet unrest" of the young girls of Copenhagen. Such a picture of tumultuous immediate life over against an essentially quiet reflectivity calls to mind "The Immediate Stages of the Erotic." A crucial difference is evident, however, in that Johannes never appears in the desperately dependent light in which A is bathed in the earlier essay. Here appears rather a reflective aesthete who is as assured and superior as he is interested. The difference in attitude stems from the seducer's knowledge that despite its intensity, the turbulence of immediacy is undeveloped. It stands in need of qualitative transformation before it can assume aesthetic significance. Only the methodic stimulation and restraint provided by his reflective management of the young girls' immediate vivacity is capable of initiating this transformation. Thus, though the characterizations in these pages of the immediate and the reflective aesthetes appear similar to those of "The Immediate Stages of the Erotic," the introduction into the Diary of considerations of quality means that here the overall "thesis" of the earlier essay is turned on its head. Whereas nature appeared there as all-sufficient and powerful, here the necessity of art predominates.

Personal Unity in Kierkegaard's Thought

The one-sidedness of these first pages of the seducer's Diary is soon strikingly redressed. In an abrupt change of tone, Johannes's placid demeanor is stimulated into frantic excitation by a passing glimpse of a girl who will in the Diary's next section be identified as Cordelia Wahl. Johannes writes:

> I scarcely recognize myself. My mind is like a turbulent sea, swept by the storms of passion. If another could see my soul in this condition, it would seem to him like a boat that buried its prow deep in the sea, as if in its terrible speed it would rush down into the abyss.[4]

Just as Johannes appears in a different light in these pages, the descriptions of Cordelia contrast profoundly with those previously provided of young girls. When Johannes next sees her, it is her calmness, her placid demeanor, that dominates his description:

> She was alone, preoccupied, manifestly not with herself but with her thoughts. She was not thinking, but the quiet play of her thoughts wove a picture of longing before her soul.
>
> [T]his preoccupation afforded infinite rest and peace in her soul. . . . Quiet peace broods over her. . . . She walked slowly, no precipitancy disturbed her peace or the quiet of her surroundings.[5]

This second complex of descriptions vividly indicates Johannes's need for "reality's gift": unsullied immediacy. Johannes not only demonstrates this need in the new warmth and life that infuses his cold, dead soul after he sees Cordelia, he explicitly states its truth.

---

[4]*Either/Or*, 1:320; *S.V.*, 2:301. The passage continues, "He does not see that high on the mast a lookout sits on watch. Roar on, ye wild forces, ye powers of passion! Let your dashing waves hurl their foam against the sky. You shall not engulf me. Serene I sit like the king of the cliff." This second half of the entry does not contradict, as it might seem to, the first half in which the turbulence of Johannes's soul is accentuated. Rather, it alludes to the second level of his enjoyment in which the seducer assumes the position of placid spectator even in relation to his own excitation. While I here emphasize exclusively the first level at which Johannes is swept up in a storm of passion, I will later return to the lookout high atop the mast who rises above, observes, and enjoys the storms below.

[5]*Either/Or*, 1:327-28; *S.V.*, 2:307.

> And should I not be content, I who regard myself as a favorite of the gods,
> I who had the rare good fortune to fall in love again? That is something
> that no art, no study, can effect, it is a gift.[6]

His exultation sets Johannes distinctly apart from the naive self-sufficiency A pretends to in "The Rotation Method." Cordelia is no mere "occasion," no mere "blank screen" onto which significance is arbitrarily projected; she is a rare gift possessing potential that marks her as distinct from other girls.

It is with an eye to this potential that Johannes recovers his composure and reasserts himself as the artist, the active developer, of feminine immediacy. His characteristic aesthetic thirst for tumultuous change dictates the goal of the development: "Her soul is to be set in motion, agitated in every possible direction; not, however, piecemeal and by sudden gusts, but totally."[7] It is Johannes's intent not only to create but also to be swept up himself in the hurricane of Cordelia's passion.

While he never loses sight of his goal, Johannes knows that he will achieve only paltry results if he pursues it with the impatience and directness of his immediate counterpart, Don Juan.

> I might attempt to raise an erotic storm, powerful enough to tear up trees
> by the roots. By its aid I might try, if possible, to sweep her out of her
> historic continuity; attempt to arouse her passion. . . . However, that would
> be all wrong from the aesthetic standpoint . . . for too much confusion is
> bad. Its effect on Cordelia would utterly fail. In a couple of draughts I should
> have swallowed what I might have had the good of for a long time, indeed,
> even worse, what with discretion I might have enjoyed more fully and
> richly.[8]

This fuller and richer enjoyment corresponds to the qualitatively more profound passion Johannes sets about to ignite in Cordelia's breast. As a reflective seducer, this is his proper sphere; his concern is not how many, the quantitative, but simply how, the qualitative.

---

[6]*Either/Or*, 1:330; *S. V.*, 2:309.

[7]*Either/Or*, 1:386; *S.V.*, 2:361.

[8]*Either/Or*, 1:362-64; *S.V.*, 2:339-41.

The Diary records in detail the demonic stratagems Johannes uses to drive the confused and anxious girl to ever higher levels of romantic tension. While these ploys vary widely, they share a profound ambivalence; they never excite without simultaneously restraining, they never heat without simultaneously cooling.

> I work to develop the contrast, I tense the bow of love to wound the deeper. Like an archer, I release the string, tighten it again, listen to its song, my battle ode.[9]

After tensing the cord of Cordelia's soul to the breaking point, Johannes takes the penultimate step in the seduction, the step before the final enjoyment, of magnifying and unleashing all the energy and passion that has been pent up over the long process of the seduction. It is a tribute to the seducer's indirectness that this last act of development is his most negative. After insinuating himself ever more completely into her soul, after taking such elaborate steps to inflame her, the seducer suddenly becomes cold and aloof. In the following passage, he describes the psychic processes this action initiates and thus tells how a titanic passion is inspired and an absolute self-surrender evoked from the unfortunate Cordelia.

> So far I would call her passion a naive passion. When the change (*Vendingen*) comes, and I begin to draw back in earnest, then she will really muster all her resources in order to captivate me. She has no way to accomplish this except by means of the erotic, but this will now appear on a very different scale. It then becomes a weapon in her hand which she swings against me. . . . Then her passion becomes definite, energetic, conclusive, logical; her kiss total, her embrace firm.—In me she seeks her freedom, the more firmly I encompass her, the better she finds it. The engagement is broken. When this happens, then she needs a little rest, so that this wild tumult may not bring out something unseemly. Then her passion gathers itself again, and she is mine.[10]

All goes exactly as Johannes's plan indicates. The seducer assumes a purely intellectual demeanor; he is enthusiastic for ideas but has "neither

---

[9]*Either/Or*, 1:345; *S.V.*, 2:323.

[10]*Either/Or*, 1:406-407; *S.V.*, 2:379-80.

eyes nor ears for her."[11] Cooling even further, he uses ironic glances to rid the girl of any notion that she may consider him her own. As predicted, her passion is qualitatively transformed and thereby greatly intensified. Whereas the above quotation begins by calling her passion naive, after putting his plan into action, the seducer writes that now "she does not rise up in naive charm, nor in immaculate serenity, but is influenced by the strong heart throbs of love."[12] Just as he promised, Johannes has taught Cordelia what it is to love. By his icy removal he has caused the immediate sexual urge to be elevated to reflective desire. An earlier passage confirms and expands this understanding of the change. Wondering whether Cordelia is a proper subject for quintessential aesthetic development, the seducer writes:

> The question is always whether her femininity is strong enough to let itself become reflective (*at lade sig reflectere sig*), or whether it is only to be enjoyed as beauty and charm; the question is whether one dare to tense the bow more strongly. Certainly, it is a wonderful thing to find a pure immediate femininity, but if one dares to attempt the change (*Changementet*), then one gets the interesting.[13]

"The change" is here associated with the coming of reflectivity. This question as to whether the girl's femininity is strong enough to become reflective is surprising as it stands. It will be remembered that Johannes views woman under the category "being for another." Explaining this category, he writes, "the being which is for another *is* not, and only becomes visible, as it were, by the interposition of another. . . . [therefore] Woman is, namely, substance [immediacy], man is reflection."[14]

Johannes's question makes sense only if it is taken to mean *not* that a femininity sufficiently strong will produce reflection (the only interpretation the present English translation allows), but rather that only a strong femininity can bear the tension caused by coexistence with its polar opposite, reflectivity. That the latter reading is correct is confirmed by Jo-

---

[11]*Either/Or*, 1:415; *S.V.*, 2:388.

[12]*Either/Or*, 1:419; *S.V.*, 2:391-92.

[13]*Either/Or*, 1:340; *S.V.*, 2:319.

[14]*Either/Or*, 1:425-26; *S.V.*, 2:397.

hannes's statements that with the seduction's culmination, the girl, as such, is destroyed. "In relation to me, she must *zu Grunde gehn*, as the philosophers say."[15] The tension can be sustained only momentarily, after which the girl becomes a woman and no longer interests Johannes. This explains the choice of the Diary's motto, *Sua passion' predominante e' la giovin principante* ("His ruling passion is the fresh young girl"). Only when this immediacy is sufficiently hardy can it coexist with reflection long enough for the seducer to enjoy the colossal turmoil produced by this elemental conflict. Herein lies an explanation of the great intensification of Cordelia's passion that follows Johannes's cold withdrawal.

This power drives Cordelia to break the engagement as an external bond; she is led to see it as a bow to conventional respectability that actually separates the two. After she is allowed a short rest in the country with friends, Johannes's servant comes to fetch the willing sacrifice to the satanic altar. As midnight approaches and the seducer hurries to claim the final prize, it is clear that he participates in the passionate exuberance he has inspired in Cordelia. "How vigorous is my soul, sound, happy, omnipresent like a god."[16]

The mutual stimulation of seducer and seduced is apparent here. Considering this moment of consummation in the context of the mediation of their opposition, however, it becomes clear that just as Cordelia's immediacy goes up into reflection, so Johannes's reflectivity descends into momentary immediacy. He writes in the Diary's penultimate entry, "Everything is symbol; I myself am a myth about myself, for is it not as a myth that I hasten to this meeting?"[17] As noted above, Kierkegaard understands myth as "the compacting (suppressed being) of the idea of eternity (the eternal idea) in the categories of time and space."[18] Thus, to

---

[15]*Either/Or*, 1:348; *S.V.*, 2:326.

[16]*Either/Or*, 1:439; *S.V.*, 2:409. "[T]he erotic energy she is developing is admirable. How interesting she is in this deep passionateness, how great she becomes, almost supernaturally so! . . . Everything is in movement, but in these elemental storms I find myself precisely in my element. . . . There is a power in her, an energy, as if she were a valkyrie." *Either/Or*, 1:419; *S.V.*, 2:392.

[17]Ibid.

[18]*J. and P.*, 2799; *Pap.* 1 A 300.

become a myth about oneself is to allow the eternal in one—spirit, and hence reflection—to be pressed back into immediacy. Henriksen confirms this interpretation, reaching the same conclusion by a different route. Noting that Johannes in a previous letter to Cordelia has contrasted myth and history, he points out that in the pseudonymous works, Kierkegaard always uses "history" to mean "continuity in the activity of the free will."

> To become a myth means to renounce freedom, to let spirit revert to flesh, where, though it does not perish, neither can it remain.[19]

A seems to have just such an incarnation in mind when he says of the seducer: "[S]ometimes . . . he assumed a parastatic body and was then sheer sensuality."[20]

This description indicates why a seduction is the only activity that can rejuvenate Johannes's soul, a soul withered from its excessive reflectivity. Vigilius Haufniensis writes that "the extremest expression of the sensuous is precisely the sexual."[21] Thus, it is in sex as in no other dimension of human life that spirit can rid itself of itself completely and revert to flesh, to immediacy.

> [I]n the culmination of the erotic spirit cannot take part . . . it cannot express itself in the erotic experience; it feels itself a stranger. It says as it were to the erotic, "My dear, I cannot be a third party here, therefore I will hide myself for the time being."[22]

---

[19] Henriksen, *Kierkegaards Romaner*, 52.

[20] *Either/Or*, 1:304; *S.V.*, 2:285.

[21] *The Concept of Anxiety*, 49; *S.V.*, 6:142.

[22] *The Concept of Anxiety*, 71; *S.V.*, 6:162. Vigilius Haufniensis continues the passage, "But this precisely is dread." He thus calls our attention to the dark underside of the tremendous passion Johannes and Cordelia achieve. The truth, which the seducer avoids confronting, is that all the power and energy developed in the moment of the girl's self-surrender and his acceptance is dread. Already in "The Immediate Stages of the Erotic," we met dread in a similar guise. "There is dread in [Don Juan], but this dread is his energy . . . the whole power of sensuousness . . . is born in dread, but this joy is precisely the demonic joy of life." *Either/Or*, 1:129; *S.V.*, 2:121. Don Juan's dread is purely substantial, that is, characteristic of the immediate. Later pseudonymous works make it clear that dread increases

The submersion of the spirit in the flesh involved in an ordinary sex act is beneath Johannes. Through his artistry, he has elevated Cordelia's immediacy to reflectivity, unleashed her passion, and by its power is able to fling himself out of reality and into the mythical. What he says of Cordelia in this respect goes equally well for himself.

> [I]n her bold flight she loses sight of . . . the mainland of reality in general so that her soul destroys an imperfect human form, in order to hasten to something higher than humanity in general.[23]

Thus, in the seduction's final moment, immediacy goes up into reflection and reflection goes down into immediacy. Difference is, if but for an instant, taken up into unity. This union constitutes the fullest possible mediation of art and nature. Appropriately, Johannes goes to Cordelia with equal praise for both principles in his mouth.

> Her beauty was a gift of Nature. I give thee thanks, O wonderful Nature. . . . Her development was my handiwork—soon I shall enjoy my reward.—How much I have gathered into this one moment which now draws nigh.[24]

Unfortunately, after that one moment, all is finished. Cordelia can no longer transport him into the mythical, the aesthetic reality "back of the world in which we live."[25] Desiring never to see her again, Johannes drives off in his carriage, ready to reenact the process with a new victim.

---

with greater reflectivity. Thus, as Johannes initiates "the change" in Cordelia and reflection encounters immediacy, he produces in her "the indescribable, fascinating anxiety which makes her beauty interesting." *Either/Or*, 1:358; *S.V.*, 2:336. This is one of the few places where Johannes acknowledges that what appears interesting to him is experienced by the girl as dread. See Henriksen, *Kierkegaards Romaner*, 39. The resulting passion in her empowers him to depart from reality and become myth, which we have already been told "precisely is dread." Thus, the tremendous power generated in the seduction issues from the paired dynamos of the two lovers' dread. See Henriksen, *Kierkegaards Romaner*, 44-45.

[23]*Either/Or*, 1:422; *S.V.*, 2:394.

[24]*Either/Or*, 1:439; *S.V.*, 2:409-10.

[25]*Either/Or*, 1:302; *S.V.*, 2:283.

The Mediation of Subject and Object

Demonstrating the occurrence of the second elimination of difference in a higher unity, the mediation of subject and object, is a task far different from the one just completed. Whereas the complementary roles of nature and art are directly described in a wealth of passages, this new investigation must proceed on the basis of a limited amount of largely indirect evidence. Furthermore, since this second mediation is apparently incompatible with the first, it is necessary to reconcile the two in the course of describing the unification of subject and object.

Earlier, I noted that acknowledging the essential role of the natural or immediate in the "romantic dialectic" also appears to involve acknowledging an element of passivity and receptivity on the seducer's part incompatible with the unqualified activity and self-enclosedness characteristic of perfect subject-object mediation. At that point, I quoted a passage from A's introduction to the Diary that suggests that the two apparently conflicting demands could be seen as compatible when the complex nature of the seducer's interaction with the world is taken into account. I quote that passage once again.

> In the first instance he enjoyed the aesthetic personally, in the second instance he enjoyed his own aesthetic personality. In the first instance the point was that he enjoyed egoistically and personally what in part was reality's gift to him and in part was that with which he himself had impregnated reality; in the second instance his personality was effaced, and he enjoyed the situation. In the first instance he constantly needed reality as occasion, as factor; in the second instance, reality was submerged in the poetic.[26]

The clear suggestion of the last of these paired descriptive statements is that the dependence on reality characteristic of the first level of enjoyment is somehow canceled in the process of dropping back to the second level. That is, as "reality [is] submerged in the poetic," the seducer "recaptures a productive relation to the events" and thereby eliminates the element of passivity and extroversion that blocked perfect subject-object mediation.

---

[26] *Either/Or*, 1:301; *S.V.*, 2:283.

Personal Unity in Kierkegaard's Thought

While recognition of the two-tiered structure of the seducer's experience promises to remove this obstacle to subject-object mediation, it appears to raise another obstacle in its place. More accurately, it appears to contradict the claim that such a mediation could take place. In describing the two levels of Johannes's enjoyment, A seems to say that the seducer is a fundamentally divided personality. One aspect of him actively pursues female prey and, according to his success, enjoys at the first level. The other remains aloof, relishing the spectacle of his alter ego's activities, and enjoys at the second level. The seducer, himself, seems to suggest just such an inner division. He writes, "[O]ne ought always to transcend [the moment] a little, so as not only to be baptismal candidate but also priest."[27] In an even more striking passage, quoted above, he first describes himself as tossed wildly about on the seas of passion and then notes that a lookout sits high atop the mast, rising above and observing the storms below. This statement presents an especially vivid image of the two levels of enjoyment and can be read quite plausibly in such a way that the distance between the lookout and the tossing ship is a figurative representation of the gap between the different components of the seducer's self.

If this were an accurate reading, "Diary of a Seducer" would represent no fuller subject-object mediation than does "The Rotation Method." As noted above, self-reflectivity in "The Rotation Method" is not absolute since the observing, describing subject and the observed agent represent different aspects of A's self. The abstract formulation of hedonic principles and their actual employment stand at a distance from each other; it would appear that the seducer is similarly divided between the observing diarist and the acting hedonist who provides material for the Diary's pages. This observation would suggest that a diarist is inherently characterized by such a division and thus that the assertion that Johannes's Diary is a formal reflection of his mediation of subject and object within himself is incorrect.

I will show that these descriptions of the two levels of the seducer's experience can, however, be read in another manner than that just suggested. The best route to this more correct reading is through a consideration of the form of Johannes's Diary and the way this form sets it apart from ordinary diaries.

---

[27]*Either/Or*, 1:338; *S.V.*, 2:317.

Typically, a diary is a book in which one retrospectively records the events of the day and, to a greater or lesser extent, one's thoughts and feelings about them. While such writings ordinarily would be more concrete than A's abstract self-assessment in "The Rotation Method," nonetheless, there is a differentiation of subject and object due to the temporal gap between the occurrence of the events and their description in the Diary. Thus, the characteristic use of the past tense in writing a diary demonstrates a relative differentiation between describer and described.

The outstanding stylistic characteristic of Johannes's Diary is precisely its almost invariant use of the present tense. A points out that though the events described occur before they are set down in writing, they are "often described with the dramatic vividness of an action taking place before one's very eyes."[28] The result is a literary reproduction of unqualifiedly reflective action. As written in the present tense, it places its readers in the midst of a world of action. As a diary, these actions are set within a context of unbounded reflection; every move Johannes makes is represented as preplanned and is accompanied by an explanation of intent. His account of his maneuvers and ploys contain no hint of immediacy or spontaneity. Here one sees the perfect identification of observer and agent, subject and object. No gap separates these two dimensions of the seducer as he appears within the bounds of his Diary.

A gap most certainly does exist, however, between the world of the Diary and the world in which the described events actually take place. The gap is, in the first and simplest sense, temporal. Even though Johannes writes in the present tense, this recording of his actions and thoughts can only have been written after the fact. More fundamentally, a gap exists between the substance of Johannes's descriptions and the events described. A explicitly indicates this gap when he writes that Johannes "constantly reproduced the experience more or less poetically. His Diary is therefore neither historically exact nor simply fiction, not indicative but subjunctive."[29]

Even without A's statement, we could arrive at the same view on the basis of internal evidence. A great number of occurrences recorded in the

---

[28] *Either/Or*, 1:301; *S.V.*, 2:283.

[29] *Either/Or*, 1:300; *S.V.*, 2:282.

Diary strain our credulity to the breaking point if taken as accurate reports of the events of Johannes's life. When the seduction demands it, doors swing open to admit him as an intimate friend of the family even though he was until then unknown to them. At just the right moment, a suitably inept suitor falls into the seducer's hands, ready to play his role in Cordelia's development. The girl dissolves the engagement just as he wishes once he becomes cold and aloof, a reaction that Kierkegaard knew, from his own unfortunate dealings with Regine Olsen, not to be universal. In short, the action too perfectly follows the seducer's plan.[30]

While it appears safe to conclude with A that the Diary is not simple fiction, it is impossible to say how much of its content corresponds to anything even vaguely similar in the world of reality. The whole demonic sequence may have been set off in Johannes's mind by the most tenuous of contacts with flesh and blood.[31] Perhaps the seducer, struck by the sight of an unidentified girl in a green cape, constructs the whole seduction in his imagination. On the other hand, A leads one to believe that there really was a Cordelia who was deceived, seduced, and abandoned by the Diary's author. In the final analysis, the Diary leaves one unable to say anything definite about its correspondence to reality except to say that it is neither a perfect copy nor altogether fictional. The world of the Diary, though inspired by actual events, exists as an independent realm. Those elements introduced from the more terrestrial realm of reality are so assimilated into this new psychic landscape that they become an integral part of it and do not betray their alien origin.

The relation of the Diary to reality is the model by which one ought to understand the relation of the first level of enjoyment to the second. The first level is one of genuine interaction with the world. It is here that art and nature play their respective roles in the creation of something aesthetically higher and better than either could give rise to alone. These interactions stimulate the poet in Johannes so that by reliving them in the world of his Diary, they can assume aesthetic proportions that are larger than life. A writes, "The fruit of the first stage is thus the mood from which the Diary emerges as the fruit of the second stage."[32]

---

[30] Aage Henriksen, *Kierkegaards Romaner*, 81-83.

[31] Ibid., 82.

[32] *Either/Or*, 1:301; *S.V.*, 2:283.

In taking "reality's gift" up into itself and imaginatively transforming it, perhaps beyond recognition, in "submerging" reality in the poetic, the movement to the second level of enjoyment cancels the element of passivity, dependence, and interaction characteristic of the first. Thus, it wins for the world of the Diary the aesthetic autonomy requisite to full subject-object mediation. This mediation is embodied in the Diary in the form of an agent who is simultaneously and indistinguishably observer.

While these mediations are completed and reconciliation is accomplished in the world of the Diary, Johannes's relation to that world must still be established. What is one to make of the gap between the world he physically inhabits and the world he imaginatively creates, between the Johannes of flesh and blood and his poetic doppelgänger? All indications are that the seducer is taken up into the world of his Diary just as are the events that stimulated its production. The seducer's practice of writing in the present tense is not merely a clever literary conceit, it is the mark of his literal reliving of the events within the poetic medium of the Diary. This reliving is, in fact, more real to the seducer than the original experience, untransformed and stained with the mundane soil of reality as the latter is. Reliving in the ideal realm of poetry, or in the language of "The Rotation Method," recollecting, affords the rich enjoyment for which Johannes lives. So completely does he throw himself into this reliving that he forgets himself in his creative act and does not so much write as live the Diary into existence. As he begins to lose self-consciousness with regard to his poetic activity, as he more and more completely becomes the character in the Diary he simultaneously writes, Johannes becomes myth, just as he describes himself in the Diary's conclusion.

Myth, according to Kierkegaard, is poetic or subjunctive statement that is taken to be indicative, that is, is mistaken for a description of reality. As Johannes evaporates into the world of the Diary, as he is taken up and transformed so that his prosaic features disappear and are replaced by poetic ones, he loses all critical distance from this poetical self and becomes identical with it. A writes, "his poetic temperament . . . is not rich enough, or, perhaps, not poor enough, to distinguish poetry and reality from one another."[33] Clearly, this absolute identification of author and character

---

[33]Ibid.

represents the fullest mediation of subject and object, describer and described, imaginable.

Thus, the terminus of both dialectics, despite their apparent incompatibility, is the same: myth. The elevation of immediacy to reflectivity caused by complete interaction of nature and art corresponds to the plunging of reflectivity down into immediacy so that it becomes myth. The infinite, spirit, is compressed into the finite, flesh. Likewise, the taking up, transforming, and canceling as debt of the real that is involved in the movement to the second level of enjoyment wins an autonomy for the resulting poetic world that allows it to forget itself as poetic so that its writer becomes unselfconsciously his own character and, thus, myth.

The independence of the aesthete from reality depicted in "Diary of a Seducer" is different from that depicted in "The Rotation Method." A close look at this difference serves to confirm the compatibility of the art-nature mediation, a compatibility already indicated by their common goal: myth.

In "The Rotation Method," independence is undialectically asserted. A claims the ability to drive back boredom solely on the basis of his art. Here in the Diary, though the gift of reality is canceled as gift, as positive contribution, as ground or cause, its memory is preserved within the poetic world it stimulated. Thus, though the Diary stands apart from reality and the extent of its correspondence to it is impossible to determine, the independent world that it represents is the scene of a complementary relation between the seducer and the seduced, between the poetic Johannes and the poetic Cordelia. Thus, the first mediation of art and nature does not conflict with the second mediation of subject and object but is taken up into it as a memory of its origins, that is, as a memory of the events that bore fruit in the mood from which, in turn, the Diary issued.

The Hegelian nature of these transactions need hardly be pointed out. The process described here as a "taking up" corresponds in all significant features to that which Kierkegaard's great German adversary, Hegel, terms *Aufhebung,* a word that signifies at once cancellation and retention. Hegel looks to this process to give ever higher and more complete mediations of opposition so that ultimately all difference is dissolved in higher unity. This culminating stage cancels its dependence on prior stages so as to embody perfect freedom but nonetheless preserves all those stages within itself in transfigured and completed form.

Since the general trends traced above through the various entries of *Either/Or* 1 converge and culminate in this final entry of the volume, the unmistakably Hegelian character of the seducer and his Diary confirms the earlier statement that the underlying structure of the work is, in many of its aspects, Hegelian. In those earlier comments, I left open the question as to whether this similarity signals a debt or a parody. Unquestionably, it signals both. The profundity of the dialectics that unfold beneath the stylistic fireworks of the book are unthinkable apart from the lessons Kierkegaard learned reading Hegel. In characteristic Kierkegaardian fashion, however, the Dane uses what he learns to contradict his teacher.

In fact, *Either/Or* 1 belongs within the group of Kierkegaard's writings that formally mimic that which they substantively attack. *The Concept of Irony* both employs and gives the theoretical basis for this ploy. Its most striking manifestations, however, are found in the two simultaneously published pseudonymous works, *The Concept of Anxiety* and *Philosophical Fragments*. In the former, Kierkegaard employs a ponderous, Latinate theological prose to oppose the theologians on the question of original sin. In the latter, he uses a deceptively simple style and responds to an unnamed interlocutor to evoke the mood of a Platonic dialogue while driving a wedge between the view contained within those dialogues, idealism, and Christianity. To support the assertion that *Either/Or* 1 similarly employs a structure suggestive of Hegel while opposing his views, I must now indicate the points of divergence from Hegel within the work.

I have already noted above that Kierkegaard's phenomenology is one of concrete representative types and paradigmatic individuals rather than of concepts, as is the case in Hegel's writings. Mackey locates the origin of this difference in presentation in the opposing responses to contradiction in the two bodies of thought. While contradiction drives inadequate concepts on to higher and more fully adequate concepts in Hegel's phenomenology, "[i]n the Kierkegaardian dialectic, each of the 'stages on life's way' *contains* its contradictions—is, in fact, the project of so containing them."[34] Thus, contradiction in the aesthete's life can drive him forward, but only as far as the most mature development of aesthetic existence. It cannot drive him on to the next stage, the ethical. Here we arrive at one of those gaps that according to Kierkegaard can only be crossed with a leap.

---

[34]Mackey, *Kierkegaard: A Kind of Poet*, 16.

Personal Unity in Kierkegaard's Thought

This is the hallmark characteristic of the existential. The dialectic of concepts described in Hegel's work remains within the realm of thought where all relations are immanent and gaps unthinkable. Thus, in viewing the developmental cul-de-sac that is the aesthetic stage, a fundamental difference from Hegel emerges.

Further fundamental differences from Hegel come to light in examining the final stage of aesthetic development. Johannes achieves mythic status by taking up into the poetic world of the Diary those aspects of reality needed as stimuli. These aspects are retained as memories within the newly created world but are so transformed that they do not constitute debts. That is, the imaginary, ideal world in which Johannes dwells sunders its direct relations of dependence to reality and becomes a completely autonomous, self-contained kingdom of the mind.

In Hegel, preceding steps in the developmental process are similarly taken up, transformed, and canceled. Such a process always leads upward to a higher order of being, whether conceptual or actual, in the German's philosophy. With Kierkegaard this is not necessarily the case. In the following description of Johannes's "liberation" from reality, A not only underlines the above assertion that the final stage of the aesthetic does not glide smoothly on into the ethical but also shows that the dialectic traced through *Either/Or* 1 leads down, not up, toward hell, not heaven.

> He who goes astray inwardly . . . soon discovers that he is going about in a circle from which he cannot escape. . . . I can imagine nothing more excruciating than an intriguing mind, which has lost the thread of its continuity and now turns its whole acumen against itself, when conscience awakens and compels the schemer to extricate himself from this confusion. It is in vain that he has many exits from his foxhole; at the moment his anxious soul believes that it already sees daylight breaking through, it turns out to be a new entrance, and like a startled deer, pursued by despair, he constantly seeks a way out, and finds only a way in, through which he goes back into himself.[35]

This description of the seducer casts a shadow over the whole of *Either/Or* 1; clearly, the developmental process depicted there is demonic. Not only does it not lead naturally and without a decisive break into the ethical,

---

[35]*Either/Or*, 1:304; *S.V.*, 2:286.

it leads away from it. As A looks anxiously ahead on the road he now walks, he sees the seducer, and despairs of there being any turning once that level of depravity is reached.[36] If the terminus of the aesthetic line of development is *not* the point from which the transition to the ethical is to be made, if one must retrace one's steps on the road to hell before getting off it, then from what point is that leap to be made? Furthermore, when does this line of development become a descent? I will seek to answer both of these questions and to uncover the fundamental disparity between the Hegelian and the Kierkegaardian phenomenologies by examining a series of problematic passages in "The Ancient Tragical Motif."

---

[36] One might ask whether this observation vitiates the assertion that the development depicted in *Either/Or* 1 is essentially different from that which Hegel describes. After all, if Johannes serves as a warning to A, if he can inspire A's ethical transformation, then there is a sense in which the aesthetic "development" (that is, descent into perdition) leads to the next stage of existence. Hegel certainly doesn't hold that no individual will find himself in a developmental dead end; not only individuals but whole civilizations reach such an impasse when they have exhausted the possibilities inherent in their natures. Then they are superseded by more advanced forms. Do we not see much the same sort of relationship between A and Johannes?

Such an attempt to align (to mediate!) Kierkegaard and Hegel fails to recognize essential disparities between Johannes's function as a warning and necessary Hegelian supercession. In Hegel, all individuals are contained within a larger context: their family, class, city, country, culture, and, ultimately, the grand movement of the world-spirit. In seeing one individual go beyond the limits of his predecessor's development, we are simply seeing the overall immanent development express itself through the "individuals" composing it. There is no such overarching and inclusive reality behind apparent individuality for Kierkegaard and, as a result, Johannes represents a real dead end. An individual human being, the ultimate reality in this finite world, has worked himself into a corner from which he cannot extricate himself; it is impossible to regard such a failure to achieve man's destiny as a creature existing transparently in its creator in Hegelian terms without fundamentally transforming it. It is a termination of development and not a mere sloughing off of dead cells within the body of an organism that lives on. If one individual can learn by observing another, that is well and good, but we must not begin to fuse the lives of these individuals so as to view them as single, immanent developmental process. For further discussion of Hegel and Kierkegaard's respective views on development, see Taylor, *Journeys to Selfhood: Hegel and Kierkegaard*.

The passages in question represent one of a number of points in *Either/Or* 1 in which A comes up against the boundary of the ethical. Here, however, he reacts atypically. In all other such encounters, A turns away from the ethical, often with a slight sneer, back to purely aesthetic concerns. At this point in "The Ancient Tragical Motif," however, he momentarily transcends his concern with a particular art form, tragedy, and even his existential position as an aesthete, to comment on the situation of the individual whose guilt is posited as sin. A writes that though "the aesthetic will put in an extenuating word for him,"[37] that is, though a consideration of circumstances, background, and so forth, will always provide some grounds for evading responsibility, will soften guilt into its aesthetic, tragic form,

> [i]t would be wrong for him to seek comfort there, for his path leads him not to the aesthetic but to the religious. The aesthetic lies behind him, and it would be a sin for him now to grasp at the aesthetic.[38]

Whereas the other encounters with the ethical are from *within* the aesthetic, in this case A stands outside both existential spheres and has a vantage point *over* this fundamental fork in the road of life. Not confined to the aesthetic, if only for a moment, and not committed to the ethico-religious as is B, he contemplates the great either-or. He recognizes that one may evade responsibility and prevail upon the tender "mother-love" of the aesthetic or one may choose the sterner "father-love" of the ethico-religious that involves accepting responsibility for one's life, acknowledging one's guilt and thereby facing one's need for divine mercy. A not only perceives this either-or, he endorses the ethico-religious side of the disjunction.

Why is it at this point and no other that A transcends the limits of aesthetic consciousness? The answer lies in this essay's position in the phenomenology of aesthetic existence that *Either/Or* 1 constitutes. "The Ancient Tragical Motif" represents the point of transition from the immediate to the reflective aesthetic. It is Kierkegaard's consistently held view that the former of these two is a universal stage in human development, both individual and social. Each individual is born as an immediate aes-

---

[37] *Either/Or*, 1:144, *S.V.*, 2:135.

[38] Ibid.

thete, just as the earliest forms of social existence involve immediate relations between the individual members and the substantial whole of society. In an early journal entry quoted in the opening section of this chapter, Kierkegaard wrote that only after an individual has gone through the stages represented by Don Juan, Faust, and Ahasverus can ethical and religious development begin.[39] In this view, not only immediate but also reflective aestheticism would constitute a universal stage of human development. It is clear, however, that Kierkegaard modifies this view before writing *Either/Or* 1. In *The Concept of Irony*, he follows Hegel in attributing to Socrates the dissolution of Greek social substantiality through the introduction of infinite reflection. But Socrates represents the standpoint of irony, the "confinium" of the ethical, and thus stands beyond the aesthetic stage. His existence shows that development may proceed directly from the immediate aesthete to postaesthetic existence, thus altogether bypassing the reflective aesthetic. This modified view lies behind A's comment in "The Immediate Stages of the Erotic" that "Don Juan . . . suggests a far more universal stage in the development of the individual's life than does [Faust]."[40]

In light of this analysis, it is clear why A is granted a heightened consciousness here at the fundamental parting of the ways, which "The Ancient Tragical Motif" discusses and represents in the phenomenological progression of *Either/Or* 1. Emerging from immediacy, one must either "leap" to a higher sphere, the ethical, by accepting responsibility and taking choice seriously, or retreat into the aesthetic by evading responsibility and refusing to choose. Subsequent essays and even subsequent parts of this essay lie beyond the point of decision; they show the road as it leads away from the fork down into the reflective aesthetic in its ever more developed and demonic forms. Thus, when understood adequately, these passages point toward fundamental differences between the Hegelian and the Kierkegaardian phenomenologies. The need for an act of will in leaping to the ethical stage indicates discontinuities in the Kierkegaardian developmental scheme unknown in the Hegelian. If this choice is not forthcoming, the aesthete "develops" into an ever more depraved being.

---

[39] *J. and P.*, 795; *Pap.*, 1 A 150.

[40] *Either/Or*, 1:102; *S.V.*, 2:78.

Personal Unity in Kierkegaard's Thought

That one may take either path marks Kierkegaard's conviction that contingency is real and choice crucial, as is reflected by the book's title, *Either/Or*.

Having followed the aesthete on his descent into the maelstrom of momentary passions and crushing despair, it is time to look to the other half of the disjunction, to those true selves who accept responsibility, resolutely choose, and in the process obey the call to be one thing.

PART III

Ways of Being One Thing

CHAPTER VI

The Common Characteristics of Unified Selfhood

In turning to the various forms of genuine selfhood, each of which in its own way hears, acknowledges, and realizes the command to be one thing, one should keep in mind the lessons learned in the preceding examination of the aesthete's rebellious manyness. There it emerged that oneness is not given to the self, that it does not characterize a self remaining in immediacy. The absence of unity in undeveloped selfhood is readily apparent in the case of the immediate aesthete. Don Juan represents prereflective life in its temporal atomism and consequent unceasing change.

The truth of this claim in relation to the reflective aesthete is less obvious, however. In the more developed forms of aesthetic existence I documented a substantial if not absolute reliance on the powers of reflection for the change and turbulence these selves demand. This demand, however, springs from the deeper immediacy of the reflective aesthete. Such a "self"[1] does not originate in choice. Rather, it develops when the possibility of choice opened by the coming of reflection is allowed to pass unused. Reflection then becomes but a characteristic or capacity of a "self" determined by its moods, desires, abilities, and circumstances, that is, by its fundamental immediacy. Thus, Judge William is justified in overlooking the relative distinction between the two main forms of aesthetic existence in his description of the decisive difference between the aesthetic and ethical stages.

> But what is it to live aesthetically, and what is it to live ethically? What is the aesthetical in man, and what is the ethical? To this I would reply: the aesthetical in a man is that by which he is immediately what he is; the ethical is that whereby he becomes what he becomes.[2]

The formula applied here to the ethical person—that he "becomes what he becomes"—can be applied equally to all genuine selves. Only by decisively departing from immediacy, and thus changing profoundly, can a self avoid the aesthete's dissolution in change and realize a unity in its life.

At first glance, this may appear disturbingly like driving out the devil by the devil's own power, but a moment's consideration will show that it could not be otherwise. When change is the prevailing condition of the self in its given state, a thoroughgoing alteration of that self is a precondition of its stabilization. Thus, the first characteristic common to all genuine selves is their origin in a profound break with their antecedent condition and their consequent reformation on a qualitatively different basis.

Kierkegaard's more general considerations of change aid in determining this transformation. Standing with Aristotle against the undialectical excesses of Parmenides and Heraclitus, Kierkegaard sees that both sameness and difference, rest and motion, are essentially involved in change. Some element must remain unchanged through the course of a change, however, so as to bind the various moments into a single process. Other-

---

[1] Kierkegaard denies that the aesthete deserves this title in the strictest sense.

[2] *Either/Or*, 2:182; *S.V.*, 3:167.

wise, the moments fall apart into simple, static difference.³ Accidental change clearly satisfies this requirement. The substance underlies and unites the various nonessential characteristics that play across its surface over the course of time. In the case of more fundamental change, the change Kierkegaard terms "the coming-into-existence kind of change (*kinesis*)," essence constitutes the binding link between the mere possibility and the actual existence of a thing.⁴

Despite the impeccably classical lineage of the two categories, a difficulty arises in placing the transformation of self discussed above in either of them. A genuine self arises out of a fundamental restructuring of the given, immediate self. This is too extensive and profound an alteration to be categorized as accidental change. While it shares with "the coming-into-existence kind of change" the distinction of ushering in something qualitatively different from that which preceded it, it differs in that it involves the transformation of an already existing human being.

Kierkegaard resolves this dilemma by borrowing and adapting yet another set of Aristotelian categories: those of primary and secondary potentiality. When a child is born, when a person comes into being biologically, he is the actualization of a potentiality. In turn, this level of actuality can be viewed under the category of possibility. In the normal course of things, the infant will become a linguistic, economic, and social being, a spouse, parent, voter, and so forth. Thus, an already existing entity can constitute the possibility of still further development; it can represent the potential for higher levels of actualization.

This pair of Aristotelian terms still does not provide the conceptual model required to understand the transformation Kierkegaard describes as leading to genuine selfhood. The developments described in the preceding paragraph are as natural to a person as is the acorn's transformation into an oak. They may be part and parcel of a life that simply "is what it is"; they may characterize one who lives his life in immediacy. That these

---

³"In so far as existence consists in movement there must be something which can give continuity to the movement and hold it together, for otherwise there is no movement." *Postscript*, 277; *S.V.*, 10:18-19. See Aristotle, *Metaphysics* 1010a 34.

⁴*Philosophical Fragments*, 90-91; *S.V.*, 6:68-69.

changes occur "in the normal course of things" demonstrates that the change involved in becoming a self does not belong to this category.

What is required is a notion of change that, while seeing it as actualizing a possibility inherent in given, immediate human selfhood, does not represent a process in simple continuity with the developments immanently involved in immediate life. This goes beyond my study's original finding that only through thoroughgoing change is the self to become unified and stable. While the profoundness of the break involved in achieving oneness is preserved, the need for continuity is given its due as well when the transformation of the self is seen as an actualization of a preexistent potentiality.

To determine further this change that is to issue in an essentially unified self, I refer again to Kierkegaard's twin principles that only the eternal is truly one and that a self reflects the object of its true attachment.[5] Only by coming to stand in a proper relationship to God (or more accurately in certain cases, the God)[6] can the self realize its task of becoming one thing. In fact, the aspiration itself would be impossible if the God-relationship did not already exist *in posse*, that is, if the eternal were not already present, albeit in unrealized form, in the self as immediately given. As Wyschogrod writes:

> Without the eternal man would be pure temporality with nothing to fear from the continuous change of time since there would be nothing in him that protests changeability and wants to maintain self-identity.[7]

Combining this insight with those already reached, it becomes apparent that all unified selves originate in a qualitative transformation of self actualizing a relationship to God that is previously present as a possibility in the self's given nature as a synthesis of the temporal and eternal.

The next task is to locate the agency behind this transformation. Since Kierkegaard consistently holds that no external influences or third parties can enter into a subject's God-relationship, it is clear that God and the sub-

---

[5]See the introduction.

[6]See Howard V. Hong, Foreword to *Philosophical Fragments*, ix-xii.

[7]Michael Wyschogrod, *Kierkegaard and Heidegger: The Ontology of Existence* (New York: Humanities Press, 1954) 84.

Personal Unity in Kierkegaard's Thought

ject are the only two candidates. If any theme emerges clearly from the many varied works of Kierkegaard, it is the depth and significance of the individual's responsibility for himself. Kierkegaard's conviction in this regard sets him in opposition to any body of thought that would assign exclusive agency to God.[8]

When in the summer of 1834 as a young theological candidate he began keeping a journal, Kierkegaard's first entries were devoted to a criticism and rejection of the doctrine of predestination.[9] In pointing out the inconsistencies and paradoxes inherent in such a doctrine, his overriding concern is to preserve for human freedom a role in determining the God-relationship. Some have asserted that Kierkegaard's emphasis upon this role is so heavy and exclusive that it eliminates from his thought any meaningful notion of grace.[10] Rejection of any strong doctrine of predestination, however, not only opens the way for real human freedom but for a living God of grace. Gregor Malantschuk comments quite perceptively on this second dimension of Kierkegaard's rejection of predestination.

> On the basis of the doctrine of predestination, God cannot be conceived of as a concrete, living, and active reality who always may enter anew into the course of world events and the life of the individual person, but only as a power that is totally bound by a plan of its own determination.[11]

Despite Kierkegaard's debt to Greek philosophy, he always views God as the acting, loving, personal deity of the Hebrews. It is in a cooperative, dialectical relationship between this God and the free human self that the self's transformation can occur. While it is true that Kierkegaard does not

---

[8]"[A]ny notion of grace that renders impossible or unnecessary man's volitional activity in faith, cannot be acceptable for [Kierkegaard]." Taylor, *Kierkegaard's Pseudonymous Authorship*, 314.

[9]*J. and P.*, 1300-1302; *Pap.*, 1 A 2, 5, 7.

[10]See, for example, Louis Mackey, "The Loss of the World in Kierkegaard's Ethics," *Review of Metaphysics* 9 (1956): 615. For rebuttal, see Vernard Eller, *Kierkegaard and Radical Discipleship* (Princeton: Princeton University Press, 1968) 126.

[11]Gregor Malantschuk, *Fra Individ til den Enkelte* (Copenhagen: Reitzels, 1978) 11. (My translation.)

credit any of the pre-Christian existence-forms with an adequate concept or development of this relationship, he sees it as so essential that all forms of genuine selfhood will echo it in at least some tenuous sense. Thus, each of the existence-forms examined in the following chapters arises from a qualitative transformation of the self in which the self's potential for a God-relationship is actualized through a dialectic of the self's freedom and God's active assistance.

This development of the contours common to all forms of selfhood worthy of that name has proceeded at too abstract a level to do justice to both halves of the synthesis that is man. I have emphasized the eternal aspect of man, first, as the given potential for a God-relationship—the *terminus a quo* of human development—and, second, as the actualization of the original potential—the goal of human development. Only when the other half of the synthesis, temporality, is included in the formula, however, can it hope to convey even an algebraic notion of what it is to be a self.

Temporal existence is essentially successive; one moment constantly gives way to the next. This quality of existence makes development possible, allowing one to leave one's unactualized self in the past and replace it with a more complete self; it also represents a challenge, because in every moment it threatens to separate one from one's achievements. Kierkegaard is quite firm in his conviction that achievements in the realm of spirit are not like financial transactions in which a right to one's legal acquisition is secure until one surrenders it willingly. Rather, each achievement must be renewed in each moment or else lost. Thus, the task of the self is not only to realize its potential but also to *repeat* this realization continually. The unity the self achieves in relating correctly to the divine One must be temporally expressed in the continuity created through the self's repetition of itself.

Repetition characterizes the forms of existence in profoundly different ways. Of the four forms of genuine selfhood Kierkegaard discusses—the ironic, ethical, immanent religious, and Christian—only the ethical and Christian are essentially characterized by repetition. The ironic and immanent religious, while conforming to the formula developed above and, thus, displaying a sort of repetition, are characterized more fundamentally by recollection. These terms betoken two very different manners of existence but may nonetheless be subsumed under the single scheme developed in the preceding pages. There are, in turn, significant differences between the respective members of each subgroup. I will sketch the general contours of the two subgroups in the remainder of this chapter and then devote the following four chapters to a more detailed description of each of the individual existence forms and their successes and failures at the project of being one thing. These analyses will show how each succeeding form remedies the fatal weakness of its forerunner, thus binding the four forms in a single line of development.

The standard contrast of recollection and repetition Kierkegaard offers through a number of his pseudonyms is that while eternity lies behind the recollecting self, it lies before the self who seeks it through repetition.[12] It is impossible on this occasion to unpack the full range of meanings present in this statement, abbreviated as it is to the point of opaqueness; however, recollection emphasizes the eternal dimension of the self in the self's original, given form, whereas repetition emphasizes the eternal dimension of the self in the self's developed, actualized form. In the first case, the self may endeavor to express as fully as possible the eternal dimension of itself, but it rests secure in the knowledge that its own exertions and the busy comings and goings of temporal existence cannot alter its preestablished relationship to the divine. In the second case, the given dimension of the self's eternality represents an opportunity of infinite significance, but it is only an opportunity. If it is allowed to pass unavailed, the self has let slip away the treasure of great worth. What matters is not what the self might have been, but what it has actually become. Clearly, recollection strips temporal existence of decisive importance while repetition accentuates temporal existence to the highest degree.

The full significance of this distinction emerges only in turning to the concrete, in examining the ways these two fundamental stances are lived. The ironist and the religious self—the two existential expressions of recollection—achieve personal integrity by constantly repudiating the finite and renouncing all pretensions to being able to accomplish anything decisive. That is, by adopting an essentially negative stance toward its temporal existence, the self achieves the only unity and consistency available to it. In contrast, the ethical self and the Christian are able—by positively interacting with God—to reconstitute, rather than simply reject, the finite,

---

[12]*Postscript*, 241, 517; *S.V.*, 9:226, 10:249-50.

temporal dimension of the self. In this way they become *positively* unified individuals.

Of special significance to this study will be the contrast of the nonessential repetition of selves related to the eternal through recollection and the genuine repetition of the ethical and Christian selves. In the former, repetition appears in its most abstract and barren form as the simple doing over and over again of the same thing. In the latter two cases, however, the fact that the finite is taken up and developed in the course of the self's actualization opens the possibility of genuinely historical existence. The individual moments of the self's life in these existence-forms coinhere and enrich each other.

CHAPTER VII

The Negative Oneness of the Ironist

In investigating, in part 2, the aesthetic stage of existence, a parting of developmental ways was located at the point where immediacy gives way to reflection. I briefly alluded to the advance toward higher forms of existence that comes with decisive resolution and acceptance of responsibility for oneself at this crossroad on life's way, but the focus of attention was on the progressive degeneration of the self that fails to avail itself of this opportunity. Down that latter road lay the absolute antithesis of unified selfhood. It is now time to show that oneness of self does, in fact, lie ahead on the road the aesthete fails to take.

A first clear indication that this is the case is Kierkegaard's statement through Judge William that the breakdown of immediacy opens the possibility for the self to win a unity hitherto beyond its reach or comprehension.

There comes a moment in a man's life when his immediacy is, as it were, ripened and the spirit demands a higher form in which it will apprehend itself as spirit. Man, so long as he is immediate spirit, coheres with the whole earthly life, and now the spirit would collect itself, as it were, out of this dispersion and become in itself transformed, the personality would be conscious of itself in its eternal validity.[1]

The movement sketched here has both negative and positive dimensions. The self's emergence as spirit, as a "personality . . . conscious of itself in its eternal validity," involves, first, a severing of all immediate links with the finite world. This act wins a negative unity for the self in that the self is removed from direct contact with the turbulence and chaos of that realm. The way is then open for the self to develop a positive unity, for the emphasis to fall on the fact that it *collects* itself, rather than on the fact that it does so *out of* a prior dispersion.

With customary thoroughness, Kierkegaard first allows the negative portion of this movement its full development as a distinct existence-form before proceeding to investigate more positively unified types of self. The self that corresponds to the negative movement is that of the ironist. This observation explains Johannes Climacus's claim that irony "follows next after immediacy."[2]

The ironic existence-form and its overcoming of immediacy's manyness can only be understood in light of Kierkegaard's conception of human consciousness and its emergence from immediacy into mature self-reflection. The understanding of man as a synthesis of finite and infinite, temporal and eternal, body and soul, underlies all Kierkegaard's anthropological investigations. Thus, man is never wholly immediate in the sense that an animal is. If he were, consciousness could never emerge.[3] Nonetheless, in its original condition as an infant, the more ideal dimensions of the self are unactualized and unmanifested possibilities buried within the too, too solid actuality of its biological being.

The self at this point is drowning in finitude and must win for itself a breath of infinitude if it is to emerge as truly human. This breath is won

---

[1]*Either/Or*, 2:193; *S.V.*, 3:177.

[2]*Postscript*, 450; *S.V.*, 10:181.

[3]*The Concept of Anxiety*, 43; *S.V.*, 6:137.

when the self's inborn dimension of infinitude manifests itself as imagination.

> As a rule, imagination [*Phantasien*] is the medium for the process of infinitizing; it is not a capacity, as are others—if one wishes to speak in those terms, it is the capacity *instar omnium* [of all capacities].[4]

Imagination renders the self infinite by freeing it from the brute here-now of unalloyed actuality. It opens the self to situations, images, events, and so forth, that are past, future, or altogether without actual counterpart. When Anti-Climacus goes on to say that this ability makes imagination the capacity *instar omnium*, he is pointing out that all uniquely human activities presuppose the ability to see beyond immediate actuality to the possibilities inherent there.

While imagination is a necessary element in envisioning possibilities, it is not a sufficient condition for it. Imagination per se is inadequately dialectical to open the self to its own possibilities. Climacus tells us, "only at the moment when ideality is brought into relation with reality does possibility appear."[5] That is, whereas the images produced by imagination simply are what they are, there is an intrinsic reference to extrinsic reality in the case of possibilities and ideals. In *De Omnibus Dubitandum Est*, this intentional quality of ideality is indicated by its close identification with language.[6]

It must be said that Kierkegaard sometimes uses the terms *ideal* and *possibility* in such a way that a relationship to reality is specifically denied. However, an inspection of these secondary uses of the terms reinforces the claim that true ideals and possibilities are characterized by such a relationship. For instance, Judge William criticizes the fantastic ideals that spring from the poet's imagination because the poet "must flee away from the world in order to rejoice in them."[7] This inability to relate to the real is

---

[4]Søren Kierkegaard, *The Sickness Unto Death*, trans. Howard V. Hong and Edna H. Hong (Princeton: Princeton University Press, 1980) 30; *S.V.*, 15:88.

[5]*De Omnibus Dubitandum Est*, 149.

[6]". . . speech is ideality." Ibid., 148.

[7]*Either/Or*, 2:214; *S.V.*, 3:196.

what prevents these projections from deserving the name *ideal* in any deeper sense. As the Judge points out, "The true ideal is always the real."[8]

Similarly, when the self's possibility is not checked against its necessity—its concrete, finite givenness—"possibility" becomes a snare that traps the self and deprives it of its ability to accomplish anything. "This self becomes an abstract possibility, it flounders around in possibility until it is exhausted, but it neither moves from the place where it is nor arrives anywhere."[9] A possibility that closes to the self all real possibilities is entitled to its name only in a derivative sense, if at all. Thus, true ideals and possibilities essentially involve a reference to reality. Only when a projection of imagination has been checked against reality and determined to be realizable can it properly be included in these categories.

With the introduction of reality as the other juxtaposed to imagination's projections, one passes to a higher determination: reflection. Reflection is not a stage in consciousness's emergence from immediacy; rather, it is a partial expression of what is involved in consciousness. According to Johannes Climacus, "The basic form of consciousness is . . . opposition." Reflection involves the two factors in this opposition—ideality and reality—apart from the active process of opposing the two, which is consciousness. Thus, reflection can be described as the possibility of consciousness.[10]

Despite its inability to exist on its own, reflection may describe the full extent to which consciousness is employed at a particular moment, as when the self is engaged in objective knowing. When the two opposed terms, reality and ideality, are to be compared, one of the two must be selected as the standard against which the other is judged. When ideality is measured against reality, the result is the project of objective knowledge, the disinterested attempt to construct a system of knowledge (the ideal) that accurately reproduces its object (the real). In objective knowledge, the knower drops out of the picture as insignificant and so we remain within the dichotomous structure of reflection.

---

[8]Ibid.

[9]*The Sickness Unto Death*, 36; *S.V.*, 15:93.

[10]*De Omnibus Dubitandum Est*, 150.

When reality is measured against ideality the picture is different. According to Johannes Climacus, the only reality that may be related to ideality without thus transforming it into ideality is one's own ethical existence.[11] Although in attempting to set up the perfect republic, make the perfect dive, or render a perfect performance of Beethoven's Ninth Symphony, a person may seem to model and measure the real after the ideal, according to Johannes Climacus, this is not essentially the case. Only when one sets about reforming one's personal existence according to one's ideals is such a relationship truly established. This activity, however, is ethical and presupposes interest, an element altogether alien to reflection. With the introduction of interest, the level of consciousness is reached. Consciousness is the self's interested, concerned relating of ideality to reality, and, as such, is trichotomous.[12]

A further determination of the terms *ideality* and *reality* reveals that consciousness for Kierkegaard is essentially self-consciousness.[13] "Reality" here represents the self as it presently is. "Ideality" denotes the vision the self has of what it could and should become. Both are equally essential parts of the self. In fact, this self actualizes itself as spirit only when it actively relates these two aspects, that is, when it is reforming its reality to correspond to its ideal vision of itself. Since the self both as real and as ideal is a synthesis of the finite and infinite, this determination of selfhood is identical with the formula proposed by Anti-Climacus: "the self is a relation which relates itself to itself."[14] It is an impressive demonstration of the constancy and early maturation of Kierkegaard's views that *De Omnibus Dubitandum Est* and *The Sickness Unto Death* cohere so closely in their respective visions of the structure of the self.

Because Kierkegaard adheres to such a demanding concept of consciousness, he labels "immediate" many forms of existence that are not usually regarded as such. Not only the infant as yet uninitiated into language, but anyone whose "actions" are mere reactions to hormones, hun-

---

[11]*Postscript*, 279; *S.V.*, 10:21.

[12]*De Omnibus Dubitandum Est*, 150-51.

[13]See John Elrod, *Being and Existence in Kierkegaard's Pseudonymous Works* (Princeton: Princeton University Press, 1975) 50-51.

[14]*The Sickness Unto Death*, 13; *S.V.*, 15:73.

ger, fear, desire, and so forth, is immediate, no matter how articulate he may be or how exhaustively he may comment on or even defend his form of existence. Such bodily determination of one's actions lacks the internal complexity of consciousness.

Even a self that in full awareness frames ideals for itself and actively goes about realizing them may be immediate. This is the case when the ideal is some finite goal, be it the earning of money, the winning of a wife, or the conquering of the world. Such a self fails to realize consciousness at two points. First, in his being both as real and as ideal, he fails to express the fact that he is a synthesis of the temporal and the eternal. As he is and as he aims to be, he is too commensurable with the earthly to manifest his divine heritage. This excessive mundaneness points toward the second inadequacy: the failure to develop a true opposition between the real and the ideal. When the ideal is qualitatively no different from the real, the two are said by Kierkegaard to collapse into each other; the duality of reflection gives way to the oneness of immediacy. One way he makes this point is in denying that any in-principle realizable ideal is worthy of its name.[15] If it were a true ideal and were to be achieved, the essential tension that is the self would be resolved and released. True or infinite reflection involves placing the self as real in relation to an infinite ideal, that is, an ideal that the self may struggle to realize all its days. Kierkegaard dismisses those selves whose ideals are finite as representing an immediacy characterized by relative reflection. He believes that most selves fall into this category. "Most people virtually never advance beyond what they were in their childhood and youth: immediacy with the admixture of a little dash of reflection."[16]

The first form of selfhood to make the quantum leap to full-fledged reflectivity is the ironic; Socrates is its perfect representative. Shortly after the collapse of the Faust project, Kierkegaard selected Socrates and, more generally, irony as the subject of his dissertation. While there are numerous points of contact between the two programs of study, the most obvious

---

[15]*J. and P.*, 1:852; *Pap.*, 1 A 221. Cited by Gregor Malantschuk, *Kierkegaard's Thought*, trans. Howard V. Hong and Edna H. Hong (Princeton: Princeton University Press, 1971) 87.

[16]*The Concept of Irony*, 57-58; *S.V.*, 15:113.

and important is the sustained interest in selves that are hidden, private, and free of immediate ties to the world around them.

Because for Kierkegaard the "determination present in all forms of irony [is that] . . . the phenomenon is not the essence but the opposite of the essence,"[17] it is apparent that irony is a qualification of subjectivity. It posits an inner self which is not only more essential than its outer but also incommensurable with it. Clearly, such a concept would attract Kierkegaard in his endeavor to describe the self's struggle to live as an infinite spirit in a finite world. As a brief investigation shows, "the simple wise man's" existential realization of irony develops what is already imperfectly present in irony as a rhetorical figure.

In ordinary discourse, in which one's words directly express their meaning, one is bound in relation to others who hear and understand and in relation to oneself in future moments. In contrast, ironic speech involves "say[ing] the opposite of what is meant."[18] The direct link between speaker, word, and hearer is sundered, leaving the speaker negatively free in relation to what he has said and to those who have heard him.

This characterization of ironic speech is not yet adequately specific, since simple dissemblance would qualify as irony as things now stand. Kierkegaard distinguishes these two quite different phenomena by referring to the ends they serve. Dissemblance misleads with a finite goal in view. To use Kierkegaard's examples, when a king disguises himself in order to check the loyalty of his officials or a policeman goes undercover in order to catch a thief, one has not irony, but dissemblance.[19]

In contrast, irony involves an internal teleology. The freedom it affords the subject over against his hearers is its own reward; to put this freedom to any finite use is to demean it. This point is best made by inspecting a degenerate if quite common form of irony. As Kierkegaard notes, "irony" is often used by one group to demonstrate its superiority to another, "just as kings and rulers speak French so as not to be understood by the commoners." Such a practice sins against irony in two ways. First, it subjects it to the task of stroking the subject's pride. Second, and perhaps worse,

---

[17]*The Concept of Irony,* 264; *S.V.*, 1:263-64.

[18]*The Concept of Irony,* 264; *S.V.*, 1:264.

[19]*The Concept of Irony,* 269; *S.V.*, 1:268.

it violates the essential hermetic spirit of irony by seeking to use it as the basis for a mutual admiration society, this when "there is as little social unity in a coterie of ironists as there is among a band of thieves."[20] A true use of irony, then, is one that frees the subject from the world of things (words) and people around him for no other purpose than for the satisfaction this freedom brings.

Though in a particular use of irony the self experiences its internality as incommensurable with the world, this experience is rendered relative by the self's ability to return in the next moment to a busy, immediate life of chasing an ever-changing set of finite goals. True realization of irony is achieved only when irony becomes not a momentary stance but a form of existence. Kierkegaard describes this qualitative transformation of irony as analogous to the intensification of doubt from its ordinary, empirical form to the hyperbolic doubt engendered by Descartes.

> Irony in the eminent sense directs itself not against this or that particular existence (*Tilværende*) but against the whole given actuality of a certain time and situation. It has, therefore, an apriority in itself, and it is not by successively destroying one segment of actuality after the other that it arrives at its total view, but by virtue of this that it destroys in the particular. It is not this or that phenomenon but the totality of existence (*Tilværelse*) which it considers *sub specie ironiae*. To this extent one sees the propriety of the Hegelian characterization of irony as infinite absolute negativity.[21]

It is now clear why Kierkegaard so closely associates infinite reflection and irony as an existence-form: the two are identical. In both cases, the self's infinitude is expressed in a withdrawal from or dissolution of all immediate ties to the finite. In neither case is there available a further principle by which the self's infinitude might be positively expressed. Thus, negative freedom is the highest determination available to such a self.

Lest I depict the negativity of Socrates in an undialectical manner, I will look more closely at the objects of his ironic destruction. This investigation will reveal that Socrates' negative activity represents a movement away from an immediacy in which the self is trapped in its finitude toward

---

[20]*The Concept of Irony*, 266; *S.V.*, 1:265.

[21]*The Concept of Irony*, 271; *S.V.*, 1:270.

more mature structures of selfhood in which infinitude is positively present.

In his master's thesis, *The Concept of Irony*, Kierkegaard analyzes the writings on Xenophon, Plato, and Aristophanes in order to support the thesis that Socrates leads ethical and religious ideals out of their previous finitude and toward, if not to, their proper infinitude. Kierkegaard points, with regard to ethical ideals, to Socrates' persistent, if always unsuccessful, attempts in the early Platonic dialogues to surpass the particularity and manyness of definition by example to find true definitions, that is, expressions of what the ideals are universally and in themselves. This attempt establishes an incommensurability between these ideals and the finite world of particulars in which they are always inadequately expressed. While it is common for readers to see these dialogues in light of Plato's later writings as pointing ahead to the theory of forms, Kierkegaard argues that their lack of successful conclusion is not simply an incompleteness to be made good by subsequent theoretical advances but a negative conclusion. That is, Socrates negatively expresses the infinite of these ideals by indicating that the existing individual can at most struggle toward them in their ideality, can but constantly depart from their inadequate, finite expressions in pursuit of them in their unreachable infinitude. The lack of positive conclusions to these dialogues, or stronger, their negative conclusions, corresponds to Socratic ignorance.[22]

Similarly, in place of the Olympian pantheon in all its rich specificity, the divine is present to Socrates only in the form of his "daimon." Kierkegaard enters into a philological investigation of the term and finds that "this word signifies something abstract, something divine, which by its very abstractness is elevated above every determination, unutterable and without predicates as it admits of no vocalization."[23] Again Socrates reaches beyond the finite toward an inaccessible infinite by moving away from the determinate toward the indeterminate. The negative infinitude of the daimon is accentuated in that it never gives positive commands, but

---

[22] "The Socratic ignorance, which Socrates held fast with the entire passion of his inwardness, was thus an expression for the principle that the eternal truth is related to an existing individual, and that this truth must therefore be a paradox for him as long as he exists." *Postscript*, 180; *S.V.*, 9:168.

[23] *Postscript*, 186; *S.V.*, 1:193.

only "warns, restrains, and urges him to abstain from something."[24] It is important to keep in mind that this apparently barren relation to the infinite and the eternal is directed toward later, more positive forms. The *Postscript* provides a useful point from which to view Socrates' relation to a purely negative divinity.

> All paganism consists in this, that God is related to man directly, as the obviously extraordinary to the astonished observer. But the spiritual relationship to God in truth, i.e., in inwardness, is conditioned by a prior irruption of inwardness, which corresponds to the divine elusiveness that God has absolutely nothing obvious about Him, that God is so far from being obvious that He is invisible.[25]

While Plato clearly follows Socrates in rejecting the perceptible gods of Greek mythology, Kierkegaard accuses him of failing to appreciate and sustain the full negativity of his mentor. When Plato moves beyond discrediting the sensuous apprehension of the divine to replacing it with an intellectual vision of the eternal order, he abandons the negative position of irony for the positive project of speculation. Further, he increasingly transforms Socrates into a speculator as the dialogues progress into the middle and later periods. But if the Platonic picture of Socrates is fundamentally misleading in this way, with what can it be replaced or even evaluated? After all, Socrates left no written record against which to check Plato's portrayals of him. Surprisingly, Kierkegaard attaches himself to an alternate portrayal that may well have contributed to Socrates' conviction and execution: that of Aristophanes in *The Clouds*. The seventh of the summary points appended to Kierkegaard's thesis for discussion at his oral defense reads, "Aristophanes has come very close to the truth in his portrayal of Socrates."[26]

Kierkegaard argues that the Aristophantic Socrates is exactly the representative of "infinite, absolute negativity," of irony as a total determination that he holds Socrates to be. Further, he supports Aristophanes' portrayal against those of Xenophon and Plato. It is in this comparison of

---

[24]Ibid.

[25]*Postscript*, 219; *S.V.*, 9:203.

[26]*The Concept of Irony*, 349; *S.V.*, 1:63.

perceptions of Socrates that Kierkegaard most vividly describes the oneness of self characteristic of the ironist.

In the highly critical and even contemptuous pages devoted to Xenophon, Kierkegaard describes his subject's approach to Socrates as "the plain historical (*den slet og ret historiske*)."[27] He sees such an approach as failing to penetrate the reality of Socrates, who, as an ironist, shows an exterior completely at odds with his essence. Thus, Socrates, whose life was devoted to leading selves up out of finitude, is mistaken by Xenophon for a comfortable denizen of finitude. The "ludicrous old geezer" he depicts is so harmless that his execution appears not so much unjust as absurd.[28]

Kierkegaard's critique of Xenophon is valuable to this study primarily for its description of the realm of finitude to which Xenophon confines his Socrates. After writing that the Xenophonic Socrates consistently determines the good according to its finite form—the useful—Kierkegaard writes:

> The useful is the external dialectic of the good, its negation, yet when torn loose as such becomes a kingdom of shadows where nothing endures but all things formless and shapeless condense and diffuse according to the inconstant and superficial gaze of the observer.[29]

Such a description of the finite dramatically underlines the earlier statement that only by distancing itself from the turbulence of temporal existence can the self hope to achieve oneness.

This is exactly the insight from which Plato's concept of Socrates takes its departure. Penetrating beneath the exterior, Socrates' student sees that his mentor concerns himself with the shifting shapes of the finite only insofar as they serve as an occasion for a movement toward the ideal.

> If one were to express in a few words the Platonic conception of Socrates, one could say that Plato has given him the Idea. Where empiricism ends, Socrates begins. His activity is to lead speculation out of the determinations of finitude, to lose sight of finitude and to steer out upon the

---

[27] *The Concept of Irony*, 182n; *S.V.*, 1:189n.

[28] *The Concept of Irony*, 53; *S.V.*, 1:75.

[29] *The Concept of Irony*, 59; *S.V.*, 1:80.

Oceanus wherein ideal striving and ideal infinity acknowledge no extraneous concern but are themselves their own infinite destination.[30]

While he correctly perceives Socrates' movement out from the finite toward the infinite, Plato's positive, poetic nature leads him gradually to forget the restraining factor that determines Socrates as an ironist rather than as a speculative philosopher. While the early dialogues show a Socrates unwilling to propose answers but anxious to scrutinize and expose as inadequate those of others, the later dialogues allow him to hold forth extensively on so many issues that one wonders that he could have been proclaimed wisest by virtue of his knowing that he knew nothing. Kierkegaard argues at length in his dissertation that this transition should be seen as the product of a waning of the direct impression of the old ironist on the young poet and a waxing of the latter's speculative bent.[31] That is, in the early dialogues Plato is so under the spell of his newly executed mentor that he is satisfied to confine his art within the limits of Socrates' distinctive existence and activity. Discussion in these dialogues leads out from the finite and manifold toward, but never to, the ideal. This portrayal evokes Socrates' essential position—irony—in which the self's infinitude is negatively expressed by its constant rejection of the finite and a constant grasping for the ever-elusive infinite.

Kierkegaard asserts that this artistic configuration is highly unstable, not because of a lack, but because of a wealth of creative talent in Plato. "In particular, a rich poetic disposition is poorly endowed to conceive such irony in the eminent sense."[32] His very surfeit of talent makes him alien to the essentially negative subject he is to portray. This natural wealth and the related temptation to reach past the negative conclusions of the early dialogues to positive results manifests itself in the changing character of the Platonic corpus.

Though the transition is gradual, Kierkegaard argues, it is qualitative. Where the regulative principle of the early dialogues is irony, that of the later ones is speculation. While Kierkegaard traces the implications of this fundamental difference in a number of dimensions, notably the nature of

---

[30]*The Concept of Irony*, 156-57; *S.V.*, 1:166-67.

[31]*The Concept of Irony*, 153; *S.V.*, 1:163-64.

[32]*The Concept of Irony*, 155; *S.V.*, 1:165.

questioning and the role of irony, the contrast emerges most clearly when he identifies the respective presuppositions of the two sets of dialogues.

> Every philosophy which begins with a presupposition naturally ends with the same presupposition. As the philosophy of Socrates began with the presupposition that he knew nothing, so it ended with mankind in general knowing nothing. The Platonic philosophy, on the other hand, began with the immediate unity of thought and being and persisted in this.[33]

As in the *Postscript*, Kierkegaard asserts that thought and being are one only within the realm of abstract thought. There, it is in fact tautological to assert their identity since the abstract expression of being is thought. When being is empirical, existential being, there is always a gap, a tension, between it and the ideal (thought). Consequently, the price of speculation's positive results, of its grasping the forms in their ideality, is a renunciation of the self's finite, existential dimension. Through the philosophical dying to self described in the *Phaedo* and other dialogues, one seeks to become the pure ego, the knowing subject, that corresponds to its object, the abstract eternal verities.[34]

> [In this] wholly subjective speculation . . . the empirical self recedes and the ideal determinations of the pure self develop, [and so] the individual to a certain extent also disappears.[35]

Kierkegaard credits Plato with an honesty and insight lacking in more modern versions of idealism in that Plato openly calls for a dying away from the finite self so as to become a philosopher rather than simply overlooking the embarrassing fact of existence from the beginning. Nonetheless, Kierkegaard profoundly disagrees with both Plato's goal and his method of reaching it. He feels that by seeking the eternal in abstract knowing, Plato "embraces the clouds instead of Juno." Worse still, the Greek tries to attain this goal through the fantastic means of ridding the self

---

[33] *The Concept of Irony*, 74; *S.V.*, 1:93.

[34] Kierkegaard writes of the *Phaedo*, "Obviously, the soul is here conceived of just as abstractly as the pure essence of things forming the object of its search." *The Concept of Irony*, 104; *S.V.*, 1:120.

[35] *The Concept of Irony*, 177; *S.V.*, 1:185.

of its actuality. Unfortunately for Plato, "actuality . . . relates in a twofold way to the subject: partly as a gift (*Gave*) which will not admit of being rejected, and partly as a task (*Opgave*) to be realized."[36]

While Xenophon portrays Socrates as a purely empirical self and Plato in his later works comes to portray him as on the way to becoming an ideal self, the true genius of Socrates is that through his ironic existence he properly expresses both aspects of himself.

> Each of these two interpreters has naturally endeavoured to render Socrates complete: Xenophon by dragging him down into the shallow regions of the useful, Plato by catching him up into the supernatural regions of the Idea. But irony is a point lying between them, invisible and extremely difficult to hold fast. On the one hand, the manifold of actuality is just the ironist's element; on the other hand, his course through actuality is hovering and ethereal, scarcely touching the ground. As the authentic kingdom of ideality is still alien to him, so he has not yet emigrated but is at every moment, as it were, about to depart. Irony oscillates between the ideal self and the empirical self; the one would make of Socrates a philosopher, the other a Sophist. Still, what makes him more than a Sophist is the fact that his empirical self has universal validity.[37]

It is this intermediate existence that Aristophanes portrays with comic brilliance in *The Clouds*. There, the unfortunate Strepsiades finds Socrates hovering in a basket over the Thoughtery.

> The ironist to be sure is lighter than the world, but he still belongs to the world. . . . [T]he basket is the foundation of empirical actuality which the ironist requires, whereas subjectivity in its infinity gravitates toward itself, is infinitely hovering.[38]

This hovering is the ironist's characteristic manner of being one thing. Although it is only "a prophecy of and an abbreviation for a complete personality,"[39] this form of existence shows all the general characteristics of

---

[36] *The Concept of Irony*, 293; *S.V.*, 1:289.

[37] *The Concept of Irony*, 158; *S.V.*, 1:168.

[38] *The Concept of Irony*, 180; *S.V.*, 1:187.

[39] *The Concept of Irony*, 177; *S.V.*, 1:185.

the unified self discussed in chapter 6. It originates in and essentially involves a qualitative break with the self as given. As I have noted, the standpoint of irony is but another expression for eminently developed reflection. This reflection decisively separates the self from its brute, given being. By bringing to light the self's incommensurability with the finite, this severing of all immediate links to finitude actualizes a given but undeveloped relation to the infinite and divine.

The above analysis bears out the earlier assertion that the ironist is characterized by an exclusively negative oneness. It remains to justify my further claims that his existence-form is essentially one of recollection, only incidentally displaying a form of repetition, and that as a result ironic existence is ahistorical.

It will be recalled that Kierkegaard's most succinct description of recollection is as an existence-form having eternity behind it instead of before it. This almost inscrutably abbreviated description refers to the fact that with recollection the self's given relation to the eternal—a relation that may or may not be existentially expressed—is emphasized, whereas with repetition time—by making everything contingent on the self's existentially expressing its relation to the eternal—is emphasized.

A self whose oneness is exclusively negative is of necessity a self characterized by recollection. The ironist saves his existence from the chaotic flux and dissolution of the finite by constantly refusing the finite any decisive importance. This self existentially expresses its inherent infinitude—its given God-relationship—by viewing all finite existence, including its own, as a disappearing moment. Clearly, such a self could never come to see in a temporal decision the basis for fundamentally restructuring its God-relationship. Thus, while the ironist believes that his existence may and even should be altered so as to express negatively his eternality, the events of temporal existence cannot, to his mind, in return change the given dimension of infinitude within the self.

Although ironic existence must be categorized as recollection, it does involve a form of repetition. That it does so is a consequence of its being a way of expressing the self's eternality. This eternality can be temporally expressed only in continuity. The true ironic self negatively displays its infinitude not occasionally, but incessantly. "Whoever has essential irony has it all day long . . . because it is the infinite within him."[40]

---

[40]*Postscript*, 450; *S.V.*, 10:181.

Because each moment of the ironist's life is a pushing away rather than a positive accomplishing, these moments fail to involve each other. Each moment of the ironist's life is *ab origine* since nothing in the preceding moment is able to support the continuation of the ironic movement in the present moment. Thus, the ironist's form of existence involves a barren and abstract repetition, the simple doing over and over again of the same thing.

The true difficulty of stably continuing irony becomes apparent when it is revealed just how divorced past is from present in this existence-form. The genius of irony is its ability to wrench the self out of its actuality and thus provide the break with the given necessary to the development of any form of unified selfhood. The self's actuality involves not only present finitude, however, but also the entirety of its past. Correspondingly, Kierkegaard writes that irony produces

> a freedom that disdains the shackles imposed by continuity. . . . [It is] a dialectic which does not feel restricted by the past nor enveloped by its ironbound consequences.
>
> [T]he outstanding feature of irony . . . is the subjective freedom which at every moment has within its power the possibility of beginning and is not generated from previous conditions.[41]

The same caustic power of irony that allows it to tear the self out of the turbulent grip of finitude thus threatens its required continuation of its original movement. According to Kierkegaard, the specific circumstances and resources of Socrates allowed him to overcome this threat and maintain himself with remarkable consistency to the very end.[42] The same cannot be said of irony's modern representatives.

In the last half of his dissertation, Kierkegaard sets out to describe and criticize the irony of the early romantic movement in Germany, concentrating on Tieck, Solger, and, especially, Friedrich Schlegel. He establishes in these pages that irony is indeed a "confinium" between existence-forms, and not itself a stable form of existence. Although Socrates rises above the aesthetic stage in its immediate form by developing reflection to

---

[41]*The Concept of Irony*, 165, 270; *S.V.*, 1:173-74, 269.

[42]"His own classicism is what makes it possible for him to sustain irony." *The Concept of Irony*, 234; *S.V.*, 1:237.

its eminent form, if this newly released reflection is not brought under control by an act of decisive resolution on the subject's part, that is, if the subject fails to pass on to the ethical stage, then ironic existence decays into reflective aestheticism.

In his dissertation Kierkegaard vividly describes this descent into reflective aestheticism, the existence-form he subsequently lets come to voice in *Either/Or* 1 and critically scrutinizes in *Either/Or* 2. Noting that after Socrates the world did not return to its previous immediacy but was irreversibly marked by reflection and the emergence of true subjectivity, he shows that the Germans depart from a very different actuality.

> But after subjectivity had exhibited itself in the world it did not disappear without a trace, the world did not sink back into its previous form of development; on the contrary, the old disappeared and everything became new. Should a new manifestation of irony appear, moreover, it must be as subjectivity asserts itself in a still higher form. It must be a subjectivity raised to a second power, a subjectivity of subjectivity, corresponding to reflection on reflection.[43]

Kierkegaard writes that just as the reflection on reflection initiated by Kant culminates in Fichte's absolute assertion of the ego, so the potentiation involved in raising subjectivity to the second degree lifts the self above all that would determine or bind it, thus establishing it as a *liberum arbitrium*, the *Unding* that has haunted the pages of philosophy and theology texts through the centuries. As above all determination, including determination by its past, such a self has no real history. Consequently, romantic ironists were infatuated with the fantastic "history" of myths and sagas.[44] One can also see in this infatuation the evaporation into the realm of possibility that comes with complete "liberation" from the actual.

Since the imaginary vistas and situations of myth and saga are enjoyed at will, they may also be changed as desired.

> At one moment it dwelt in Greece under the beautiful Hellenic sky. . . .

---

[43]*The Concept of Irony*, 260; *S.V.*, 1:260.

[44]*The Concept of Irony*, 294; *S.V.*, 1:289.

At the next moment, it concealed itself in the virgin forests of the Middle Ages. . . . At the next moment it chose something else.[45]

The self that lives its life in such an arbitrarily chosen sequence of imaginings is dissolved in discontinuity. That such an existence is the romantic ironist's aim is made unmistakably clear by a reading of Schlegel's *Lucinde*. Not only is the piece formally disunified, its hero-protagonist, Julius, is the apotheosis of temporal atomism.

> Everything that he loved and thought of with love was isolated and disconnected. In his imagination his whole existence was a mass of unrelated fragments. Each fragment was single and complete, and whatever else stood next to it in reality and was joined to it was a matter of indifference to him and might as well not have existed at all.[46]

It is apparent that the romantic ironist is the reflective aesthete. Both abandon actuality in order to embrace possibility and consequent manyness of self. This manyness must still be contained within some form of unity for the self to be designated as self at all, even one whose name is legion. The only available mediation of the discrete moments is in boredom, the empty continuity the aesthete struggles so agonizingly to disrupt.[47]

When viewed in light of *The Concept of Anxiety*, the sudden changes and the boredom of the romantic ironist clearly indicate his difference from Socrates and increase one's understanding of the reflective aesthete's agenda with change. Virgilius Haufniensis writes that the demonic is the sudden and the contentless or boring. He defines the demonic as "anxiety about the good."[48] Thus, while Socrates is directed toward the good through

---

[45]*The Concept of Irony*, 294-95; *S.V.*, 1:290.

[46]Friedrich Schlegel, *Lucinde*, trans. Peter Firchow (Minneapolis: University of Minnesota, 1971) 78. See also p. 81.

[47]*The Concept of Irony*, 294-302; *S.V.*, 1:290-98. For more on the idea that the aesthete's continuity is boredom, see Søren Kierkegaard, *Repetition*, trans. Howard V. Hong and Edna H. Hong (Princeton: Princeton University Press, 1983) 150-76; *S.V.*, 5:132-53. Here, Constantine Constantius attempts a repetition and finds only boredom.

[48]*The Concept of Anxiety*, 123; *S.V.*, 6:205.

his irony, the romantic ironist or reflective aesthete is directed away from it, retiring in anxiety. These opposing orientations trace back to the fundamental difference between the given actualities the two types of ironist neutralize. Socrates destroys the already sick and dying world of immediate society, thus making room for higher forms of social, ethical, and religious life. The romantic ironist, however, emerges in a world that is post-Easter. In Kierkegaard's view, the coming of Christ essentially altered the world. While this world has much wrong with it that must be opposed, the indiscriminate negation involved in total irony opposes the good there also. For instance, one cannot undialectically oppose the institution of marriage, despite its all too infrequent proper realization, without attacking the view upon which it is based of man as spirit. Thus, the irony of Schlegel, his creation, Julius, and their counterpart in Kierkegaard's pseudonymous authorship, Johannes the seducer, takes the form of a *Rehabilitation des Fleisches*. "What it seeks is a naked sensuality (*Sandselighed*) in which the spirit is a negated moment."[49]

This explanation casts considerable light on the dark selves of the aesthetic stage. What appears in the restless and even frenzied erotic pursuits of these characters and even more vividly in the contemporary human bestiary is anxiety seeking to escape itself and its divine heritage in an oblivion of flesh.

---

[49]*The Concept of Irony*, 307; *S.V.*, 1:301.

CHAPTER VIII

Duty and Continuity: The Historical Oneness of the Ethical Self

Irony's instability and ultimate collapse into reflective aestheticism point the way to the next form of selfhood: the ethical. The ironic self's break with its immediacy is too exclusively negative. Though the self emerges as synthesis, it is as yet unposited; that is, it is only a synthesis of two negatively related moments. Elrod writes:

> Ironical consciousness expresses the tension in the relation between the claims of finitude and infinitude, but the self, as yet, has not become an active relation of the two.[1]

---

[1] John Elrod, *Being and Existence in Kierkegaard's Pseudonymous Works*, 130; Hermann Diem further explains this failure by tracing it to the excessively intellectual character of Socrates' relation to the eternal. "Socrates first isolates thought and endeavors to attain by thought alone an understanding of the ideal, he arrives

Recollection and, consequently, ahistoricity mark such an incompletely unified self. As ahistorical, the successive moments of the ironist's life fail to cohere and involve each other. In this failure lies the ironic self's ultimate downfall.

If the ethical self is to avoid such temporal dispersion and realize its aim of living historically—the characteristic ethical understanding of the imperative to be one thing—it must fundamentally reinterpret the qualitative change out of which all unified selves emerge. The purely negative passage from unconscious existence in the finite to irony's reflective hovering must give way to an acceptance and qualitative transformation of the self's concrete givenness. The first, most abstract definition of repetition describes just such a transformation.

> The dialectic of repetition is easy, for that which is repeated has been—otherwise it could not be repeated. . . . When one says that life is a repetition one says: actuality, which has been, now comes into existence.[2]

It is within this framework that the ethical self is first expressed. Its expression is based on its genesis, but it also indicates its structure and differentiates it from aesthetic selfhood. Accentuating both the centrality of decision and the self-directedness of the ethical stage, Judge William writes that one becomes a genuine self by choosing oneself. His description of this choice shows that its structure is that of repetition as defined above.

> In this case choice performs at one and the same time the two dialectical movements: that which is chosen does not exist and comes into existence with the choice; that which is chosen exists, otherwise there would not be a choice. For in case what I chose did not exist but absolutely came into existence with the choice, I would not be choosing, I would be creating; but I do not create myself, I choose myself. Therefore, while nature is created out of nothing, while I myself as an immediate personality am created

---

at definitions which are so abstract that they cannot subsequently be brought into any vital connection with the other aspects of the ego, i.e. will and feeling.'' Hermann Diem, *Kierkegaard's Dialectic of Existence*, trans. Harold Knight (London: Oliver and Boyd, 1959) 23.

[2]*Repetition*, 149; *S.V.*, 5:131.

out of nothing, as a free spirit I am born of the principle of contradiction, or born of the fact that I choose myself.[3]

This choice is not of good or evil, but rather of good and evil as determinants by which to live one's life. It is the decision to accept responsibility for oneself, the decision to place oneself in a moral universe; it is the choice of ethical existence as one's own. Its alternative is aesthetic existence, but not the choice of aesthetic existence. Every self begins as an immediate aesthete but becomes a reflective aesthete only by failing to determine itself through decisive choice when the onset of reflection makes such choice possible. Thus, Judge William writes, "the aesthetical is not the evil, but neutrality (*Indifferentsen*)."[4]

Because it takes one out of a prior aesthetic existence, there is a negative dimension to this absolute choice of oneself. This negativity, however, is not directly expressed in either the ordinary sense of the word *choice* or in the above description. Nonetheless, the negativity so one-sidedly displayed by the ironic self is not simply rejected but is taken up into the more dialectical ethical self. Judge William indicates the essential role of negativity in ethical selfhood when in pleading with A to choose himself, he first calls on him to despair.

It appears quite strange, at first sight, that Judge William would call on A to despair. He has written only pages before that "every aesthetic view of life is despair,"[5] obviously intending this remark as a criticism of A's manner of existence. In order to clarify the meaning of his demand, he undertakes an analysis of despair, moving from its least to its most developed forms, thus attempting in a preliminary fashion the task Anti-Climacus undertakes in *The Sickness Unto Death*.

Having already shown that one may be in despair without knowing it, Judge William states that the despair he counsels is not despair over something particular and finite, despair over one's given position in life, or even the universal despair of A. While ethical despair is just as all-encompassing as this last, most developed form of aesthetic despair, it differs qualitatively in that it is chosen, not suffered; actively willed, not passively

---

[3] *Either/Or*, 2:219; *S.V.*, 3:200.

[4] *Either/Or*, 2:173; *S.V.*, 3:159.

[5] *Either/Or*, 2:197; *S.V.*, 3:180.

endured. Judge William describes this despair as "a deed which requires all the power and seriousness and concentration (*Samling*) of the soul."⁶

This despair is the negative dimension of choosing the self. In the transformation brought about by this choice, one arrangement of the given elements of the self is supplanted by another. More specifically, as one enters the ethical stage, the determinants of aesthetic existence—desire, talent, mood, natural bent, and so forth—are dethroned. Similarly, the aspect of the synthesis to which these factors relate, the finite, is deprived of its status as the exclusive regulator of the self's behavior. While its power is taken from it, the finite itself is not destroyed or rejected. Rather, it is taken up into a new configuration of self. Thus, one cannot accurately speak of the self's despair over itself without noting that the same movement is the choice of a new self.

> So then choose despair, for despair itself is a choice. . . . And when a man despairs he chooses again—and what is it he chooses? He chooses himself, not in his immediacy, not as this fortuitous individual, but he chooses himself in his eternal validity.
>
> [T]his self of which I despair is a finite thing like every other finitude, whereas the self I choose is the absolute self, or myself according to its absolute validity.⁷

What is this absolute or eternally valid self that the ethical individual chooses and, in so doing, ushers into existence? Judge William answers that it is freedom, which, he writes, "is the most abstract of all things, and yet at the same time is the most concrete."⁸ This contradictory characterization of freedom marks the discussion's passage from the univocal realm of immediacy to the dialectical realm of true selfhood. But what does this dialectical description of the self signify?

The key to deciphering Judge William's rather algebraic, though unabbreviated, comments is the Kierkegaardian theory of the self sketched

---

⁶*Either/Or*, 2:212; *S.V.*, 3:194.

⁷*Either/Or*, 2:215; *S.V.*, 3:196; see Elrod, *Being and Existence in Kierkegaard's Pseudonymous Works*, 135n.

⁸*Either/Or*, 2:218; *S.V.*, 3:199.

in chapter 6. All of the pseudonyms work within this understanding of the self, though they range widely in their use and comprehension of it.

According to Kierkegaard, the conscious self is a relation of the real and the ideal. The ideal arises through the exercise of imagination, the capacity *instar omnium*, which infinitizes the self. While imagination opens the possibility of true selfhood by opening the self to possibility, it is as dangerous an element of the self as it is powerful. The reflective aesthete or romantic ironist loses himself altogether in the realm of possibility conjured forth by imagination and fails to give the finite, concrete aspect of his self its due. In healthy, Socratic irony, the self manages to keep its finitude while becoming conscious of the ideal, but it is unable to unite the two. It is unable to because the ideals Socrates strains toward are abstract and thus do not refer to his concrete, individual existence. The perfectly good, true, and beautiful defy embodiment in the changeable and intractable medium of finite existence.

The ideal assumes a different form in the synthesis that is ethical selfhood because it is much more closely related to its counterpart, the real. Judge William writes that by despairing and choosing itself, the self is infinitized.[9] This clearly refers to the projection of ideals. The formation of these ideals specifically in a reflection on the self as real orients them toward the real in a way hitherto unseen. The ideal, in this case, is a projection of what the self really may become, not a will-o'-the-wisp fantasy.[10] The self is neither this ideal nor the reality from which it is projected. It is the interested, active relation of the two through which the real is brought to correspond to the ideal.

> This self which the individual knows is at once the actual self and the ideal self which the individual has outside himself as a picture in likeness to which

---

[9] *Either/Or*, 2:225, 227; *S.V.*, 3:205, 207.

[10] "Ethical ideality emerges not through abstract thinking, contemplation, or intuition but through the unconditional requirement upon the individual to be himself. If ideality were derived in this former manner, reality would be directed toward an ideal alien to it, whereas, for Kierkegaard, the ideal is discovered in the real." Elrod, *Being and Existence in Kierkegaard's Pseudonymous Works*, 116.

he has to form himself and which, on the other hand, he nevertheless has in him since it is the self.[11]

This passage explains why Judge William characterizes the self as both the most abstract and the most concrete of all things. Further, it describes the first two elements of the series of repetitions constitutive of ethical existence. In the projection of possibilities, the self as real is "repeated" in the self as ideal. In turn, this ideal self is to be "repeated" in the medium of existence, that is, it is to be realized.

The active relating of real to ideal in the ethical self gives that self its characteristic historicity. An essential part of choosing oneself in one's eternal validity is accepting one's reality. One accepts not only one's present finite aspects (abilities, gender, appearance, nationality, and so forth) but also one's entire past. Since a true ideal is infinite, it is impossible that one's past life conforms altogether to the requirements of the ethical. Thus, the choice of oneself is always the choice of oneself as guilty. It is, therefore, also an act of repentance.[12]

In the repentance characteristic of the ethical stage, the real—past and present—is taken up as a task, as duty. The self in reflecting on itself, blemishes and all, projects possibilities that it must then realize. Through the central aspects of ethical existence—repentance and duty—the self is constituted as historical. Its whole past is gathered into its present as the real that must be chosen and appropriated. In the process, the self's future becomes present in the form of the ideals that are projected in this ethical reflection on the given. Thus, all the moments of the ethical self's life stand in internal relation to each other, co-inhering and involving each other.[13]

The historicity of the ethical self becomes still more apparent when the discussion passes from this static description of each moment's involvement with every other moment to the active process by which the historical self presses on into its future, carrying its past with it. As time passes and the self realizes its ideal, that is, restructures its existence to conform to its ideal picture of itself, the ideal becomes the real and, in turn, the basis for

---

[11]*Either/Or*, 2:263; *S.V.*, 3:239.

[12]*Either/Or*, 2:262; *S.V.*, 3:238.

[13]*Either/Or*, 2:144-45; *S.V.*, 3:134-35; see Taylor, *Kierkegaard's Pseudonymous Authorship*, 213, and Mackey, *Kierkegaard: A Kind of Poet*, 53.

a new projection of ideality that the self must struggle to realize. This process has no cessation internal to it but continues as long as ethical self does. Judge William cryptically describes its dynamics in the following passage.

> In the resolution is posited another thing, but at the same time this other is posited as overcome. . . . The historical factor here consists in the fact that this other comes forth and acquires its validity, but precisely in its validity is seen to be something which ought not to have validity, so that [the self], tested and purified, issues from the movement and assimilates the experience.[14]

In this "law of motion," lies a third and more concrete form of repetition characteristic of the ethical self. As in the ironic self, the decisive movement must be repeated in every moment. The ironic self, however, is capable only of a barren and monotonous abstract repetition in which each moment simply does over again that which was done a moment before. In contrast, the ethical self's repetition builds on the previous moment's accomplishments. It assimilates rather than rejects the reality brought about in the previous moment's struggle. It thus makes true history possible in which the self's activity creates for itself an ever richer life.

With this last description of the ethical self as a historical unity born of repetition, this discussion reaches the limit of its development of the original, abstract "choice of choice" from which ethical selfhood emerges. The only form this temporal repetition can take at this level is the self's responsible reacceptance of itself in each succeeding moment. As thus expressed, it is so abstract and contentless a repetition that it lacks altogether the dimension of growth and enrichment characteristic of true repetition. In order to uncover the historical aspect of the ethical self, this investigation must move to the level of concrete, actual choices, the resolutions by which the self that has chosen to choose, that has taken responsibility for its life, gives that life content.

In moving from the abstract to the concrete, I reverse the progression of Judge William's thought and, to that extent, misrepresent his treatment of the ethical stage. The "choice of choice" described in the preceding pages is the subject of a letter entitled, imposingly enough, "Equilibrium Between the Aesthetical and the Ethical in the Composition of Personal-

---

[14]*Either/Or*, 2:100; *S.V.*, 3:94; see also *Either/Or*, 2:254-55; *S.V*, 3:231.

ity." This is the second of two long letters that make up the bulk of *Either/Or* 2. Judge William's primarily practical interest is reflected in his placing the much more concrete "Aesthetic Validity of Marriage" at the volume's beginning. My project of comparing the structures and forms of unity of varying Kierkegaardian selves justifies this reversal of the Judge's procedure. The task is now to turn to the first letter and examine one way in which the basic structure of the ethical self is concretely, existentially expressed.

As the titles of both letters suggest, Judge William is anxious to show that the aesthetical is not eliminated but harmoniously included in ethical existence. This retention is in keeping with my observation that the genesis of the ethical self lies in a transformation and development of the earlier life of the self, rather than a simple rejection or negation of it. Since that earlier life is one of immediate existence, the Judge must show that marriage is the ethical expression and completion of immediate love.

Why does Kierkegaard again have pseudonymous characters bring to life a stage of existence through a written expression of that stage's characteristic form of sexual relationship? Familiar and reductionistic biographical considerations aside, the presence of a common theme in the widely varied writings facilitates comparison between the various stages. Further, this topic no doubt best elicits personal and not simply intellectual interest on the part of his audience.

While these considerations cast light on the prevalence of this theme in the pseudonymous works in general, there are specific reasons why it is the ideal subject for Judge William to use in presenting the ethical stage. Most individuals have experienced at some time the all-consuming quality of romantic love. While the object of a romantic passion lies within the manifold realm of finitude, there is at least a promise of oneness in a self that can so wholeheartedly devote itself to another human being. Another pseudonymous character, Johannes de Silentio, goes so far as to make that capacity for such devotion a condition of further development as a person.

> [T]he knight will have the power to concentrate the whole substance of his life and the meaning of actuality into one single desire. If a person lacks this concentration, this focus, his soul is dissipated in multiplicity from the beginning, and then he never manages to make the movement.[15]

---

[15]Søren Kierkegaard, *Fear and Trembling*, trans. Howard V. Hong and Edna H. Hong (Princeton: Princeton University Press, 1983) 43; *S.V.*, 5:41.

Further, the historical unity of the ethical self is best expressed in marriage, the ethical transfiguration of immediate love. Like the general ethical duty of taking responsibility for oneself, the duties accepted in the marriage vow are without specifiable satisfaction in the present moment or temporal limit; marriage is an infinite task.[16]

Still more fundamental in explaining the Judge's choice of marriage as the most representative aspect of ethical selfhood is Kierkegaard's perception of the essential link between man's existence as a sexual creature and his capacity to have a history. As Vigilius Haufniensis rather abruptly puts it: "without sexuality, no history."[17] This statement is true, first, of men considered as a race. Only because the individuals that constitute a race are bound to each other by generational links does the race have a history.[18] Such linkage is a necessary but not a sufficient condition of having a history, however. That more is required is apparent from the inability of any nonhuman species of animal to have a history in the Kierkegaardian sense.[19] Only when the individuals making up the race are themselves historical creatures can the race have a history.[20]

This conclusion brings one to the second and more profound sense in which sexuality is the basis of history. Just as no beast can have a history, so such an honor is denied angels.[21] Neither has a history because neither is a synthesis but is either simply of the temporal or simply of the eternal order. Man, however, is of both; this duality is most evident in his character as a sexual being.[22]

---

[16]See Taylor, *Kierkegaard's Pseudonymous Authorship*, 206.

[17]*The Concept of Anxiety*, 49; *S.V.*, 6:142.

[18]*The Concept of Anxiety*, 73-74; *S.V.*, 6:163-64.

[19]*Philosophical Fragments*, 94; *S.V.*, 6:70.

[20]I am unable in this context to discuss Kierkegaard's views on the relation of the individual to the race. However, such an investigation would show this claim to be a reasoned conclusion and not a fallacy of composition.

[21]*The Concept of Anxiety*, 49; *S.V.*, 6:142.

[22]"The sexual is the expression of the prodigious *Widerspruch* [contradiction] that the immortal spirit is determined as *genus*." *The Concept of Anxiety*, 69; *S.V.*, 6:160.

In eating, one fulfills a physical need; in reading poetry, the psychical is given needed attention. In loving another person, however, the needs of both soul and body may be simultaneously satisfied. Ideally, in this case, these needs cease to be distinguishable. As the synthesis that one is achieves such positive expression—or, to use Kierkegaard's terminology, as one posits (*sætte*) the synthesis—one emerges as spirit, an outcome that in Kierkegaard's view is our hope and destiny. Correspondingly, any failure to achieve this destiny manifests itself in a disharmony between the bodily and psychical dimensions of love, warping it into a caricature of itself. This makes clear why Kierkegaard emphasizes the sexual in his investigation and portrayal of the various ways man lives out his existence as synthesis.

Understanding man's sexuality as the essential meeting point of his two dimensions, it is possible to appreciate more fully Vigilius Haufniensis's assertion of sexuality's special connection with history. In positing (positively uniting the elements of) the synthesis, the timelessness of eternity and the *nunc stans* (eternal now) of exclusively temporal existence give way to the ecstatic moment of historical existence.

> Only with the moment does history begin. . . . The moment is that ambiguity in which time and eternity touch each other, and with this the concept of *temporality* is posited, whereby time constantly intersects eternity and eternity constantly pervades time. As a result, the above-mentioned division acquires its significance: the present time, the past time, the future time.[23]

This understanding of history permits a deeper understanding of the change by which ethical existence emerges from immediate or aesthetic existence. It has been shown that this transition is a transformation rather than a rejection of the given, finite dimension of the self. It is now clear that it involves the interpenetration of the self's two dimensions in such a way that the self develops historically. In addition, my placing ethical existence under the category of repetition is borne out here. The self must realize itself as spirit within time and, at least partially, through its temporal dimension. That the self so realizes itself accentuates the importance of decision within time for the self that "has its eternity before it," that is, who must seize or else forfeit eternally its divine heritage.

---

[23]*The Concept of Anxiety*, 89; *S.V.*, 6:177.

Judge William devotes much of his writing to a discussion of one particular decision: marriage. In "The Aesthetic Validity of Marriage," he begins by defining marriage in terms of the finitude that it is to take up and transform. "What properly constitutes it, gives it its substantial content, is obviously love (*Elskov*)." [24] Judge William is careful to distinguish this immediate love from that which is often called love in ordinary speech but that lacks the infinitude of true love. All forms of sexual love arise out of the sensuous inclination that marks the self as finite, temporal, and embodied; true, immediate love—or as he more often and descriptively terms it, first love (*den første Kjærlighed*)—has eternity within it.

> In spite of the fact that this love is essentially based upon the sensuous, it is noble, nevertheless, by reason of the consciousness of eternity it embodies; for what distinguishes all love from lust is the fact that it bears an impress of eternity.[25]

This impress manifests itself in both possible dimensions of the eternal's presence in time: the intensive and the extensive. In his third and final discourse, "Observations on Marriage," the Judge writes that "love (*Forelskelsen*) is nature's profoundest myth."[26] Because myth for Kierkegaard and his pseudonymous characters signals the compression of the eternal into a moment in time, it is clear that he here refers to the plentitude of the moment for two new lovers. The present is so full that past and future are forgotten in an eternal now; this represents the intensive dimension of first love's eternality.

Johannes the seducer's elaborate maneuvers in relation to Cordelia are all designed to culminate in such a moment as well. He can never really achieve that moment, however, because his love, even at its fullest moment, lacks the extensive dimension of eternity characteristic of first love. Johannes the seducer is aware that the "eternal" moment will pass and his love with it. First love, in contrast, is not only certain that, as love lyrics so endlessly testify, it will last forever, it is certain that it has always been,

---

[24]*Either/Or*, 2:33; *S.V.*, 3:35.

[25]*Either/Or*, 2:21; *S.V.*, 3:25.

[26]*Stages on Life's Way*, trans. Walter Lowrie (New York: Schocken Books, 1967) 121; *S.V.*, 7:106.

in the sense that this union of kindred souls is seen as a *harmonia praestabilita* (pre-established harmony), fated to occur since time's beginning.

> Like everything eternal [first love] has the double propensity of presupposing itself back into all eternity and forward into all eternity.[27]

Despite first love's confidence in its eternity, it lacks the resources to sustain itself. In a world constantly in flux, it finds itself challenged by changes in the lovers' moods, fortunes, appearances, locations, and so forth. The danger is that the death of an "eternal" love will so transform the lovers that, thenceforth, their longing for the opposite sex will take an exclusively finite, temporal form devoid of the element of eternity that separates love from lust. "Love," in this eventuality, falls within a continuum having the promiscuity of the one-night-stand as its minimum and serial monogamy as its maximum. In both cases, sensual desire is stamped as lust by the self's knowledge that the attraction will end in time.

First love's lack of the resources for preserving its stamp of eternity, its inability to maintain itself over time, shows, according to Judge William, that it finds its fulfillment and culmination only in marriage.[28] The two immediate lovers enter this new estate by a choice that is structurally identical to, but far more concrete than, the original choice of choice through which one is posited as an ethical being. The chosen, in this case, is the immediate love the two have come to feel for each other. By choosing this love, by accepting responsibility for it, they profoundly change it as well as their general relationship to the world around them. Judge William discusses at length how marriage moves one's existence from idiosyncratic individuality to universality, how it frees the self from its "close reserve," from egocentricism, thus allowing it to reveal itself. While these are important themes, this investigation demands special attention to marriage's transformation of love and thus to the transformation of the loving self from an ahistorical to a historical form.

In taking the wedding vow, one's relation to one's love becomes active. Whereas originally love was something that simply happened to one, perhaps catching one by surprise and even at an inopportune moment, that

---

[27]*Either/Or*, 2:43; *S.V.*, 3:45.

[28]*Either/Or*, 2:47; *S.V.*, 3:49.

love now is actively taken up as duty. Just as the original, abstract choice of oneself alters the self's relation to time, so this acceptance of love as duty is, in the first analysis, an acceptance of the task of keeping it alive and healthy through time.[29] Thus, married love has within it a "law of movement," a dynamic projecting of itself into the future, which marks it as a historical love.[30]

While marriage places new demands on the self, it also offers new resources by which these demands may be met. In fact, the existence of the demand, the stern "you shall," acts as the self's anchor in those times when it questions its ability to sustain its love.

> Love drives out fear; but yet when love is for a moment fearful for itself, fearful of its own salvation, duty is the divine nutriment love stands in need of; for it says, "Fear not, you shall conquer," speaking not futuristically, for that only suggests hope, but imperatively, and in this lies an assurance which nothing can shake.[31]

The break with immediacy involved in the ethical life of marriage is clearly evident in this sureness born of duty. One of the marks of the immediate self is that it is entirely present in its moods. That is, it does not so much decide to act, as outwardly reflect in its behavior the feelings it presently experiences. Since moods and feelings are notoriously evanescent, the life of such a self will be discontinuous and disunified. These emotions are no basis for marriage, which is to be maintained even when romantic feelings have momentarily run dry. For the self to act as a faithful, loving spouse even when it doesn't feel much like one requires that this self stand apart from and above mood and respond instead to the idea of obligation, to the memory of the vow it took.[32] The spouse's break with immediacy is more clearly seen when it is described not simply as a rising above mood but as resignation.[33] That is, sometimes one's immediate urges

---

[29]*Either/Or*, 2:144; *S.V.*, 3:134.

[30]*Either/Or*, 2:62; *S.V.*, 3:62.

[31]*Either/Or*, 2:149; *S.V.*, 3:138.

[32]*Either/Or*, 2:234-35; *S.V.*, 3:213-14.

[33]*Either/Or*, 2:37; *S.V.*, 3:39.

will not only fail to coincide with duty, they will conflict with it; hence, when married one must refuse to act on sexual desire felt for anyone other than one's spouse. There are, of course, similar examples pertaining to all the other dimensions of human life as well.

The ethical self's resignation, its resistance to the illicit urgings of its feelings and emotions, does not represent the destruction or exclusion of its immediacy; it is simply its removal from a place of authority. The self, thus freed from slavery to its whims, moods, and passing desires, is able to achieve the essential continuity necessary to a positive expression of its existence as a synthesis. Now that the self stands sure in the present in its task of renewing itself in the future on the basis of its decision in the past, it has achieved a simultaneity of its three temporal aspects. This achievement expresses the self's eternality through its refusal to dissolve into the multiplicity of discrete moments that is time. Thus, ethical selfhood represents the first positive interpenetration of time and eternity in the Kierkegaardian "phenomenology."

> [This internal history] is an eternity in which the temporal has not vanished like an ideal moment, but in which it is constantly present as a real moment. . . .
> [The married man] has not fought with lions and ogres, but the most dangerous enemy: with time. But for him eternity does not come afterwards . . . , he has had eternity in time, has preserved eternity in time. . . . He solves the great riddle of living in eternity and yet hearing the hall clock strike. . . .[34]

In achieving such a historical existence, the ethical self surpasses its ironic predecessor in being one thing. Socrates realizes no more than a negative unity; by asserting the self's infinitude he distances himself from the chaos of the finite. Judge William, in contrast, uses the infinite to transform, tame, and unify the finite, thus bringing into existence the positive, historical unity of the ethical self.

What is the explanation of these selves' qualitatively different attitudes toward their finitude? Why does the Judge see his given immediacy as a task and not simply a point of departure? Why should the self choose itself? It is impossible to answer these questions if only the self's relation to

---

[34]*Either/Or*, 2:140-41; *S.V.*, 3:130-31.

itself is considered. Only when a new level of relation, the God-relationship, is considered does the vast difference between the ironic and the ethical selves make sense.

As Anti-Climacus states in the opening pages of *The Sickness Unto Death*, every relation of the self to itself is simultaneously a relation to the power that established it. This is not to say that every existence-form appreciates the religious significance of its manner of being; many selves are so underdeveloped or mired in despair that their improper relationship to God is present to them only as an incomprehensible anxiety.

All four forms of genuine selfhood possess at least some awareness of their God-relationship. In Socrates, the divine manifests itself as the purely abstract and purely negative daimon; it presents itself exclusively as the not-finite. Socrates' "communion" with this daimon, as abstract as it is, reflects itself in his understanding of his incommensurability with the finite world in which he dwells. This realization is the truth of ironic religiousness and is repeated in some form at each of the higher levels of selfhood; the existence of the God-relationship establishes man's uniqueness. Because his vision of the divine is exclusively negative, however, Socrates is unaware of God's positive dimension as creator, as the power that establishes the self and the cosmos. Because of this blind spot, the ironic self seizes undialectically on the self's uniqueness and incommensurability with the finite world. It looks on the part of itself it shares with the world, its finite givenness, as a burden to be cast off. In fact, it expresses its infinitude by repeatedly casting off this aspect of itself, by ironically depriving the finite of significance.

Judge William's positive relation to his finitude is the counterpart of his recognition of God as creator. Clearly, Kierkegaard does not attribute to the Judge a complete appreciation of the significance of existing before God. Nonetheless, at every turn the letters testify to the foundational role God plays in ethical selfhood. This role is especially apparent in the concrete examples the Judge selects to illustrate his form of existence. Marriage is of course continually presented as the substance and paradigm of ethical life. Why would the Judge select a commitment made during a religious ceremony—before a priest, a congregation, and ultimately God—unless he sought to make explicit and visible the divine component in ethical resolution that is usually implicit and private? His extensive comments on God's role as the founder and sustainer of the marriage covenant and his diagnosis of A's aversion to marriage as dread of divine authority underline this conclusion.[35]

The second letter's concrete examples not only confirm the role of divine authority in ethical life, they also best illustrate the Judge's "theology." In "Equilibrium," Judge William often returns to his earliest experiences of obligation to capture the unalloyed spirit of the ethical. These vignettes always include an authority figure, usually William's father. In the most illuminating of these episodes, the Judge describes his entrance into Latin school. The father, having purchased his son's schoolbooks, places them in the young man's hands and says, "William, when the month is up, you are third in your class."[36] The task established and the means for its completion provided, William is left to himself. He is allowed to play and study as he wishes, never questioned about his homework, neither encouraged nor threatened. That his father nonetheless keeps an eye on things and that one day there will be an accounting so impresses the child with a sense of duty that he never loses it.

The dominant feature of Judge William's theology is its vision of man's positive role in developing himself and, more specifically, in establishing the self's historical continuity. God is seen exclusively as the provider of possibilities; he so constitutes the self that it is capable of ethical activity. He then remains as witness, lending that activity its requisite seriousness. All actualization of these God-given possibilities, however, is left to the individual. It is in this reliance on man's ability to realize his divinely imposed duties and not in the exclusion of God from a foundational role that ethical religiousness is inadequate.

The ethical self's advance in the project of being one thing—the achievement of historical existence—can be attributed to two factors. First, the ethical self adopts a positive relation to its finitude, accepting the given as its project. This acceptance gives concreteness to the self and allows the development characteristic of true history. Implicit in this acceptance is the second factor in the ethicist's success: a positive relation to God. In issuing positive commands, rather than simply warning and discouraging as in the case of Socrates' daimon, God directly contributes to the self's develop-

---

[35]*Either/Or*, 2:46-62; *S.V.*, 3:47-62.

[36]*Either/Or*, 2:273; *S.V.*, 3:248.

ment as historical. That the given is given by God, is assigned by him as task, and is kept unceasingly within his omniscient awareness not only makes possible the ideal of lifelong commitments but also sustains the self in endeavoring to fulfill them.

Ethical existence originates not simply in the combination of a positive relation to finite existence and to God but, more specifically, in the conflict and tension engendered in a self that simultaneously sustains both these relations. Neither a purely earthly nor a purely divine being is capable of ethical endeavor. Rather, the ethical is born in the tension of simultaneous involvement in both realms and the resulting consciousness of the disparity between what one is and what one ought to be.

While this tension is the source of ethical existence, it also threatens to pull it apart at the seams. Because of the profound differences between the factors involved, the synthesis of the physical and the spiritual, the aesthetic and the ethico-religious, which ethical selfhood represents, is never secure and easy. The Judge's first two letters reflect what must be described as oblivious self-confidence, but in his "Observations on Marriage" there is an undertone of anxiety and an explicit, if still inadequate, recognition of this tension that indicates a deepening self-consciousness.

This last contribution by the Judge reveals that just as the synthesis of the temporal and the eternal is best manifested in man's sexuality, so is the tension between the two. Thus, marriage is not only the triumph and characteristic expression of ethical life; it contains the seeds of its ultimate collapse as well. In keeping with its compound, dialectical nature, marriage faces not a simple but a double challenge. Judge William writes:

> So marriage is threatened from two sides: if the individual has not put himself into a relationship of faith to God as spirit, paganism haunts his brain as a fantastic reminiscence, and then he cannot enter into any marriage; or, on the other hand, . . . so soon as one thinks of God as spirit, the relation of the individual to God becomes so spiritual that the psycho-physical synthesis wherein the strength of Eros lies readily disappears from sight . . . so neither in this case can he marry.[37]

While Judge William vigorously defends against both threats in "Observations on Marriage," other pseudonymous works show both to be fatal

---

[37]*Stages on Life's Way*, 106; *S.V.*, 7:92.

to the ethical project. It proves to be impossible to do justice to one aspect of the synthesis without slighting the other. Kierkegaard's pseudonymous characters go about making this clear in two ways. First, by concentrating on the idea of God, by allowing him to emerge fully "as spirit," ethical existence is shown to commit the sin of lese majesty against the deity. The ethical self presumes both in limiting God to a set mode of interaction with man and in supposing that mere mortals are capable of positive cooperation with the Almighty, of "coming to the aid of the Deity." Alternately, a deeper exploration into the true character of the given, finite dimension of human nature reveals it to be less amenable to ethical transformation than the Judge believes.

These two failures of the ethical self's theories and aspirations are intimately connected; a close analysis of the first leads to the second. Nonetheless, there is good reason to examine them separately. Each represents a particular challenge to the self in its quest for oneness. To each of these challenges corresponds an answering form of selfhood. Therefore, in each of the following sections, I pursue each failure of ethical existence through to a new form of selfhood.

Both of these new forms of selfhood are described by Kierkegaard as religious. With the collapse of the ethical self's confidence in its ability to consolidate itself as a unity, God emerges as much more than a mere creator of possibilities. In a later religious work, Kierkegaard writes:

> As He is the truth, thou dost not learn to know from Him what the truth is, to be left then to thine own devices, but thou dost remain in the truth only by remaining in Him.[38]

If "the truth" is replaced with the related description of God, "the One," this passage serves nicely to indicate where the Judge has gone astray.

---

[38]*For Self-Examination*, trans. Walter Lowrie (Princeton: Princeton University Press, 1944) 24; *S.V.*, 17:47.

CHAPTER IX

Oneness as Repentance: The Unity of the Religious Self

The theology implicit in Judge William's writings is one of positive cooperation between God and man. God is the creator and sustainer of ethical possibilities that human beings, in turn, are charged with actualizing. His view would appear to meet Kierkegaard's early stated and always maintained demand that neither divine assistance nor human initiative excludes one another in the process of salvation, or more appropriately here, in the emergence of genuine selfhood.

Unfortunately for the Judge, this straightforward concept of cooperation is totally inadequate when the parties involved are a finite human being and God. Because Judge William's main interest is in securing a positive role for man, he manifests this inadequacy exclusively in a slighting of God's omnipotence. If humans are to develop themselves as unified, historical persons, there must be a specified, understood, and relatively constant course of action that will bring them to this end; that is, God must relate to persons only through a preestablished set of moral laws. Such a restriction of God effectively excludes him from the ethical self's frame of reference, since his essence is his freedom from all restriction. Like the smile left behind by the Cheshire Cat, the moral laws are all that remain when God vanishes from the Judge's confining embrace. Johannes de Silentio writes that if duty to God is identical to the duty to obey his universal moral dictates,

> [t]he whole of existence of the human race rounds itself off as a perfect, self-contained sphere, and then the ethical is that which limits and fills at one and the same time. God comes to be an invisible vanishing point, an impotent thought; his power is only in the ethical, which fills all existence.[1]

God does not long suffer such human-imposed restriction. Already in "Observations on Marriage," the Judge anxiously defends ethical existence from the threat presented to it by the religious exception. Forced as he is to admit that God has a right to demand of an individual acts lying outside the universal, he cancels this concession by stipulating the conditions that must be met before one can justifiably consider oneself so summoned; that is, he brings the individual back under the universal. The following section of *Stages on Life's Way*, "Guilty, Not Guilty," shows that no such introduction of epicycles suffices to preserve the ethical understanding of existence and its corresponding attempt at oneness. It is, however, in *Fear and Trembling* that Kierkegaard most strikingly illuminates his belief that God's interaction with his creation refuses to be channeled exclusively through the medium of universal ethical laws.

Johannes de Silentio's excursion in "dialectical lyric" is inspired by the biblical account of the Akedah, the sacrifice of Isaac. Cutting through the pious sugarcoating within which this story has been encased by centuries of homiletic banalization, Johannes powerfully evokes the tremendous conflicts and horrible torments that are inseparable from such a trial. Here, God not only summons Abraham out of the universal into a life as

---

[1] *Fear and Trembling*, 68; *S.V.*, 5:63. This conflation of God and the ethical order is shown in miniature in Judge William's statement that as a youth he saw his father as "an incarnation of the rule." *Either/Or*, 2:274; *S.V.*, 3:248.

an exception, he commands an action specifically forbidden by the ethical: murder.

The choice posed here is clear: either one must refuse the account of the affair offered in Genesis, deny Abraham the title "father of faith," and brand him a homicidal madman, or else accept that there is a "teleological suspension of the ethical." In neither case can Judge William's ethical stage stand. If one chooses the former, one must admit to preferring a godless universe to one in which the ethical order may be summarily suspended. To do so, however, deprives the Judge of the theological principles upon which he founds his view of ethical existence.

If, on the other hand, the possibility of a teleological suspension is acknowledged, the ethical plainly comes to grief. The individual's absolute duty to God is now more than a euphemism for an absolute duty to obey the universal moral laws. God may summon an individual into an immediate relation to him that not only lies outside the medium of the universal but that demands that the individual act contrary to the moral laws. In such a case, the self exists qua individual, self-revelation is impossible, and a happy relation between its finite and infinite dimensions is precluded. These characteristics the Judge has seen and condemned in the aesthetic self. In this case, however, they signal a self not lower, but higher than the universal. This is a thought that the ethical self simply cannot think. In turn, this inability signals its failure or refusal to think God's omnipotence.

Does the mere *possibility* of a teleological suspension sound the death knell for ethical existence? Granted, an individual called into the immediate presence of God may resort to the comfortable categories of the universal only in defiance of God and as a surrender to temptation. But what of the vast majority of men who never receive such a call? Is it not their duty to remain within the universal, to live in the manner the Judge describes, perhaps respecting, but certainly neither understanding nor envying, those both blessed and cursed by direct contact with the living God? Does not Abraham himself return from Mount Moriah to life on the plain? Does he not resume his former ethical life as soon as his trial is over?

Rather than proving the provisional validity of the ethical, Abraham's return points toward a higher form of existence: paradoxical religiosity or religiousness B. He earns his title "father of faith" not by his willingness to sacrifice his son—Johannes de Silentio states that he could follow Abraham in this resignation of his whole earthly, immediate life[2]—but in his reacquisition "by virtue of the absurd" of all that he had lost. The "knight of faith" is the subject of my next section. Before proceeding to examine this self that, with the help of God, is capable of such a simultaneous withdrawal and return, I will examine the self that manages only the first half of the movement: the "knight of infinite resignation."

Johannes de Silentio not only discusses but is such a knight. His situation is striking because he is never personally tested in the manner Abraham was. Rather, his fascination as a dialectician-poet with Abraham's trial, his vicarious experience of God's dreadful command, his repeatedly unsuccessful attempts to understand Abraham's return to the finite, immediate life, are sufficient to drive Johannes de Silentio out of the comfortable and gregarious life of the ethical stage into the isolation of one who has given up all that is finite but must continue to exist within it nonetheless.

In Johannes de Silentio appear the tracings of the next self in the Kierkegaardian hierarchy: the self of religiousness A. That Johannes de Silentio is robbed of his immediacy by what for him is merely the *possibility* of a teleological suspension indicates that it is not the extraordinary call by God itself, but rather the thought of a truly absolute God, that so alters his existence.

In each of his developments of the self of religiousness A, Kierkegaard begins simply by positing a self that seeks to understand itself as existing before such an absolute God.[3] That such an understanding produces a specifically religious self bears out my earlier claim that the ethical self can sustain neither its self-understanding nor its aspirations in the face of a decisive conception of God. When the self grasps the overwhelming thought that God is interested in its existence, its infinite dimension is emphasized, and the carefully tended balance between the two dimensions, the finite and infinite, is disrupted. This accentuation of the infinite shatters the immediacy on which the ethical depends. Furthermore, the universal laws by which the ethical self lives are now seen to be both too much and too little. Fulfilling the demands of a legal code is seen as altogether insufficient to

---

[2]*Fear and Trembling*, 34-35; *S.V.*, 5:33.

[3]"The cornerstone of the religious life is the conviction that *God is*." Mackey, *Kierkegaard: A Kind of Poet*, 100.

express the infinite debt of obedience the finite self owes its infinite creator. In turn, the self's unavoidable failure to express infinite obedience posits the self as guilty; thus, it cannot even fulfill the universal moral demand for righteousness.

This impotence, and the self's corresponding understanding that it can do nothing by itself, leads to a reinterpretation of the task of being one thing. Whereas Judge William aspired "to come to the aid of the Deity," to make use of the God-given opportunity to establish himself as a unified, historical self, the self of religiousness A looks to God alone for its help and contributes only by understanding that it can contribute nothing at all. Instead of seeking to build its oneness within the finite through its own activity, instead of seeking to bring to historical expression the "eternality" of immediacy, the religious self[4] looks beyond the finite to God, the sole locus of oneness and unchangeability.[5]

In the eighteen edifying discourses Kierkegaard published under his own name in 1843 and 1844, he presents his richest and most varied discussion of immanent religiousness. These discourses testify to his creative genius, working and reworking as they do a single, simple theme with seemingly inexhaustible originality. Read as a group, they provide a complete picture of this form of existence as well as an earnest admonition that we make it our own. This very richness, however, leads me to base my discussion of religiousness A on the sparer and more theoretically oriented presentation found in the *Postscript*.

In "Existential Pathos," Johannes Climacus gives a three-step development of the self that exists in "an absolute relationship to the absolute." Not only do these pages present a single, more succinct, and more philosophically oriented discussion, they are the ideal point of departure for this investigation because at each of the three levels, the religious self is shown to be engaged in the task of being one thing. I will occasionally supplement my discussion of this section with references to *Purity of Heart is to Will One Thing*, a later discourse that also traces the development of the religious self from its given relationship to God to its decisive expression.

---

[4]I will use this term throughout to indicate the self of immanent religiousness.

[5]Søren Kierkegaard, *Edifying Discourses: A Selection*, trans. David F. Swenson and Lillian M. Swenson, ed. Paul Holmer (New York: Harper and Row, 1958) 16; *S.V.*, 4:26.

Joahnnes Climacus begins by defining the religious self as one that stands in "an absolute relationship to the absolute." He has arrived at this definition by a circuitous and "unscientific" course of argument and satire in which he shows that subjective appropriation, not objective certainty, is the proper goal of an existing individual. Because "truth is subjectivity," because "the more passion the more self," human existence is seen to culminate in that most interested of all relationships: the interest of the individual in his eternal happiness.[6] Because the object of this relationship can equally be described as God, one reaches the formula, "an absolute relationship to the absolute." This is the highest determination of selfhood possible on a strictly human or, as Kierkegaard puts it, immanent basis.

The focusing of self that goes with such an absolute commitment, such a "willing of one thing," is the first expression of the personal unity of the religious self. This expression is incomplete as it stands, however, since it is the essence of an absolute relationship to continue itself through time.

> To relate oneself with existential pathos to an eternal happiness is never expressed by once in a while making a great effort, but by persistence in the relationship, by the perseverance by which it is put together with everything; for therein lies the art of existing, and here perhaps it is that men are most lacking.[7]

This connection between the continuity and unity of the religious self and its formulaic description as standing in "an absolute relationship to the absolute" is underlined and made concrete when it is shown to be implicitly contained within Kierkegaard's assertion that "Purity of Heart is to Will One Thing." In the book of this title, Kierkegaard argues that only the Good (= God = the Absolute) is truly one. Because the self takes on the essential character of the object of its willing, it can be pure in heart—that

---

[6]"The development or transformation of the individual's subjectivity, its infinite concentration in itself over against the conception of an eternal happiness, that highest good of the infinite—this constitutes the developed potentiality of the primary potentiality which subjectivity as such represents." *Postscript*, 116; *S.V.*, 9:108. This represents religiousness A's version of the two-tiered process of actualization that we have seen to be common to all four forms of true selfhood recognized by Kierkegaard.

[7]*Postscript*, 476; *S.V.*, 10:207.

Personal Unity in Kierkegaard's Thought

is, one—only when it wills the Good. Not only the object—the what—of this willing but also its manner—its how—is essential to its becoming one thing. The self is only one when it wills the Good "in Truth." When Kierkegaard spells out what he means by this phrase, we see how very close he is to the formula of the *Postscript*: "If, then, a man in truth wills the Good, then HE MUST BE WILLING TO DO ALL FOR IT or HE MUST BE WILLING TO SUFFER ALL FOR IT."[8]

This development of the idea of "an absolute relationship to the absolute" leads to its immediate corollary: such a self also stands in "a relative relationship to the relative." In requiring an absolute commitment, the absolute shows itself to be a jealous God. No other interest or combination of interests can be allowed to figure over against the one, absolute interest; a qualitative distinction must be made between obedience to God and all other concerns.

In the "Initial Expression," the first of the three parts of "Existential Pathos," Johannes Climacus vehemently attacks the attempts of his contemporaries to mediate this distinction. While his attack is obviously directed at Hegel and, especially, at the Danish Hegelian theologians, Judge William's thought and action are also based on just such a mediation. He identifies marriage, vocation, and other manifestations of the universal human as the media within which he may adequately express his God-relationship. Johannes Climacus, obliquely referring to Abraham's terrifying experience, specifically rejects any such assumption of harmony between religious and ethical duty.

> The principle of mediation either allows the relationship to the absolute *telos* to be mediated into relative ends or else lets it flow, as being abstract, exhaustively into the relative ends as its concrete predicates. . . . But the relationship to the absolute *telos* cannot pour itself exhaustively into the relative ends, because the absolute relationship may require the renunciation of them all.
>
> Mediation is a rebellion of relative ends against the majesty of the absolute, an attempt to bring the absolute down to the level of everything else, an attack upon the dignity of human life, seeking to make man a mere servant of relative ends.[9]

---

[8]*Purity of Heart is to Will One Thing*, 122; *S.V.*, 11:78.

[9]*Postscript*, 363, 375; *S.V.*, 10:97, 109-10.

Since no individual begins his life in such a relative relationship to the relative, immediacy involving as it does direct ties between the subject and the finite world, entering an absolute relationship to the absolute requires a profound break with the self's previous condition. Such a radical departure from immediacy is a common feature of all selves that set about the task of being one thing. Whether called resignation or renunciation, the religious self's movement from immediacy to its developed state is marked by a deeply negative relationship to the finite.

> In his immediacy the individual is rooted in the finite. But when resignation has convinced itself that he has acquired the absolute direction toward the absolute *telos*, all is changed, and the roots have been severed. He still lives in the finite, but he does not have his life in the finite. . . . He is a stranger in the world of the finite.[10]

This negative relationship to the finite world that the self must nonetheless inhabit so long as the self exists is structurally similar to the ironic existence of Socrates. By the same token, it differs profoundly from the ethical self's retention and transformation of its finitude. Like Socrates, the religious self is called upon to express temporally its negative oneness by persistently repeating its departure from its finite circumstances.[11] Johannes Climacus bases his claim that religious life is essentially and unavoidably one of suffering on the constantly renewed pain of this unceasing renunciation of one's immediate desires and impulses.[12]

One might argue that this description of religiousness A is one-sided; not a negative but a relative relationship to the relative is required. As this formula stands, it sounds more similar to the ethical self's call for the removal of the finite from control than to the ironist's total rejection of finitude.

---

[10]*Postscript*, 367; *S.V.*, 10:102. "[I]n existence, the beginning must be made by exercising oneself in the relationship to the absolute *telos*, and by taking power away from immediacy." *Postscript*, 386; *S.V.*, 10:119-20.

[11]"The significance of the religious suffering is that it is a dying away from immediacy; its reality consists in its essential persistence." *Postscript*, 446; *S.V.*, 10:177.

[12]*Postscript*, 390-400, 412; *S.V.*, 10:124-33, 144.

This impression is supported by Johannes Climacus's rejection of monasticism.[13] As a critic of the modern mediating mentality, he cannot but admire those whose passion for the absolute leads them to surrender their earthly lives. The monastic movement errs, however, in its belief that the religious renunciation of the world should be externally expressed. This erroneous belief in turn leads to the even more serious misconception that through such sacrifice one earns merit in the eyes of God.

As befits its description as "the religion of hidden inwardness," religiousness A calls on the individual to conceal his absolute relationship to God within an incognito of ordinariness. While such an existence threatens to slip unawares into spiritlessness, into the reality rather than simply the appearance of conformity, it is the only consistent application of the refusal to mediate between the earthly and the divine. Monasticism only thinks through this refusal halfway; implicit in its attempt to express the the God-relationship externally is an assumption of commensurability between the two realms.[14] Johannes Climacus concludes that

> the task is . . . to exercise myself in the relationship to the absolute *telos* so as always to have it with me, while remaining in the relativities of life.[15]

Just as an adult may wholeheartedly enter and even inspire the games of children without playing as a child, so the religious self is called to live its life among the busy games of the adult world.[16]

The religious individual's awareness that finite concerns lack ultimate significance in no way dampens his enthusiasm for pursuing them. Rather, he casts aside all thought of results and dedicates his efforts to the greater glory of God. Only when every thought of accomplishment and merit is foreign to him does he stand self-consciously as a finite self before the in-

---

[13]How different Johannes Climacus's rejection of monasticism is from that of Judge William!

[14]"The cloister wishes to express inwardness by means of a specific outwardness which is supposed to be inwardness. But this is a contradiction, for being a monk is just as truly something external as being an alderman." *Postscript*, 366; *S.V.*, 10:101.

[15]*Postscript*, 364-65; *S.V.*, 10:99.

[16]*Postscript*, 370; *S.V.*, 10:104-105.

finite God.[17] That the self can accomplish nothing of itself—that it is nothing before God—is a consequence of the qualitative distinction between God and man. Religiousness A is the simultaneous self-annihilation and self-fulfillment involved in the repeated appropriation of this truth about the creature's existence before its creator. Johannes Climacus cites this recognition as a second basis for the essential connection between religious existence and suffering.[18]

On the basis of this "Initial Expression," it would be oversimplistic and possibly wrong to describe as negative the religious self's relationship to the finite. This changes, however, upon passing from the ideal drawing of consequences from the original postulate of "an absolute relationship to the absolute" to its existential realization. As Johannes Climacus informs the reader in turning to the "Essential Expression," "the task must now be understood more closely in its concrete difficulty."[19]

Already in "The Initial Expression," Johannes Climacus remarks with characteristically ironic understatement that "it is not an easy thing to maintain an absolute relationship to the absolute *telos* and at the same time participate like other men in this and that."[20] In the second section, he relentlessly exposes all attempts to evade this difficulty, to get around it with a little thoughtlessness and a touch of dishonesty, until it is apparent that continually to maintain both relationships is beyond human capacity. Whatever its ideal character, in the realm of existence an absolute relationship to the absolute involves a negative relationship to the relative.[21]

Johannes Climacus sets about juxtaposing the real and the ideal with devilish merriment and an adherence to concrete detail that might cause infuriated readers to cry with Gorgias, "By heavens, you literally never

---

[17]*Postscript*, 421; *S.V.*, 10:154; see also *Postscript*, 362, 414, 452; *S.V.*, 10:97, 146, 183.

[18]"And even if it could be done at a stroke, because the individual is an existing individual, he will encounter suffering in the repetition." *Postscript*, 412; *S.V.*, 10:144.

[19]*Postscript*, 386; *S.V.*, 10:119.

[20]*Postscript*, 365; *S.V.*, 10:99.

[21]*Postscript*, 447n; *S.V.*, 10:178n.

Personal Unity in Kierkegaard's Thought

stop talking of cobblers and fullers and cooks and doctors, as if we were discussing them."[22] Rather than speaking of the ideal in its pristine abstractness, he places it in the mouth of His Reverence, the parson, as he delivers his Sunday morning sermon to the flock. "You must not depend upon the world, and not upon men, and not upon yourself, but only and alone upon God; for a human being can of himself do nothing."[23] The congregation responds to this orthodox message with equally orthodox nods, whether of approval or drowsiness, I will not attempt to say.

Though this pious maxim is easy to understand while sitting in a pew, it is rather more difficult to live by during the other six days of the week. Johannes Climacus sends forth his spy to see how his countrymen are faring with this task. Time and again, the spy's conversations and observations reveal a wide gap between professed belief and actual behavior. The humorist's chuckle is not inspired by the gap itself so much as by the utter failure of the concerned selves to perceive it. The ability of these individuals to act in a way directly at odds with the words that are still fresh on their lips betokens an effective separation of ideal and real. Like our finest china, we save thoughts of our God-relationship for Sundays and special occasions, making use of plainer but more functional principles for daily use.

An absolute relationship to the absolute can never exist in such an on-again, off-again manner. Its specific nature is the unbroken continuity that always marks the presence of the eternal in a temporal being. Thus, if the religious self is to maintain a relative relationship to the relative, its relationship to God must self-consciously penetrate every moment of this engagement with the finite.

Johannes Climacus runs aground on the rocks of triviality in every attempt to accomplish this feat. It is possible to think God together with a momentous event, with a moral resolve, and, in his role as the righteous judge and forgiving father, even with a moral failure. But can one simultaneously sustain an absolute relationship to God and enjoy an outing at Deer Park? Our initial reaction is that to join the thought of God to so trivial a matter is sacrilege. This reaction, however, indicates that our thought

---

[22]Plato *Gorgias* 491a.

[23]*Postscript*, 417; *S.V.*, 10:149-50.

remains at the level of the ethical. It is an attempt to place the action in the moral category "the indifferent" and thus make the question of its connection with our God-relationship moot. This reaction stems from the ethical self's relation to God exclusively through the medium of universal laws. If one obeys the law, one expresses obedience to God. If one disobeys the law, one rebels. This moral scheme, however, leaves all the actions that are neither required nor prohibited to our discretion. The absence of any further significance to the event frees the ethical individual to sport freely, to abandon himself to his immediate impulses, when he takes his family out for an afternoon at Deer Park.

The religious self, however, is called to exist as an individual before God and, thus, must regard such a retreat into the universal as a temptation. But how terrible to think the most serious and strenuous of thoughts and at the same time to engage in the most lighthearted of enjoyments! And yet, this he must do. If he refuses to indulge in such frivolous pursuits because they are irreconcilable with his pious meditations, his only consistent recourse is to don a cowl and find a barber who can tonsure him (no mean feat in nineteenth-century Copenhagen!). "If the religious man is to be in any way peculiar in his behavior outwardly, then the cloister is the only energetic expression therefor; the rest is only botchwork."[24]

How, then, can our religious friend enjoy an afternoon at Deer Park? Constant thought of God so lames his immediacy that he cannot really enter into the spirit of the excursion. He may be physically present among the other vacationers, he may show no outward differences from them, but inwardly he is "*distrait.*" Like a ghost at a feast, he must wistfully observe his fellows enjoy an immediacy forever denied him.

> What the conception of God or an eternal happiness is to effect in the individual is, that he transform his entire existence in relation thereto, and this transformation is a process of dying away from the immediate. This is slowly brought about, but finally he will feel himself confined within the absolute conception of God; for the absolute conception of God does not consist in having such a conception *en passant*, but consists in having the absolute conception at every moment. This is the check on his immediacy, the death verdict which announces its annihilation.

---

[24]*Postscript*, 422; *S.V.*, 10:154.

Personal Unity in Kierkegaard's Thought

[T]he absolute consciousness of God consumes him as the burning heat of the summer sun when it will not go down, as the burning heat of the summer sun when it will not abate.[25]

As a last attempt to save the religious self from utter alienation from the finite world, Johannes Climacus appeals to the very humility that existence before God commands. He notes that "one ingredient in the lowliness of a human being is that he is temporal, and cannot endure to lead uninterruptedly the life of the eternal in time." Is it not arrogance to lament one's need for recreation? Is it not far more fitting to make the trip to Deer Park, thus expressing "[t]he humility that frankly admits its human lowliness with humble cheerfulness before God, trusting that God knows all this better than man himself"?[26]

As plausible as this may sound, Johannes Climacus soon enmeshes it in a hopeless tangle of reflection. If it is true that one needs recreation, does one need it this afternoon? Is the little excursion absolutely needed or is it self-indulgence? Either one slides quickly and carelessly over this question, in which case one ceases to stand in an absolute relationship to the absolute, or one is immobilized by its ultimate unanswerability. It is no wonder that Johannes Climacus concludes his extensive inquiry into the possibility of such a seemingly simple venture by saying that others may answer for themselves, but he simply cannot maintain an absolute relationship to the absolute and enjoy an afternoon at Deer Park. Despite its ideal expression, an absolute relationship to the absolute effectively excludes anything but a strictly negative relationship to the relative. It is the inevitability of this negative relationship that causes Johannes Climacus to say that suffering is the essential expression of religious life.

In "The Decisive Expression," the self's distance from the originally posed task looms even greater. "[P]lunging deeper into existence," the religious self discovers that its suffering is further determined as guilty suffering. Unable to combine any sort of positive relationship to the finite with its absolute relationship to God, the religious self is now forced to admit its total inability to meet the demands of this latter relationship as well.

---

[25]*Postscript*, 432-33; *S.V.*, 10:163.

[26]*Postscript*, 439-40; *S.V.*, 10:170-71.

Thus things go backwards: the task is presented to the individual in existence, and just as he is ready to cut at once a fine figure (which only can be done *in abstracto* and on paper, because the loose trousers of the abstractor are very different from the strait-jacket of the exister) and wants to begin, it is discovered that a new beginning is necessary, the beginning upon the immense detour of dying from immediacy, and just when the beginning is about to be made at this point, it is discovered that there, since time has meanwhile been passing, an ill beginning is made, and that the beginning must be made by becoming guilty and from that moment increasing the total capital of guilt by a new guilt at a usurious rate of interest.[27]

Johannes Climacus lays particular weight here on the role of temporality in the self's determination as guilty. However, the unavoidable time lag between the posing of a task and its completion is but one manifestation of a more general inability of a finite self to more than approximate obedience to an ideal command. Before God, however, obedience is never more or less without becoming disobedience. Thus it is that guilt obeys a qualitative and not a quantitative dialectic. The slightest deviation or shortcoming places the individual in a position of absolute guilt before God.[28] Since the self's finitude makes this inadequacy unavoidable, it is apparent that guilt is an expression, the decisive expression, of the existence of a finite being before God. "[T]here is a ceremonial rule that says that when the finite spirit would see God, it must begin as guilty."[29]

This insight was already expressed by the unnamed Jutlandish parson in the "Ultimatum" with which *Either/Or* 2 concludes. This "sermon"[30] takes as its subject "The edification implied in the thought that as against

---

[27]*Postscript*, 469; *S.V.*, 10:200.

[28]*The Concept of Anxiety*, 30; *S.V.*, 6:126.

[29]*The Concept of Anxiety*, 109; *S.V.*, 6:192.

[30]The "Ultimatum" fulfills the formal requirements of a sermon—it is preached by an ordained minister as part of a sacred service in a Christian church—but its content is strictly immanent religious. Kierkegaard is very careful to distinguish between his own immanent-religious productions, which he calls edifying discourses, and the sermon, which not only requires an ordained minister but also a paradoxical religious content. See *Postscript*, 229-30; *S.V.*, 9:214-15.

Personal Unity in Kierkegaard's Thought

God we are always in the wrong."[31] Judge William chooses to send the sermon on to his young friend A with an endorsement of its contents, but it represents the decisive dismissal of the ethical self's pretensions of contributing positively to its own "salvation" (maturation as a genuine self).

This discovery of guilt brings us to the paradoxical heart of immanent religiosity. Just as a relationship to eternal happiness expresses itself within existence as suffering, a relationship to God manifests itself in guilt consciousness, that is, in an awareness of one's absolute distance from God. Johannes Climacus describes this representation of the positive by the negative as "the constant criterion of the religious sphere."[32] He writes:

> A revelation is signalized by mystery, happiness by suffering, the certainty of faith by uncertainty, the ease of the paradoxical-religious life by its difficulty, the truth by absurdity.[33]

It is in "an eternal recollection of guilt," a continual reappropriation of awareness of absolute guilt before God, that religious selfhood reaches its fullest development. Correspondingly, it is here that we find the most decisive expression of this self's manner of being one thing. First, the religious self's concentration on guilt means that it "thinks one thought" rather than scattering itself among many thoughts as does the immediate self.[34] Second, this focusing of self must be continually repeated, thus lending the self a form of continuity over time.[35]

A glance at *Purity of Heart* underlines these findings. This discourse focuses on the link between standing in the absolute relationship to the absolute and being one thing. In fact, it argues that the two are ultimately identical. Kierkegaard develops the idea of being one thing in great detail

---

[31] *Either/Or*, 2:343; *S.V.*, 3:318.

[32] *Postscript*, 387; *S.V.*, 10:120.

[33] Ibid.

[34] *Postscript*, 473; *S.V.*, 10:204.

[35] *Postscript*, 474; *S.V.*, 10:205.

and concreteness but concludes by saying that this purity of heart lies only in the humble confession before God that one has not been one thing.[36]

Thus the religious self, like the ironist, displays an exclusively negative oneness. In both cases, this negativity has two dimensions. First, both cut themselves off from any real contact with the finite: the ironist by means of infinite reflection, the religious self by means of absolute resignation of its immediacy. Second, the two selves express their status as existing individuals by relating only negatively to the infinite, which they nonetheless consider their essential aspect. In constantly professing his ignorance, Socrates imparts an abstract, intellectual expression to this negative relationship. Since "guilt is . . . the most concrete expression of existence,"[37] since it involves not only the mind but also the will and emotions of man, the religious self, with its perpetual mea culpa, shows a definite advance over its ironic predecessor in achieving a unified *existence*.

Because the religious self continually strives to eliminate its immediacy and continually repents its failure to do so completely, in no real sense can it have a history. The self's finitude, including its past, is always abandoned rather than appropriated, transformed, and retained, and so the self always finds itself beginning again from the beginning. Thus, while its relationship to the eternal must express itself in continuity, in the constant repetition of its characteristic movement, the negativity of this movement precludes any enrichment of one moment by its preceding moments. As in the case of the ironist, time for the religious self is to be understood not in terms of a biological metaphor such as growth, but rather from the image of identical beads strung along a thread.

A negative relationship to the finite, a barren repetition, and a lack of any real history are the marks of the self of recollection. The religious individual is therefore such a self, for it not only displays all these characters but also may be described as "having its eternity behind it." Kierkegaard uses this image to convey the recollecting self's accentuation of the given dimension of its God-relationship. Unquestionably, the religious individual strives to express in its existence its relation to the divine; that is, it

---

[36]*Purity of Heart*, 216; *S.V.*, 11:138; see Louis Mackey, "The Analysis of the Good in Kierkegaard's *Purity of Heart*," in *Experience, Existence and the Good*, ed. T. C. Leib (Carbondale: Southern Illinois University Press, 1961).

[37]*Postscript*, 470; *S.V.*, 10:200-201.

struggles to actualize its potential for such a relationship. The potential itself, however, is the decisive element. It represents a bond to the eternal that no temporal action can alter. Even guilt, the strongest expression of the self's removal from God available to the religious self, does not essentially change the self it characterizes. Rather, it is the existential expression of the underlying, unalterable relationship between God and man.

> Though the consciousness [of guilt] be ever so decisive, it is nevertheless the relationship which sustains the disrelationship. . . . the eternal happiness and the exister do not so repel one another that it comes to an absolute breach. . . . In the consciousness of guilt it is the selfsame subject which becomes essentially guilty by keeping guilt in relationship to an eternal happiness, but yet the identity of the subject is such that guilt does not make the subject a new man.[38]

When nothing the self does can "make him a new man," the struggle Johannes Climacus describes as required of an existing individual seems odd. In his description of the humorist, he provides a wonderfully concrete image to illustrate this curious nature of religious striving.

> [T]he humoristic explanation of existence . . . assumes that when existence is apprehended as a process of walking along a way, the distinctive and remarkable fact about existence is that the goal lies behind one—and yet one is compelled to walk forward, for walking is the image for existence.[39]

While the *Postscript* account of the religious self has been used because of its succinctness, the discussion now requires an even sparer statement of this form of selfhood. In his earlier work, *Philosophical Fragments*, Johannes Climacus provides a clear view of the basic principles of religiousness A. In *Philosophical Fragments*, Johannes Climacus describes "the Socratic standpoint" as the view that every human being "is his own center, and the entire world centers in him, because his self-knowledge is a knowledge of God."[40] This is a clear statement of the basic tenet of im-

---

[38]*Postscript*, 473-74; *S.V.*, 10:204-205.

[39]*Postscript*, 402; *S.V.*, 10:135.

[40]*Philosophical Fragments*, 14; *S.V.*, 6:16.

manent religiousness, which sees the God-relationship as existing within the individual and needing only to be discovered. The absolute significance of this preexisting relationship overshadows the when and the how of the self's arrival at a knowledge of it. "From the standpoint of Socratic thought every point of departure in time is *eo ipso* accidental, an occasion, a vanishing moment. The teacher is no more than this."[41]

Seeking not to disprove immanent religiousness but to distinguish it from Christianity, Johannes Climacus asks what would be implied if the self did not have the truth within it but was alien to it and, in fact, constantly receding from it. In this case, the Teacher and the moment he brought the Truth to the self would be of essential importance. Before this occurred, however, the self's alienation from the Truth would prevent it from realizing its predicament. Though believing itself in possession of the Truth, its actual estrangement from it would manifest itself in anxiety, in an indeterminate sense that something was dreadfully amiss.

Johannes Climacus strays beyond his stated goal of simply juxtaposing and contrasting the two views when he notes such an anxiety in Socrates. In reference to *Phaedrus* 230a, he writes:

> The connoisseur in self-knowledge was perplexed over himself to the point of bewilderment when he came to grapple in thought with the unlike; he scarcely knew any longer whether he was a stranger monster than Typhon or if his nature partook of something divine. What then did he lack? The consciousness of sin, which he indeed could not more teach to another than another could teach it to him, but only the God—if the God consents to become a Teacher.[42]

At first glance, this claim that Socrates lacks an adequate consciousness of sin might seem odd. After all, "the Socratic standpoint" is decisively expressed in an eternal recollection of absolute guilt before God. In the Kierkegaardian vocabulary, however, guilt and sin are qualitatively different concepts. Guilt is the expression of an existing self's God-relationship. Sin,

---

[41]*Philosophical Fragments*, 13; *S.V.*, 6:15. "In religiousness A there is no historical starting-point. The individual merely discovers in time that he must assume he is eternal. The moment in time is swallowed up by eternity. In time the individual recollects that he is eternal." *Postscript*, 508; 10:240.

[42]*Philosophical Fragments*, 58; *S.V.*, 6:46.

however, represents a sundering of a self's relationship to God that immanent religiosity cannot think. This inability stems, first, from the fact that sin involves an essential disrelationship between God and man that is not from eternity but originates within time.[43] This contradicts the tenet of religiousness A that no one can "become a new man" on the basis of temporal action or failure to act. The profound scandal to immanent religiousness, however, is that the "new man" who results from sin is cut off from God. The idea of such a separation strikes at the central axiom of this existence-form.

Johannes Climacus writes in the *Postscript* that the religious self's opaqueness to itself, which results from its inability to think its defining characteristic, its existence as sinner, manifests itself in its thought about guilt. In religiousness A, guilt is seen as rooted in man's existence as a finite and temporal creature. As Vigilius Haufniensis points out and Johannes Climacus admits, such guilt is really not guilt because all responsibility must be laid upon God, who so created man. But then Johannes Climacus argues that rather than exonerating man from guilt, such a defense constitutes self-incrimination.

> To him who is essentially innocent it can never occur to cast guilt away from him, for the innocent man has nothing to do with the determinant we call guilt. . . . [T]o will essentially to throw off guilt from oneself, i.e. guilt as the total determinant, in order thereby to become innocent, is a contradiction, since this procedure is precisely self-denunciation. . . . *[Q]ui s' excuse s' accuse.*[44]

However effective these observations are in dispelling any pretensions to innocence, they do nothing to explain its loss. Johannes Climacus slides nimbly over this mystery, proceeding in the remainder of the section as if nothing were amiss with the notion that guilt is simply a decisive expression for a finite existence before an infinite God. While he does later show that with the appearance of sin, paradoxical religiosity must supplant religiousness A, he never progresses beyond a juxtaposition of the two views. He never analyzes the religious self's existence in light of its deepest, unrecognized reality: sin.

---

[43]*Postscript*, 517; *S.V.*, 10:249-50.

[44]*Postscript*, 470-71; *S.V.*, 10:200-201.

The tracings of such an analysis appear in *The Concept of Anxiety*. There is some difficulty in using this work to supplement the description of religiousness A in the *Postscript* because Johannes Climacus and Vigilius Haufniensis use somewhat different categories. However, Vigilius Haufniensis—"the watchman of Copenhagen"—identifies and more closely examines the mystery of guilt as it applies to the self of immanent religiosity. The self's opaqueness to itself with regard to this guilt, its vague sense of fallenness, which its intellect refuses to acknowledge, gives rise to the anxiety Johannes Climacus has already noted in Socrates.

> The anxiety found in Judaism is anxiety about guilt. Guilt is a power that spreads itself everywhere, and although it broods over existence (*Tilværelse*) no one can understand it in a deeper sense.[45]

Just as the demonic energy of the seducers Don Juan and Johannes arises from anxiety, so it appears that the religious self's immolation of itself in a perfervid repentance arises from anxiety as well. Though the self described in the following passage differs in some details—notably in its explicit recognition of sin—from the religious self of the *Postscript*, the outlines of the latter self are evident in this horrifying picture of repentance gone mad.

> Sin advances in its consequence; repentance follows it step by step, but always a moment too late. It forces itself to look at the dreadful, but like the mad King Lear . . . it has lost the reins of government, and it has retained only the power to grieve. At this point, anxiety is potentiated into repentance. The consequence of sin moves on; it drags the individual along like a woman whom the executioner drags by the hair while she screams in despair. . . . Sin conquers. Anxiety throws itself despairingly into the arms of repentance. . . . In other words, repentance has gone crazy.[46]

In closing his essay on anxiety and the sin that occasions it, Vigilius Haufniensis indicates the only exit from this labyrinth of madness: "[H]e

---

[45]*The Concept of Anxiety*, 104; *S.V.*, 6:190.

[46]*The Concept of Anxiety*, 115-16; *S.V.*, 6:199-200.

who in relation to guilt is educated by anxiety will rest only in the Atonement."[47] His statement points on to the culminating form of selfhood: that of the Christian believer.

---

[47]*The Concept of Anxiety*, 162; *S.V.*, 6:240.

CHAPTER X

Unified through Faith: The Oneness of the Christian Self

In chapter 8 I noted that both the comparative success and ultimate failure of the ethical self can be traced to the dynamic tension that results from its attempt to maintain simultaneously a positive relationship to its finitude and to God. While the Judge correctly perceives that such a synthesis of the self's temporal and eternal dimensions is the highest goal of human development and the way to essential oneness, he relies too heavily and one-sidedly on the self's own activity in positing this synthesis. He does so because his conceptions of both elements in the synthesis are inadequate.

In the preceding section, I traced the emergence in Kierkegaard's authorship of a decisive concept of God and the corresponding notion of the self and its project. The anxious hysteria of repentance in which this development culminates points toward the second inadequacy of the Judge's thought: his assumption that human immediacy is fundamentally innocent. As a reading of other pseudonymous works reveals, this immediacy has a still more profound determination than as finite: the worm of sin gnaws secretly at the heart of the bud. The first hints of this revelation are to be found, as previously in the case of the God-relationship, in Judge William's nervous, defensive maneuvers in "Observations on Marriage."

After only vaguely stating in *Either/Or* 2 that in ethical resolve immediacy is not destroyed but "taken up into a higher concentricity," the Judge feels the need in "Observations on Marriage" to argue at length for and describe in much greater detail this compatibility. This changed attitude springs from his recognition that ethical activity and immediacy are *prima facie* mutually exclusive. He writes, "[R]esolution presupposes a reflection, but reflection is the destroying angel of immediacy."[1]

The Judge rescues his project out of this seemingly hopeless impasse by distinguishing between two types of reflection. Reflection is the juxtaposition of the real and the ideal. While the real is given, the ideal may have one of two fundamental natures: the abstract or fantastic and the concrete or ethical. When the ideal is abstract or fantastic, it is formed without any specific reference to the real, and the real is then judged against it. For example, upon falling in love, one may compare the real object of one's affections with an ideal romantic partner, be that ideal generated by one's imagination, one's readings, the latest productions of Hollywood, or, worst, the incessant assaults of Madison Avenue. In such a movement away from reality toward the abstract ideal, reflection does indeed destroy immediate love. Even if the one tested is found altogether adequate—an unlikely eventuality—one continues in the relationship not as an immediate lover, but as one who has struck a good deal in the purchase of a horse.

Judge William contrasts this life-destroying reflection with ethical or concrete reflection. Here the ideal is projected from the given reality when that reality is accepted as task. Ethical reflection does not lure one away from reality into the impotent alienation of a fantasy life, but opens the way for a pursuit of the possibilities inherent in the given reality. In the case of

---

[1] *Stages on Life's Way*, 155; *S.V.*, 7:141. "The ethical always presupposes reflection and, thus, a conscious consideration of the action and its motives. A spontaneous behavior [*Livsytring*, literally 'life utterance'] understood as an action has nothing to do in any real sense with the ethical. Spontaneity lies within the realm of immediacy and, strictly speaking, cannot be ethically judged." Malantschuk, *Fra Individ til den Enkelte*, 34. (My translation.)

immediate love, ethical reflection does not extinguish its flame but tends it and shelters it from the blasts of a hostile world.

Even if one concedes that such a form of reflection is theoretically possible, the Judge's project nonetheless makes demands altogether exceeding human capacity. Who among us is able to resist completely the temptation to cast an evaluating glance at this new acquaintance of the opposite sex to whom we feel strangely drawn? Who would want to resist since the alternative is blind commitment on the basis of a first infatuation? Rather than constituting a necessary condition of stable, ethical marriage, such a "leap" is a recipe for marital disaster, as all too many divorce-court records testify. Judge William's concept of love does not allow the reasonable option of evaluating first, committing later, because immediacy is forever gone if once interrupted by intrusive reflection. By the same token, if the Judge's stipulations are legitimate, a momentary lapse into comparative reflection will burst the bubble of even a correctly begun and long-maintained love relationship.

Judge William eloquently describes how marriage's transformation of immediate love from given to task protects and sustains that love. He fails, however, to say how to parry any attacks from within. Whereas the preceding chapter examined the external threat to the ethical self's project, the existence of a transcendent God, now we are face to face with its fatal inner weakness: the immediacy on which it is based is too fragile to survive in the world of reflection within which every normal, adult human being lives.

The project the Judge sets forth may seem naive when considered in the abstract, but it appears mockingly cruel when one remembers that his description of it is not theoretical but part of an exhortation directed to A. Judge William pleads with his reflective friend, A, to preserve an immediacy he has already lost; the Judge is no bearer of hope, but a counselor of despair.

A either is, or gives himself out to be, so deeply mired in reflective aestheticism that such admonitions amuse rather than disturb him; therefore, one must turn to the young man of *Repetition* to see the collisions resulting from a combination of the Judge's ideal and the aesthete's reality.

The young man begins well enough by the Judge's standards, falling hopelessly into a profound immediate love with a girl who returns his feelings. Inflamed by the heady wine of this love, the young man's natural poetic bent asserts itself, causing him to see his beloved not as a particular, concrete human being but as *Das Ewig-Weiblich,* the ideal embodiment of feminine perfection. "[S]he was merely the visible form, while his thoughts, his soul, sought something else that he attributed to her."[2]

By thus embracing the clouds instead of Juno, the young man is hopelessly removed from his concrete lover, even when he stands in the closest physical proximity to her. Constantine Constantius explains to his readers that the young man recollects his love, observing it as though it were already far in the past, even as his lover anxiously awaits their next meeting. Kierkegaard vividly captures this state of reflective removal in the picture he paints of the melancholy youth incessantly repeating lines from Poul M. Møller's "The Old Lover."

> *Then to my easy chair,*
> *Comes a dream from my youth.*
> *To my easy chair,*
> *A heartfelt longing comes over me for you,*
> *Thou sun of women.*[3]

Rather than cultivating this state of removal as A recommends in "The Rotation Method," the young man longs to break out of his "poet-existence," return to his concrete lover, and bring this love to ethical expression in marriage. In short, he would readily follow Judge William's advice if he could. But this option is closed to him because he lacks the immediate love upon which marriage is founded.

Before examining the options open to such a self, Kierkegaard explores through the young man the idea that a return to first immediacy and a corresponding reopening of the ethical option might be possible. After considering, then rejecting, the bizarre aesthetic machinations recommended by Constantine Constantius, he attempts this *redintegratio in statum pristinum,* this repetition of first immediacy, by personally identifying with Job. Despite the great differences between the scheme proposed by Constantine and that adopted by the youth, both involve recovering the loved one by first losing her. Also, in both cases this loss is related to the young man's placing himself in the wrong.

---

[2]*Repetition,* 141; *S.V.,* 5:124.

[3]*Repetition,* 136; *S.V.,* 5:119.

There is a truth in this last dimension of the proposed plans to regain first immediacy that neither the young man nor his confidant are in a position to appreciate and that renders impossible the youth's longed-for restitution to his original state. Both Constantine and the young man fail to understand this being in the wrong as an essential determination, as the most profound condition of one's existence. Constantine recommends hiring a seamstress to pretend to be the youth's mistress, thus rendering him a scoundrel in the eyes of all Copenhagen and, more importantly, in the eyes of his lover. Clearly, this guilt is mere appearance, in no way touching the youth's reality.

After breaking away from the pernicious influence of Constantine, the troubled youth seeks to grasp the fact that, like Job, he is eternally in the wrong before God. Here, guilt characterizes him more essentially but still only insofar as he is a finite being existing before the infinite God. He fails to see that unlike the righteous Job, whose sufferings are at Satan's hand and thus of external origin, his loss of immediacy is his own responsibility. This blindness manifests itself in his failure to take responsibility for the suffering he is causing. Constantine writes, "He was aware that he had made her unhappy, and yet he was conscious of no guilt (*Brøde*)."[4]

Consistent with the young man's lack of self-knowledge and Constantine's even more restricted purview, this essential difference between the youth and Job never comes to view in *Repetition*. Only in the simultaneously published *Fear and Trembling* is there an explicit discussion of this contrast. In this latter work, the earlier juxtaposition is repeated in the persons of the Merman and Abraham, except that here the guilty party, the Merman, is conscious of his guilt.[5] While Abraham, like Job, is able by virtue of the absurd to regain what he lost, to return to immediate life, guilt blocks the way for the Merman as it did for the youth. When Abraham's test is past and the teleological suspension suspended, he returns to life as it is lived on the plain; once more he can conduct himself according to the universal dictates of the ethical. The suspension of the ethical through guilt, which manifests itself in the inability of the youth and the Merman to enter

---

[4]*Repetition*, 138; *S.V.*, 5:121.

[5]See Gregor Malantschuk, "Stadier i Frihedens Bevægelse hos Søren Kierkegaard," in *Frihed og Eksistens*, 249.

into marriage with their respective loves, is no such temporary condition, however. This guilt stamps their being deeply and is, in fact, its fundamental determination.

It is in the discovery that this fundamental guilt, which is later further accentuated by being revealed as sin, characterizes not only the Merman and the youth, but all of Adam's children, that the ethical project is "shipwrecked."[6] To be sure, the ethical is not so naive as to deny the fact of guilt or to overlook the discrepancy between what is and what ought to be. Since, however, its fundamental presupposition is that man does possess the ability to realize the ethical task, the ethical must regard these errors as nonessential.[7] This perception manifests itself in Judge William's undialectical grasp of the significance of sin. He quite rightly points out that the value of the human self is infinitely accentuated by its potential to fall under this category. "It is a glorification of human life that all that pertains to it is referred to the category of sin."[8] In contrast to Anti-Climacus, he fails to note that while the possibility of sin is man's infinite advantage, its actuality is his infinite burden.[9] When the Judge does acknowledge that sin is a sign of human weakness, he immediately affirms that it can be overcome with resolution.[10] Drawing a useful comparison with epistemology, Vigilius Haufniensis writes:

> As all ancient knowledge and speculation was based on the presupposition that thought has reality [*Realitet*], so all ancient ethics was based on the presupposition that virtue can be realized. Sin's skepticism is altogether foreign to paganism. Sin is for the ethical consciousness what error is for knowledge of it—the particular exception that proves nothing.[11]

---

[6]*The Concept of Anxiety*, 17; *S.V.*, 6:116.

[7]"Ethics points to ideality as task and assumes that every man possesses the requisite conditions." *The Concept of Anxiety*, 16; *S.V.*, 6:115.

[8]*Either/Or*, 2:93; *S.V.*, 3:89.

[9]*The Sickness Unto Death*, 15; *S.V.*, 15:74.

[10]*Either/Or*, 2:98; *S.V.*, 3:94.

[11]*The Concept of Anxiety*, 19; *S.V.*, 6:117-18.

While this optimism about the human condition is the basis for ethical endeavor, the repeated process of resolution and failure makes the self increasingly recognize the depth of its guilt. Thus, the collapse of the ethical caused by bringing the self to the threshold of the discovery of sin can, in a sense, also be described as its culmination.[12] That its collapse can be a culmination supports the widely held view that Kierkegaard's ethical stage is an unstable form of selfhood; it naturally develops toward immanent religiousness if the self is honest with itself. Just as a recognition of God's omnipotence forces this movement, so the self's awareness of its guilt leaves it no alternatives besides religious existence and despair.

> [W]hen the single individual by his guilt has come outside the universal, he can return only by virtue of having come as the single individual into an absolute relation to the absolute.[13]

First in *Philosophical Fragments* and then in *Postscript*, Johannes Climacus juxtaposes the two profoundly different forms this absolute relation to God may take: the Socratic or immanent religious and the Christian or paradoxical religious. As a humorist and therefore below both these forms of existence, Johannes Climacus never tries to decide between the two, being content to separate and distinguish that which loose thinkers have conflated. He does write that Christianity is an advance over immanent religiosity in that it brings the existing subject to the highest possible pitch of passionate inwardness; only when Anti-Climacus, Johannes's Christian counterpart, appears is it made clear that the Incarnation has forever closed the possibility of immanent religiosity. The disjunction is now starkly set: either faith, or offense and despair; *tertium non datur*.[14]

In leading to this, the fundamental either/or in Kierkegaard's thought, Anti-Climacus brings the authorship to a close. The long maiuetic process begun in *Either/Or* six years and many books earlier finds "its definite point

---

[12]"In the struggle to actualize the task of ethics, sin shows itself not only as something which belongs accidentally to the accidental individual, but as something that withdraws deeper and deeper as a deeper presupposition." Ibid.

[13]*Fear and Trembling*, 98; *S.V.*, 5:89.

[14]*The Sickness Unto Death*, 125-31; *S.V.*, 15:174-80.

of rest at the foot of the altar."[15] This statement, however, represents but one side of the Janus-faced Anti-Climacus. He not only closes the pseudonymous authorship but opens, ideally if not chronologically, Kierkegaard's "second authorship." The ambiguities associated with this final pseudonym and his works are symptomatic of their position at the boundary line between Kierkegaard's two literatures. That Kierkegaard sends forth *The Sickness Unto Death* and *Training in Christianity* under another's name makes these works continuous with the first authorship. The reason for this pseudonymity is quite different, however. Although he had intended to publish them under his own name, Kierkegaard later decided that these works portrayed a rigorous and ideal Christianity that he himself had not realized. Whereas previously he used the pseudonyms to set himself apart from existential stages he had already passed through and left behind, here his use of pseudonyms is an admission of his shortcomings as a sinful human being.

The Sickness Unto Death is stylistically and methodologically continuous with the first authorship, recalling especially *The Concept of Anxiety*. *Training in Christianity*, though it also accentuates the scandalous, paradoxical nature of Christianity developed at length in Johannes Climacus's writings, proceeds in the sober, concrete, and piercingly direct style of the second authorship.

The scope of the latter writings precludes anything but a general summary of their development of the place of oneness, of unity and continuity, in the life of faith. Such a sketch, however, will round out this survey of the four positive responses to the imperative to be one thing Kierkegaard describes. Such use of the late religious writings conflicts with studies that stress the differences between the two authorships to the point of denying the relevance of one in the study of the other.[16] The differences, especially in matters of method and style, are great. However, I agree with Elrod that a common theory of the self runs through both authorships.[17] In particular, this continuity includes Kierkegaard's concern with continuity and unity.

---

[15]*For Self-Examination*, 5; *S.V.*, 17:27.

[16]See, for example, Taylor, *Kierkegaard's Pseudonymous Authorship*, 368n.

[17]John Elrod, *Kierkegaard and Christendom*, 131n.

In fact, the presence of this theme in all his various and varied writings strongly confirms its foundational role.

The late religious works' content as well as exhortative style is predicated on the conviction that an individual's eternal happiness or unhappiness is to be decided within time. This conviction is in agreement with Johannes Climacus's assertions that Christianity is characterized by repetition; the eternal lies before the self through decision rather than behind it in immanence.

This observation leads once again to the structural similarity of the ethical and Christian selves. This similarity extends far beyond a common belief that the self's decisions in time determine its essential nature. Repeatedly, recognizable but profoundly altered elements of the Judge's thought reappear in the second authorship. These elements are perhaps most evident in *Works of Love*. Because this work treats the same theme as *Either/Or* 2, love, similarities and differences between the ethical and Christian selves vividly emerge.

As I showed above, the ethical self's unity is historical. It achieves this character by positing itself as a synthesis, by fusing time and eternity, "by living in eternity while hearing the hall clock tick."[18] Marriage is its paradigm because in it, as in no other facet of ethical life, the two sides of man interpenetrate each other; as the ethical development of sexuality, body and soul express themselves through each other, and spirit is posited. This positing gives rise to an essential oneness of self that manifests itself, intensively, in a coinherence of each moment of the ethical self's life with every other such moment, and extensively, in a persistence in the chosen task, a continual renewal of commitment and repetition of response.

Like its ethical counterpart, the Christian self owes its essential oneness to its positive unification of its finite and infinite dimensions. But what difference lies within this similarity! Where the ethical self seeks the meeting of heaven and earth in a spiritualized sexuality, the Christian self finds its unthinkable realization in the Paradox, the God-man, Jesus Christ. By believing in, by becoming contemporaneous with, by following and imitating Christ, the self repeats this incarnation within itself; God's gracious act of redemption, when accepted, heals the inner wound of sin and allows

---

[18]*Either/Or*, 2:141; *S.V.*, 3:131.

the self to relate to itself properly and truly, to exist as it was created to exist: simultaneously finite and infinite, temporal and eternal.

The possibility of such a positive synthesis in both its ethical and Christian forms traces directly to another shared feature of these selves: they are posited in being set under obligation. Only because these selves are assigned their given situations as task are they able to return to the finite and allow it a positive place in their lives after the necessary sundering of immediate ties to it.

In chapter 8 I showed that the movements of withdrawal and return in which ethical selfhood originates are really two aspects of one movement; immediate ties to the finite are severed as the self accepts the finite as task. My review of the authorship has shown that this self's reliance on its own ability to grasp the finite is ill-founded. Sin renders an impotent, worldless repentance, the maximum to which the self can aspire on its own; this self exists under a suspension of the ethical because it lies outside the universal in guilt. Only the redemptive action of Christ allows man to return to his proper place of life under obligation, the true, positive freedom.[19] No thought of merit can be associated with a positive response to this renewed possibility of obedience to God's commands. The possibility itself is an undeserved gift of God's grace, and response, the expression of thankfulness.[20]

---

[19]Malantschuk, "Stadier i Frihedens Bevægelse hos Søren Kierkegaard," 249.

[20]While this is not the place for an extended discussion of Kierkegaard's notion of grace, a word or two seems warranted by the widespread sense that it does not enjoy a central place in Kierkegaard's thought but is eclipsed by the demands for contemporaneity and imitation. In fact, Kierkegaard stands squarely in the Lutheran tradition, rejecting any idea of "works-righteousness." "Yes, I certainly do realize very well that to want to build one's salvation on any works, to dare to come before God with anything like this, is the most abysmal sin, for this means a scorning of Christ's Atonement." *J. and P.*, 1469; *Pap.*, X^1 A 507. Though unwavering in his belief that man is saved only through God's grace, Kierkegaard perceives that an undialectical appropriation of this reformation theme leads to the spiritlessness of Christendom. Only when our reliance on grace is inspired by a full sense of our failure to measure up to the demands placed on us can grace truly be grace. It becomes simply a permission for self-indulgent laziness when this dialectical tension is not maintained. (See *J. and P.*, 1486; *Pap.*, X^4 A 618.) A read-

Though mention here of task, obligation, obedient response, and so forth, implies that the Christian self moves in the same categories as does its ethical counterpart, actually, "all things are become new." In place of the law, with its many rigid commands, Christ has given a single commandment: love. It is in describing this life of love that Christ commands and makes possible that Kierkegaard most clearly speaks of the essential oneness of the self of faith.

The consolidation of the many demands of legalistic ethical codes into the single command to love reflects itself in the selves that obediently respond. Where the ethical self busily moves from one duty to another, sometimes finding itself torn between conflicting obligations and always falling short of completely satisfying its demands, "Love is the fulfilling of the law" (Romans 13:10). A single, simple way of being satisfies in its infinitude the multiplicity of demands the law makes.

This life of love expresses its essential oneness both intensively and extensively as did the ethical self. Kierkegaard writes that in fulfilling the law, love meets "in part a demand for inwardness and in part a demand for perseverance."[21] Because the decision of faith, the only entrance to the life of love, is a positing of the self's relation to the eternal, it implicates the past and future of the self. The self's past is repented and its future committed to the constant renewal of the movement of faith. So integral is this implication of the future to the decision of faith that subsequent apostasy reveals that the decision, no matter how genuine the individual believed it to be, was only appearance. As Anti-Climacus puts it, because of the element of the eternal in the dialectic, despair at any moment of a person's life reveals that that life has been in despair in every previous moment.[22]

---

ing of his "second literature" shows clearly that Kierkegaard throws himself passionately into the task of reasserting this missing dimension in the spiritual life of "Christendom." In so doing he does not deny or exclude grace but rather strives to make a place for it by awakening in a complacent people a true awareness of the depth of their need. Again we see that only in light of his pedagogical purpose (or here, pastoral strategy) can we appreciate Kierkegaard's writings. To read them as espousing abstract philosophies or theologies is to misread them.

[21]*Works of Love*, 132; *S.V.*, 12:129.

[22]*The Sickness Unto Death*, 24; *S.V.*, 15:83.

This extensive oneness of the Christian self—its essential continuity—manifests itself most vividly in Christian love. Repeatedly in *Works of Love*, Kierkegaard describes this love's persistence in the face of changes in the world. Whether separated from the loved one by distance, hate, or even death, true love continues unchanged.

Kierkegaard believes such imperturbability is possible because in Christianity, love is a duty.

> [T]he 'you shall' makes love free in blessed independence; such love stands and does not fall with variations in the object of love; it stands and falls with eternity's law, but therefore it never falls.[23]

This theme has already been seen in Judge William's writings, but it is subtly different in *Works of Love*. For the ethical self, historical continuity is an explicit project. Its importance to this self is evident in the Judge's repetitive remarks that his love is durable while aesthetic love is transient. For the ethical self, the extensive dimension of its unity is most important and forms the basis of its intensive oneness; the ethical self gathers its past into its present in repentance so as to project an ideal picture of itself, which it moves toward as its future. The coinherence of each moment with every other moment derives from the dynamic running through them from past to future. Thus, the ethical self is quintessentially a historical self.

While the Christian self is historical in Kierkegaard's sense of the word—that is, it determines its essential character within time—its intensive oneness is most important and forms the basis for its quality of extensive oneness. The intensive oneness of the Christian self, its essential unity in a given moment of time, also traces directly to its existence in obligation before God. As an essential dimension of his redemptive action, God restores the creature, man, to his proper place in the created, finite order. Above all, this position is one of obedient recognition of God as creator and lord. But this recognition cannot be expressed directly. It must be lived out in the world in which the self finds itself. God makes such a life possible by assigning the given as the self's task. Here again, the Incarnation is reflected in the life of the believer; he becomes the child of God not by abandoning actuality but by going down into it as deeply as possible, by accepting it as it is, without illusion, by becoming perfectly present in it.

---

[23]*Works of Love*, 53; *S.V.*, 12:43-44.

Personal Unity in Kierkegaard's Thought

In this movement the self becomes the most complete unity possible within the realm of existence. Its radical oneness and unqualified presence emerge most perfectly in the Christian self's relations to that most important element of the situation in which it finds itself: other human beings. In place of the discriminating love of the natural man, which is internally divided between giving itself in love and judging to make sure the other is really lovable, the command to love we see, when heard, dispels all doublemindedness and sets the Christian self immediately and wholly about the business of expressing this love. Herein lies the essential link between the central idea of Kierkegaard's Christian ethics, the neighbor (*Næste*), and the theme of personal unity. Human love (*Elskov*), no matter how total it may appear, is internally divided. The "Shadowgraphs" of *Either/Or* 1, with their portraits of three deceived women, prove this point. In each of the three cases, a deception causes the woman's love to oppose itself, thus producing an eternal round of reflective suffering. In Kierkegaard's view, the possibility of such self-opposition reveals the essential disunity of all human love.

The concentration of the self in undivided love caused by the command to love strikingly affects the temporality of the Christian self. Anti-Climacus writes that the more the self accepts the infinite task, "the more personally present and contemporaneous it becomes in the small part of the task that can be carried out at once."[24] Following Jesus' exhortation to take no thought for the morrow, the Christian self's temporal horizons contract to leave it wholly within the moment. But it is within the moment that time and eternity meet.

By living in the moment, by expressing its relationship to God, by becoming wholly present in the given situation, the self achieves the most absolute oneness possible for it. Where the ethical self achieves unity in time by enduring as a continuity through it and is to this degree dispersed among its nonsimultaneous moments,[25] the Christian self lives as an eternal being within time, as the Paradox writ small. Presence and its corre-

---

[24] *The Sickness Unto Death*, 32; *S.V.*, 15:89.

[25] "Only the eternal can be and become and remain contemporaneous with every age; temporality, on the other hand, divides within itself, and the present cannot become contemporaneous with the future, or the future with the past, or the past with the present." *Works of Love*, 47; *S.V.*, 12:37.

sponding concept, the moment, are the common denominators of time and eternity, a fact Kierkegaard notes is captured in Latin's description of the divine as *praesens*.[26] At this point of intersection, human beings may display the oneness of Him in whose image they were created. As Wyschogrod writes, "The 'now' is that non-componental entity which reflects in the medium of time the absolute non-componentiality of pure Being."[27]

Thus this investigation has come full circle: the dialectic of development began in a timeless immediacy, and there it finds its end. And yet, the second immediacy is different from the first. The opaque consciousness of the prelinguistic infant gives way, in the full course of development, to the self that reposes transparently in its creator. In between lies the wide domain of reflectivity, a domain that varies in distance from the ideal of oneness, but that ultimately and by its nature is divided.

It is impossible to contemplate this progression from immediacy to reflectivity and back to a higher immediacy without thinking of Hegel. Clearly, Kierkegaard's thought shows the positive influence of his great German antagonist as well as the more blatant marks of disagreement. In fact, the two sides of Kierkegaard's relationship to Hegel are inseparable. In the individual works Kierkegaard often imitates the style and form of a philosophy or theology whose content he is attacking. The same pattern plays itself out on a larger scale in his writings as a whole. Kierkegaard learns and uses much in reading Hegel but employs his thus-acquired insights to articulate a profoundly antithetical message: Where the demands of perfect unity lead Hegel to envision an all-consuming synthesis, Kierkegaard finds in the command to be one thing a demand for the integrity of the individual.

---

[26]*The Concept of Anxiety*, 86; *S.V.*, 6:175.

[27]Wyschogrod, *Kierkegaard and Heidegger: The Ontology of Existence*, 126. See also pp. 98-100.

CONCLUSION

Having completed this survey of the Kierkegaardian corpus as it reflects its creator's absorption with the idea of unity, it is time to take stock of results. At the most basic level, I have compiled descriptions of the various unities that appear in Kierkegaard's writings. These range from the "external" unities present in successful art and science to the whole gamut of existential expressions of essential oneness.

As noted in the introduction, no mere compilation of such descriptions is able to convey the role the idea of unity plays in Kierkegaard's thought. It is necessary to appreciate the connection between these various forms of oneness, to see the dialectic leading from one concern with oneness to the next, in order to understand the theme's presence in the writings surveyed.

This study began by situating the young Kierkegaard in the intellectual milieu of Copenhagen in the 1830s. Here his dim, unarticulated interest in personal unity is enlightened, sharpened, and enriched by contact and conflict with current thought about art and science. In this period before his launching of the authorship, Kierkegaard defines his lifelong interest in the individual self and rejects the systematic unity of science as the model for human oneness. His early interest in art and in the organic, personal unity that art displays allows him to avoid a false dichotomy between lifeless systematization and orderless subjectivism. In working out how art, especially the novel, is organized by a life-view, he lays the foundation for his later work on the stages of existence.

Part 2 of this study traced the development of Kierkegaard's early studies of art as they lead him to the idea of the aesthetic stage of existence. This paradoxical stage forces clarification of the idea of a life-view. In Don Juan and Johannes the seducer, we see figures who press the muddled aestheticism most of us practice most of the time through to its final, impossibly consistent realization. Inconsistency, discontinuity, and manyness are the characteristics such selves consistently display. Thus, Kierkegaard makes it clear that not only a life-view, but a particular sort of life-view, is required of the self that would be one thing. Further, by conjuring forth this demonic form of life at the very beginning of the authorship, he provides a dark backdrop against which all subsequent forms of selfhood appear more distinctly.

In part 3, I determined the general characteristics of the truly unified self and described the four ways Kierkegaard believes these abstract determinations can be existentially expressed. These four existence-forms were seen to fall into two groups according to the way they achieve their distinctive oneness: the ironic and religious selves are negatively one, constantly departing from the Heraclitean realm of finite existence for the unobtainable reaches of the ideal, while the ethical and Christian selves achieve a positive oneness in which their relationship to the eternal transforms their finite dimension. It was a central concern of these chapters to demonstrate the developmental relationships existing between these four forms of selfhood. As the study progressed from the ironic to the ethical to the immanent religious and finally to the Christian self, it became apparent that each form's characteristic expression of oneness overcomes the fatal weakness of its predecessor's form of oneness. Thus, only with the Christian self is the demand for oneness fully met.

When the individual parts and chapters are considered together, they can be seen to form a basis for establishing the idea of personal unity at the center of Kierkegaard's concerns. This theme's appearance in all forms and phases of Kierkegaard's writings has been repeatedly documented here. In addition, I indicated the idea's foundational role by showing that close attention to it allows one to perceive structure and meaning where disorder and ambiguity ruled previously. Such a discovery of order was achieved first in a close reading of *Either/Or* 1 and then in a survey of the widely varied works describing the four forms of unified selfhood. This, as it were,

Personal Unity in Kierkegaard's Thought

microscopic and macroscopic vindication of my claim's heuristic value should establish its truth.

In establishing the pervasiveness of this theme, I take a position in the long-running debate over the unity or disunity of the body of writings Kierkegaard left. While there *are* profound differences in style, method, and content within these writings, there is at the level of basic intuitions and intents a profound continuity from the earliest to the last writings. Kierkegaard's affinity for indirection makes this the level at which continuity should be assessed.

In the preceding chapters, I was often forced to assess the significance of apparently Hegelian structures within the Kierkegaardian writings. In every case I wished to recognize the debt Kierkegaard owes his German adversary without forgetting that no ploy is more characteristically Kierkegaardian than the use of an opponent's own weapons to slay him. This ploy has been shown in relation to individual works; it is also present in the authorship as a whole. The development Kierkegaard there portrays is in sum and detail recognizably Hegelian—but its meaning, spirit, and character are altogether at odds with Hegel's views. Further work must be done to illuminate this thoroughly dialectical relationship. It is my hope that such work will free us from both Thulstrup's overemphasis of Kierkegaard's independence from Hegel and Taylor's occasional exaggeration of the Dane's debt.

Finally, I would like to think that this study points in its own feeble way to the amazing richness of Kierkegaard's writings. Like all works of genius, there is an inexhaustibility to the writings this strange man produced in such a few, intense years. It is our task as students of Kierkegaard to take up these texts ever anew, to view them from new angles, to ask of them new questions. If we fail in this, if we succumb to the scholastic senility and academic rigidity that always threaten those who seek to read the texts carefully and who look for help from other such readers, then God grant us another such gadfly as Kierkegaard to come and tease, ridicule, and infuriate us back to our senses.

Index

Aesthetic stage, 41-105; ahistoricity of, 60-61; development of idea of, 41-48; immediate form of, 56-64; mediation of subject-object split, 94-105; reflective self-production of change, 74-79; relation to Hegel, 99-102; synthesis of art and nature, 86-93

Aesthetic theory: aesthetic vs. ethical criticism, 34-37; relation of art to artist, 19-37

Af en Endnu Levendes Papirer, 22-27

Ahasverus, 46-48, 50, 104

Anderson, H. C., 22-26, 29-37

Antigone, 66-69, 73

Anxiety, 67-68, 92-93n, 134, 174-75

Aristophanes, 125-26, 130

Aristotle, 110, 111

Billeskov-Jansen, F. J., xix, 53

Blicher, Steen Steenson, 26-29, 37

Boredom, 75-76, 134

Brandt, Frithiof, 23

Christianity: as an existence-form, 177-90; relation to philosophy, 42

Concept of Anxiety, 100, 118, 134-35, 145, 146, 168, 174-75, 190

Concept of Irony, xvii, 100, 104

Concluding Unscientific Postscript, 8, 18, 21, 111, 118, 126, 159-75

Consciousness, 120-21

Crites, Stephen, 22, 24, 25, 35-37

De Omnibus Dubitandum Est, 58, 119-21

Despair: aesthetic, 77, 101-102; ethical, 139-40

Don Juan, 46, 49, 50, 56-64, 88, 104, 109

Edifying Discourses, 159

Either/Or, 48-105, 137-54, 185; choosing oneself, 138-39, 150-51; ethical stage of existence, 137-54; and God-relationship, 151-54; historicity, 142-50; and marriage, 144-50

Faust, 6, 45-48, 50, 104, 122
Fear and Trembling, 144, 156-58, 181-82
For Self-Examination, 154, 183-84
Freedom, 132, 140

Gilleleje journal, 3-10, 14-15, 41, 42
God-relationship, 112-14, 126, 151-54, 155-75, 177-90
Goethe, 11, 43, 45-46
Grace, 113, 186n
Guilt: contrasted with sin, 172-75, 182; immediate vs. reflective, 65-68; religious, 167-75
Gyllembourg, Thomasine, 26-29, 37

Hegel, G. W. F., xvn, 6, 26, 54, 70-71, 74, 85, 99-105, 190, 193
Henriksen, Aage, xviin, xix, 23, 85, 93n
Høffding, Harold, 16

Ideality, 119-21, 141, 178-80
Imagination, 119, 141
Immediacy, 117-18, 121-22
Immortality, x-xiv
Intuition of unity, 12, 14
Irony: as an existence-form, 117-35; defined, 123-24; degeneration into romantic aestheticism, 134-35

Jørgensen, Marete, 19, 25, 34-37

Kant, Immanuel, 11, 16, 133

Life-view, 22, 26-27, 34, 44

Mackey, Louis, xix, 80-81
Malantschuk, Gregor, 9, 113

Marriage, 144-50
Master-thief, 45
Møller, Poul Martin, xviiin, 12, 180
Mood, 28-29, 149
Music as expressing immediacy, 56
Myth, 43-44, 91-92, 98-99

Occasion, 79-81

Paradox, 70, 185-86
Philosophical Fragments, 100, 111, 171-73, 183
Plato, xiii, 125-30, 164-65
Poet-existence, 51
Predestination, 113
Purity of Heart, xi-xiv, 159, 160-61, 169-71

Recollection, 76, 114-16, 138, 170
Religious stage of existence, 155-75
Repentance: ethical, 142; religious, 167-75
Repetition, 60, 114-16, 138, 142-43, 170, 185
Repetition, 179-82

Schelling, Friedrich, 11
Schlegel, Friedrich, 11, 43, 132, 134-35
Schleiermacher, Friedrich, 43
Sexuality, 57-58, 92, 144-46
Self: as substance, xi, 17; as synthesis, x, 114, 118, 146, 185-86
Sibbern, F. C., 11-15
The Sickness Unto Death, 119, 120, 121, 139, 151, 184, 187, 189
Sin, 172-75, 182-83
Socrates, 122, 124-35, 150, 151, 164-65, 172
Stages on Life's Way, 147, 153, 156
Steffens, Henrik, 11

Taylor, Mark, 193
Thulstrup, Niels, 6, 193

Tragedy, 64-69
Training in Christianity, 184
Treschow, Niels, 16-17
The Two Ages, 21n, 24

Unhappy Consciousness, xvn, 70-71
Unity: artistic, 19-37; general characteristics of personal, 109-16; scientific, 10-18

Works of Love, 185-90

Xenophon, 125-27

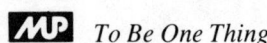 *To Be One Thing*

Interior typography designed by Margaret Jordan Brown
Binding designed by Alesa Jones and Margaret Jordan Brown
Composition by MUP Composition Department

Production specifications:
    text paper—60-pound Warren's Olde Style
    endpapers—70-pound Gainsborough White Text
    cover (on .088 boards)—Holliston Kingston 35417 Natural finish
    dust jacket—70-pound Gainsborough White Text
        Printed PMS 173 (burnt orange)